THE SOUTHWOLD
RAILWAY
1879 – 1929

With best wishes,

[signature]

Fig 1: A mixed down train passing through Deadman's Covert between Blythburgh and Walberswick stations. This image was used by the Railway Company on the 1914 Timetable because it was one of the most attractive sections of the 8.5 mile route.

THE SOUTHWOLD
RAILWAY
1879 – 1929
THE TALE OF A SUFFOLK BYWAY

DAVID LEE   ALAN TAYLOR
ROB SHORLAND-BALL

PEN & SWORD
TRANSPORT

AN IMPRINT OF PEN & SWORD BOOKS LTD.
YORKSHIRE – PHILADELPHIA

First published in Great Britain in 2019 by
Pen and Sword Transport
An imprint of
Pen & Sword Books Ltd
Yorkshire - Philadelphia

Copyright © Rob Shorland-Ball, 2019

ISBN 978 1 47386 758 1

Typeset by Aura Technology and Software Services, India
Printed and bound in India By Replika Press Pvt. Ltd.

Pen & Sword Books Ltd incorporates the Imprints of Pen & Sword Books Archaeology, Atlas, Aviation, Battleground, Discovery, Family History, History, Maritime, Military, Naval, Politics, Railways, Select, Transport, True Crime, Fiction, Frontline Books, Leo Cooper, Praetorian Press, Seaforth Publishing, Wharncliffe and White Owl.

For a complete list of Pen & Sword titles please contact
PEN & SWORD BOOKS LIMITED
47 Church Street, Barnsley, South Yorkshire, S70 2AS, England
E-mail: enquiries@pen-and-sword.co.uk
Website: www.pen-and-sword.co.uk

Or
PEN AND SWORD BOOKS
1950 Lawrence Rd, Havertown, PA 19083, USA
E-mail: Uspen-and-sword@casematepublishers.com
Website: www.penandswordbooks.com

CONTENTS

PRINCIPAL REFERENCE SOURCES

David Lee has researched the history, operation, rolling stock, management, staffing and memories of the Southwold Railway for many years. He envisaged a book about the Railway being, essentially, an academic treatise with all the details of his research in the text and each reference numbered then detailed at the end of each chapter.

I share David's interest in the details of the Railway's history and operation, but I am a story teller so we have compromised. The principal sources are listed here and all can be visited – often online. A researcher who reads this book and then wants to see David's original notes and follow up interests this book has generated is advised to contact the Curator of Southwold Museum. David has agreed that his many files, pages of notes and albums of pictures should eventually be deposited under his name in the Museum Archives. Likewise, I have deposited many of the scans I have made from David's files at the Museum and am very grateful for the help I have received there.

Read and enjoy – and, if you wish, research more and explore.

Rob Shorland-Ball

Principal sources are:

- *Story of Southwold*. M. Janet Becker, Editor. F. Jenkins. 1948
- *The Southwold Railway*. Eric Tonks. Published by author. 1950
- *The Southwold Railway*. Alan R. Taylor. Eric S. Tonks. Ian Allan. 1979
- *Memories of the Southwold Railway*. A. Barrett Jenkins. John W. Holmes. 2012
- *Branch Line to Southwold*. Vic Mitchell. Keith Smith. Middleton Press. 1984
- Principal File References – The National Archives, [TNA] Bessant Drive, Kew. TW9 4DU
- Local File References – Suffolk Record Office, Gatacre Road, Ipswich. IP1 2LQ
- The British Newspaper Archive www.britishnewspaperarchive.co.uk
- Ian Bunting has researched *Halesworth Times* for any Southwold Railway references
- Southwold Museum, 9-11 Victoria Street, Southwold. IP18 6HZ
- GOOGLE online search engine <www.google.co.uk>

MEASUREMENTS and CURRENCY
This book is an historical work so the pre-decimal form of UK currency and imperial measurements will be used throughout. Conversions, if necessary, can be obtained from the GOOGLE search engine

ACKNOWLEDGEMENTS

When researching the past history of a subject or a company, information may be obtained from a number of sources including The National Archive, Local Record Offices, Museums, Government and Local Authority sources, undertakings with any connections with the subject, or online search engines.

All these sources have contributed to this book but David Lee, a long-time resident and researcher in the Southwold area, has also been able to track down contacts whose forbears worked for the Southwold Railway. A number of them, usually by correspondence, have contributed memories and sometimes pictures or papers so are thanked and acknowledged here:

A. Barrett-Jenkins *(the late)*	–	Photographer, Alderman and Mayor of Southwold
G. Beard	–	W.J. Fisk, SR Foreman Goods porter
M.A. Bottomley *(the late)*	–	W.G. Bridal, SR Station Master Southwold
J. Chambers	–	H. Ward, SR Secretary
		C.C. Chambers, SR Contractor
		W.C. Chambers, SR Director
H.J. Ecclestone	–	H. Ward, SR Secretary
N. Elson	–	W.G. Jackson, SR Locomotive Foreman
T. Evans	–	E. Stanley, SR Clerk-in-Charge Walberswick Station
B. E. Girling	–	B. E. Girling, Last Southwold Station Master
Institution of Civil Engineers	–	A.C. Pain and C. Pain – both served as SR Engineers and Chairmen
M. Messenger	–	A.C. Pain, SR Engineer and Chairman
D. Negus	–	Technical information on locomotives and rolling stock
S. Pain	–	A.C. Pain, SR Engineer and Chairman

PART I

BEGINNINGS

CHAPTER 1

SOUTHWOLD RAILWAY – PREAMBULATION

Rob Shorland-Ball

My Oxford English Dictionary [OED] defines 'preambulate' as 'To walk in front' and I am honoured to walk in front of David Lee and the late Alan Taylor in telling the story of the Southwold Railway.

I have known Southwold since the 1940s when as a 4-year old, just after the Second World War, my mother took me there to enjoy the seaside. We lived in Cambridge, not too far from Southwold, but getting there meant a rather complex rail journey as far as Halesworth and thence by bus. Or in a hired car from Cambridge. The missing railway link was the Southwold Railway which closed in 1929 and, by the end of the 1940s, was only a scar on the landscape, several derelict buildings, some bridges and many memories. As soon as I was old enough in the early 1950s I explored these remains, photographed some of them (**Fig 2**), and researched the memories because railways have always fascinated me and here were the remains of an unusual narrow-gauge railway.

I did not meet David Lee until the 1980s, when I was Director of the Museum of East Anglian Life in Suffolk and David was – and still is – the Honorary Librarian at Southwold Museum. I explained my interest in Southwold and the Railway and David, with the wry smile and impish humour I have come to cherish, said, 'You know, I rode on the Southwold Railway'. He explained that as a 4-year old, sitting on his mother's knee, he travelled to Southwold but remembers little more than that there was not much to see because it was pouring with rain.

Fig 2: Southwold Station building in the early 1950s.

My museum career, and my affection for Southwold, kept me in touch with David. When in 2015 I was commissioned to research and write a book about the Railway my first contact was with David, still very much alive in his 90s. I knew that he planned to write a definitive book on the history and operation of the Southwold Railway and that he has always been an exhaustive and very meticulous researcher into subjects which interested him. Some of his booklets have been published by Southwold Museum, but he believed that the Railway needed a fully illustrated and extensive book.

I was concerned David might feel that I should not take over his project but, at our first meeting, he acknowledged that I could be a means to his end. I had a commission from a publisher and was therefore committed to delivering text and pictures for what has become this book. In our subsequent meetings, at David's house in Southwold, we explored my knowledge of the Railway and agreed a list of contents. David showed me what he had already written and the several hundred pictures and paper artefacts he had accumulated.

People stories have generally underpinned my writing, so I suggested to David that I would like to introduce our book with a brief biography of him. Though he is an unassuming man, and initially resisted my suggestion, I guessed he would have some interesting stories to tell:

'I was born on 9 April 1922 and christened David Mark Lee; the 'Mark' was a family memory of my grandfather, Sir John Mark, who was Mayor of Manchester in the 1890s. Schools were Stubbington House Prep School and then Uppingham – but that did not do me any good!

'I was still at school at the beginning of World War Two. I left in July 1940 and after a failed attempt to get into the Royal Marines I joined up in January 1941 as an Ordinary Seaman RN. After initial training I joined HMS *Norfolk* for convoy escort work then more training at HMS *King Alfred*, a training depot for RNVR officers, and passed out as Sub Lieutenant Lee, RNVR in June 1942.

'There followed training at Chatham as a High Angle Control Officer (HACS) on a British anti-aircraft fire-control system used by the Navy from 1941. HACS calculated the necessary deflection to reach a target flying at a known height, bearing and speed. There followed sea-going service on HMS *Argonaut* then HMS *Nigeria* and finally to HMS *Tulip* which took me to the Far East and to Singapore on air-sea rescue work. I was demobbed in June 1946 so that is the end of that story!

'My interest in railway operation was fulfilled by clerical employment for fifteen years on the GWR, then BR Western Region and finally 4 more years with BRB in the Passenger Rolling Stock Section. I resigned in 1965 because the Beeching cuts were making my long-term railway future a little doubtful so I moved with my wife and family to Southwold to become an antique furniture repairer and restorer. From 1969 to 1989 I owned and managed an antiques business in the front of the High Street house which is still my home.'

I have 'pruned' David's life story but I hope it gives a flavour of the man who has researched and contributed much of this book. However, I made clear in our subsequent discussions that this was to be *our* book, not just David's book, and I have explained to him that I must judge what twenty-first century readers, and our publisher, would consider to be readable, saleable and a good story about a Railway which was a Suffolk byway.

A byway in the OED is a little-known area of knowledge and the Southwold Railway fits that definition:

- A 3ft gauge railway – an unusual gauge found only elsewhere in the UK for passenger-carrying on the original Ravenglass & Eskdale Railway, acknowledging that the 3ft gauge Isle of Man Railways is outwith the UK.
- A railway company in rural Suffolk which was managed from a London office with which, for many years, there was no telephone connection so instructions and decisions were communicated by letter from Secretary Ward.

Just such a letter is **Fig 3** which I have re-created from David Lee's extensive collections. At first sight the Secretary is applying standard railway operating procedures and insisting that they must be followed.

However, the final sentence of the first paragraph reveals a little more; other evidence suggests that one of the Railway's regular passengers, whom the driver and guard would recognise, was hurrying for the last down train of the day so the train was 'detained' for him. What we do not know is who reported this practice to Secretary Ward but perhaps another passenger, in a hurry to get home and frustrated by a 'regular' who got special treatment, felt that the driver and guard should be 'severely dealt with'. This incident is typical of many rural railway byways where the staff were keen to help their passengers but where Head Office, often many miles away, had other views.

I knew our second author much less well than I know David Lee and I was unable to develop my knowledge of Alan Taylor – whom I met several times – because he became very unwell and died on 16 January 2017 aged 91. Like David and me, Alan had a long interest in the Southwold Railway and his name may be best known as co-author with Eric S. Tonks for *The Southwold Railway*, Ian Allan, 1965 and subsequently a revised edition in 1979. For this book, Alan has contributed Chapter 2 and was very supportive of the whole endeavour in which a number of images from his extensive photograph collection were promised to me for publication; I hope those pictures, which are acknowledged to him in the List of Illustrations, may be another tribute to Alan.

David Lee recalls Alan and writes:

'We became acquainted in the 1950s when I was staying in Southwold and Alan came over from Beccles to discuss his research into Southwold Railway history and to exchange photographs. We kept in touch periodically and discussed some of our continuing researches. I was very pleased when Alan became President of the Southwold Railway Trust (see Chapter 18) in 2011 and he was encouraged, despite his ill health, by the prospect of a recreated Southwold Railway. Rest in Peace, Alan.'

When David Lee and I discussed the contents of this book we had differing viewpoints. As a geographer, and with ready IT access to a number of sources, I enjoy well-written words but also think in terms of map extracts and pictures which should speak for themselves in telling a story. David, without a computer but with an indefatigable skill at detailed research, thought more in terms of words

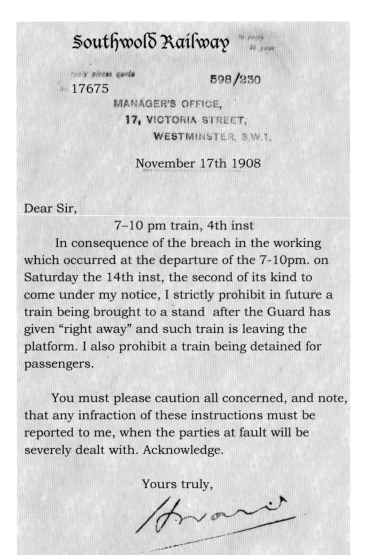

Fig 3: A peremptory letter from Secretary, and subsequently Manager, H. Ward in London to the operating staff in Suffolk.

and sometimes very detailed statistics plus a number of pictures from his files, each with a detailed caption.

My solution is what follows; many words, some maps, many pictures and captions wherever the words cannot embrace the illustrations so they complement each other. But I believe it is very important that an interested researcher should be able to access all of David's work. He has agreed, therefore, that all his research files and associated papers, plus my scans of all the pictures he and others have made available, should be deposited in the Archives at Southwold Museum one day in the future. In due course they can be seen, by appointment, in the excellent Search Room there. The contact is the Curator at: <curator@southwoldmuseum.org> or telephone 07708 781317.

Fig 4: SR No 1 *SOUTHWOLD* heading the 6.30pm mixed down train at Halesworth. 3 July 1920.

We hope that this book will be an enjoyable tale about a Suffolk railway byway, wandering across the marshes and through the wooded coverts between Halesworth and Southwold. And that readers who want to discover more will visit Southwold Museum, explore David Lee's collection which will be accessible there for current and future generations and, perhaps, contribute more research and their own discoveries.

If there are mistakes in the text we would be pleased to hear of them and, since I am happy to accept responsibility for them please contact me at robsb@wfmyork.demon.co.uk and I will share them with David in Southwold.

David Lee   Rob Shorland-Ball

CHAPTER 2

PROPOSALS FOR A RAILWAY TO SOUTHWOLD

Railways of northern East Anglia, 1840 – 1859

Railway promotions in the Blyth valley, 1860 – 1876

[Text by Alan Taylor, copied and compiled from David Lee's Research Notes obtained by him from TNA and other sources – see pages 7 and 8]

Southwold, in the nineteenth century, was a small coastal town with a population of a little over 2,000 situated in East Suffolk, south of Lowestoft and north of Dunwich. This latter, in mediaeval times, had been a thriving town and port but nearly all of it had been lost to the inroads of the sea. Southwold was close by the mouth of the River Blyth and was served by a harbour in that river. The river's valley extended to the Southwold hinterland via Halesworth, a small market town.

Fig 5, a 1960 sketch map, shows the river winding its way through extensive marshes to the sea at Southwold. The contours show there was very little land above 50ft, so the construction of a railway should not require extensive civil engineering – and consequent cost. If the local landowners were keen to see a railway through, or near, their property and were persuaded that it could improve the local economy, a railway proposal might be successful.

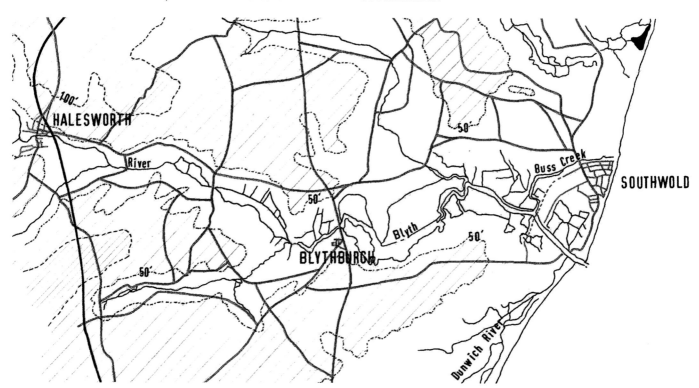

Fig 5: 1960 sketch map, shows the River Blyth winding its way through extensive marshes to the sea at Southwold.

But why was there such a Suffolk byway as the Southwold Railway? This can best be explained by the development of rail systems in East Anglia and the subsequent isolation of Southwold. The Great Eastern Railway Company was incorporated by the Great Eastern Railway Act of 7 August 1862. The purpose of the Act was: 'To amalgamate the Eastern Counties, the East Anglian, the Newmarket & Chesterford, the Eastern Union and the Norfolk Railway Companies, and for other purposes'. The ECR had previously leased and absorbed the constituent Companies which morphed into the GER in 1862 but the ECR was never financially stable and lacked holistic management. The GER Act was an expression of parliamentary good sense in bringing together in one Company a diverse miscellany of company management and operational practices. The Sketch Plan of the Great Eastern System (**Fig 6**) shows the network of standard gauge main lines, and some branches, but Southwold is isolated.

The first railway in Eastern Suffolk and Norfolk was the Yarmouth and Norwich Railway which opened on 30 April 1844 and became the Norfolk Railway in 1845. By 1849, Norwich was connected to London via Cambridge.

In 1844, Sir Morton Peto – an entrepreneur, railway developer and civil engineer – bought the ailing Lowestoft harbour and began developing the Lowestoft Railway and Harbour Company (LR&HC) which joined the Norfolk Railway at Reedham and was taken over by the Norfolk Railway in 1846 and this in turn came under the control of the Eastern Counties Railway (ECR] in 1848.

The next line of the ECR system, the Halesworth, Beccles and Haddiscoe Railway (HB&HR), opened for traffic to Halesworth on 4 December 1854. *The Southwold Diary of James Maggs (1818-1876)*, Boydell Press, Suffolk Records Society, 2007 records: '1854 Decr 20 – Fish first sent from here [by road] to Halesworth Railway Station.'

Southwold was now less than 9 miles from a standard gauge main line railway at Halesworth.

In 1854, the HB&HR became the East Suffolk Railway and obtained authority to build southwards from Beccles to Woodbridge with branches to Leiston, Snape and Framlingham. By 1860, this extension was complete to Woodbridge with standard gauge branches to Framlingham, and to Aldeburgh via Leiston and a goods-only line to Snape to serve Snape Maltings.

Yarmouth, Lowestoft and Aldeburgh were now connected to the railway system but Southwold was still isolated. Southwold, with no direct rail link, was connected to the outside world by public omnibuses to Darsham.

Of the population of about 2,000, many felt that their town was important enough to be served by its own railway. As a result, a number of proposals were made with this in mind. In 1855, the Mayor of Southwold, Alfred Lillingston, presented a petition to the East Suffolk Railway requesting that a branch be constructed to Southwold, but the request was rejected.

The *Suffolk Chronicle* of 11 October 1856 carried the following report:

'SOUTHWOLD – Oct 9th PROPOSED BRANCH RAILWAY At a very important and highly influential meeting, held at the Town Hall, in this Borough, on Friday, the third inst. presided over by the Mayor (Alfred Lillingston, Esq.,) and attended by the members of the Town Council, the Town Clerk, . . . and many other of the inhabitants and visitors interested in the welfare of the town, proposed:

'… to take into consideration the best means of promoting a railway as a branch from the East Suffolk Line at Halesworth.'

It was resolved:

'That the inhabitants do hereby give, and the Mayor and Corporation are also requested to give their warmest support to the project; and that, in the event of the railway passing through the Corporation property, the Corporation be invited to take payment for the value of their land required for the railway in paid-up shares of the Company.'

Also resolved:

'That a committee . . . (with powers to add to their number), be appointed for the purpose of inviting all persons having an interest in the trade and prosperity of the town, to take shares, as an earnest of their approval of the project.'

It was also agreed that copies of the resolutions should be submitted to the Right Honourable the Earl

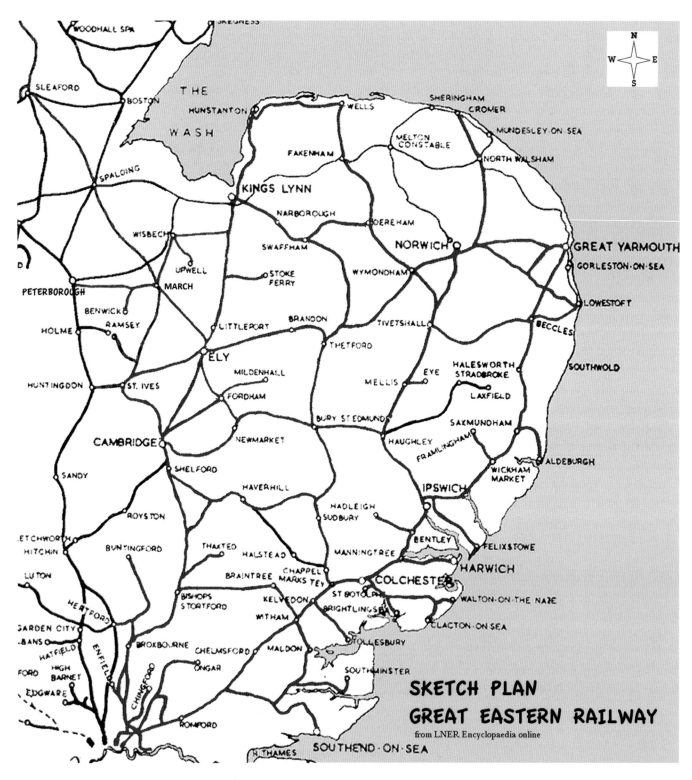

Fig 6: The network of GER lines serving East Anglia. The Southwold Railway is not shown because it was a narrow gauge independent company. Note that the non-GER Mid Suffolk Light Railway is included and is heading towards Halesworth and, its promoters hope, to Southwold.

of Stradbroke, Sir Edward Sherlock Gooch Bart MP, Sir John Blois Bart, Sir Fitzroy Kelly MP, and other Gentlemen residing in the neighbourhood, with a request that they will give their support to the same. Most cordial thanks were voted to Alfred Lillingston, R.A. Broomar, and G.J. Mayhew, Esqrs, for their exertions in furtherance of the proposed railway, and to the former gentleman for his kindness and ability in presiding at the meeting. A subscription list for shares was subsequently presented, and, we understand received general support.

In reference to the above meeting another correspondent says:

'The meeting decided in favour of the proposed plan, the only opposition being that of the Rector, whom, we are told, thought himself justified in that course as the line would bring an influx of Sunday visitors to the town, and thus, by offering facilities for travelling on that day, exert a "prejudicial effect on their morals."

Maggs' diary contains a cutting dated 11 October 1856, possibly from the *Ipswich Journal*, also reporting the October meeting. The cutting emphasises that a railway and improvements to the harbour would greatly improve the prosperity of the local fishing industry and the welfare of the town.

However, little, if any, progress was made and despite the East Suffolk Railway's success with branch lines, the Eastern Union Railway (soon, with the ESR, to be part of the GER) was not persuaded that branch lines were remunerative (**Fig 7**).

In 1859, further representations were made by people in Southwold to the East Suffolk Railway for a connecting branch line but the request was again turned down. However, there was a real public desire for a rail connection to Southwold and the story is best told in the vigorous *reportage* of the local press.

On 14 August 1860, the *Halesworth Times* carried the report:

'PROJECTED RAILWAY. Those at all acquainted with the Eastern coast will bear ample testimony to the natural advantages possessed by Southwold as a seaport and, as a place of resort for invalids and pleasure seekers, we know of no place comparable.

'Owing to the want of public spirit amongst the inhabitants the town has fallen into a state of desuetude and decay, whilst towns like Lowestoft and Aldeburgh, with not a tithe of Southwold's natural benefits, are in a state of comparative prosperity. But we hope the end of these things is approaching, and that Southwold will soon be able to vie with either Yarmouth, Lowestoft or Aldeburgh.

'A project is on foot for establishing railway communication via the East Suffolk Line, at Darsham or Halesworth. We trust the scheme will be taken up with energy and spirit by the inhabitants. Now or never must be the cry: "*With a long pull and a strong pull, and a pull altogether*," and the thing may yet be a *fait accompli*. Lord Stradbroke has been waited upon, we understand, and is favourably disposed towards the undertaking.'

In September 1860, the *Suffolk Mercury* newspaper reported that a memorial had been prepared by the

---

from: **THE SUFFOLK CHRONICLE**
OR IPSWICH GENERAL ADVERTISER AND COUNTY EXPRESS

March 3rd 1855

EASTERN UNION RAILWAY COMPANY

The half-yearly meeting of this Company was held on Tuesday at the London Tavern;
Mr D Waddington MP in the chair.

Mr Tozer and other proprietors expressed themselves strongly against the system of constructing branch lines and extensions, and urged the propriety of local parties making them at their own cost instead of at the cost of the Company. The past experience of branch lines in their district showed them to be a ruinous drain upon the Company.

The dividend in 1853 amounted to 12/- per share but in 1854 it only amounted to 10/- 6d per share.

Fig 7: Notice from the *Suffolk Chronicle . . etc.* expressing concern about EUR proposals to build more branch lines in East Anglia. 3 March 1855.

Southwold Town Clerk for presentation to Sir Morton Peto, who had been involved in the development of Lowestoft, was the contractor for constructing the East Suffolk Railway, and a Director of that Company.

A September report in the *Halesworth Times* stated:

'With scarcely an exception the whole town are very anxious that this projected line should be carried into effect. There can be no doubt that the formation of such a line would give immence [sic] impetus to the trade of the town, and restore it to its proper position, as one of the most important ports on the Suffolk and Eastern coasts.

'One of the advantages of the projected line would be the cheapness with which it could be constructed – it being estimated that from £3,000 to £4,000 per mile would be the actual [cost], the principal portion of which might be expected to be almost entirely subscribed for by the residents of the town.'

Progress seemed to be slower than the keenest advocates might wish but the *Halesworth Times* of 13 November 1860 reported on a meeting with Sir Morton Peto which was very positive:

'SOUTHWOLD – PROPOSED RAILWAY

'The proposed railway from this old seaport still continues the engrossing topic of conversation here, and considerable anxiety is manifested that it may ere long become a *fait accompli*. The principal inhabitants of the town, headed by the Mayor Alfred Lillingston, Esq, had an interview with Sir Morton Peto, on Tuesday last, at the Angel Hotel, Halesworth, in connection with the proposed scheme, and were most politely received by the honourable baronet.

'The Mayor, in the name of the deputation, stated the facts of the case, clearly pointing out to Sir Morton the immense advantages that must accrue not only to the town of Southwold and the neighbourhood around but to the share-holders as well. Immense quantities of fish were caught off this coast, and, provided greater facilities were granted by means of direct railway communication with London and other large towns, a very great impetus would be given to the trade of the port, and a much

more extended and extensive business would be carried on. New enterprises would be embarked on and he had no doubt but very important results would follow.

'Other members of the deputation pointed out to Sir Morton Peto the advantages that would accrue from the formation of this line. Sir Morton Peto listened most attentively to the various statements of the deputation and in reply assured them he would assist them in the undertaking to the best of his ability. It appeared to him that the cost of the proposed railway would be about £60,000. The heaviest item in the amount would be the construction of the bridge over the river – if of solid masonry the cost would be not less than £10,000, and if a swing bridge, the amount required would not be less than £16,000. The honourable baronet seemed very favourably disposed, and stated that if the deputation would guarantee half the amount he himself would undertake to furnish the remaining £30,000.

'The question then arose whether the junction should be at Darsham or Halesworth, and could the consent of Lord Stradbroke be obtained for the passing of the line through his estate? The general feeling appeared to be in favour of the junction being formed at Halesworth.

The deputation, after thanking Sir Morton Peto for his urbanity and patience in listening to their statements, then withdrew.

'There is a tide in the affairs of towns as well as men that followed at the flood leads on to fortune – and this seems to be the turning point in the history of Southwold. Now or never if the inhabitants wish to see the old seaport taking its proper position as one of the best, and pleasantest, and most prosperous of places on the eastern coast. Surely there is enough of public spirit in the old town not to let this opportunity slip, but to put fourth all its energies for the accomplishment of an enterprise which must prove highly advantageous in every point of view.'

A printed circular letter, dated December 1860, but with the originator not stated, was distributed in the district. It read:

'I have the pleasure of informing you that a project has been set on foot to connect this town by means of a Branch with the East Suffolk Railway, relative to which an interview was sought with Sir Morton Peto, Bart MP who estimated the cost of such Branch Railway at £60,000, and stated that upon its being shewn to him that £30,000 was subscribed he should be willing to enter upon the necessary arrangements.

'A Public Meeting was subsequently convened in Southwold Town Hall, the Mayor, Alfred Lillingston Esq presiding, at which the desirability of the undertaking was admitted, and evinced by the Gentlemen present entering their names upon the Subscription List, and upwards of £1,000 was subscribed in the Room, and a resolution passed that "Application should be made to Gentlemen possessing property, and having interest in the Town to enable them to aid the undertaking by adding their Names to the Subscription List."

'I need scarcely remind you that the want of Railway Accommodation has been long felt in this Bathing Town, and has deterred many Families from visiting it, who would otherwise have been only too desirous of availing themselves of the opportunity of pleasant temporary Marine Sojourn.

'I have therefore to solicit your co-operation by allowing your name to be placed on the List, and request the favor [sic] of your informing me the amount of the Subscription you desire to be added, in.

'I am, Your obedient Servant,' *A N Other*

What success this appeal had is not known, but it is known that Sir Morton Peto became more involved with the finances of the East Suffolk Railway and was also beset by financial difficulties so thus was unable to continue support for the Southwold branch project. Without his support, the project failed.

In 1862, the East Suffolk Railway was absorbed by and became part of the Great Eastern Railway, which owned and operated most of the railway lines in East Anglia.

The Blyth Valley Railway Company came on the scene in the mid-1860s with a proposal to build a Standard Gauge line connecting with the East Suffolk Railway at Halesworth and roughly following the course of the River Blyth to Southwold. On 8 November 1865, the *Halesworth Times* reported:

'SOUTHWOLD – PROPOSED RAILWAY

'There is at length a probability that our old town will once more be allied with the living world by means of railway communication. But for the appalling [sic] of some, and the opposition of others, Southwold might now have held a place second to none on the Eastern Coast. Nature has marked out the spot as a harbour of refuge, and the advantages it possesses as a watering place ought long ago to have secured it more facile means of communication with the outer world. But, perhaps, better late than never, although several rivals have sprung up – yet it is to be expected that ere long the sound of the whistle will re-echo along the valley of the Blyth.

'The past week has given indications that the project is intended. Mr. Bruff, the engineer, and assistants have been busy in surveying the lands between this town and Halesworth via Blythburgh and Wenhaston and, although the exact route has not yet been determined on, we may feel assured that the junction will be at Halesworth, where a large traffic in heavy goods will be carried on throughout the year.

'We trust all the inhabitants of the Borough will bestir themselves in the matter, and not again let slip an opportunity so favourable for the well being of the old town.'

On 12 December 1865 the *Halesworth Times* next reported:

'BLYTH VALLEY RAILWAY

'We understand the preliminary survey of this line has been completed.

'The Corporation of Southwold have fallen in with the project, and have offered 9 acres of land upon the most reasonable terms, the amount realised between £500 and £600 to be taken in shares. We also understand that the land belonging to Sir John Blois [around Wenhaston] has been amicably arranged, and the probability is that in about 12 months or 15 months from this date the sound of the whistle will be heard along the valley of the Blyth. There can be no doubt there will be an immense amount of traffic on this line. We repeat what we have often said that no finer port can be found on the Eastern Coast. It is the nearest point also to Holland.'

An advertisement (**Fig 8**) was published on the front page of the *Halesworth Times* on 19 December 1865 and the back page of the same issue reported:

'LOCAL INTELLIGENCE
'THE BLYTH VALLEY RAILWAY
'A meeting of the promoters of this line, which is favoured by owners of land and the inhabitants of the district will, as per advertisement, be held at Southwold on Thursday next. Mr. Bruff, Civil Engineer, speaks favourably of the scheme which will, when completed prove, we doubt not, of great advantage to this town [Halesworth] as well as to Southwold.'

The 26 December 1865 issue of the *Halesworth Times* reported this meeting at length. There follows an edited version of this report and subsequent press reports and letters to the Editor which are worth reproducing here because they set out very precisely the mid-nineteenth century reasons for what was eventually to become, albeit under a different name, the Southwold Railway and why it took a long time to gain Parliamentary approval and to build the line. This account is the nineteenth century equivalent of Facebook and Twitter today. It illustrates how news travelled, and opinions were influenced, at that time when gossip from carters moving from place to place, public meetings, daily newspapers, Royal Mail and the Uniform Penny Post were the principal means of communication:

'BLYTH VALLEY RAILWAY
'A public meeting was held in the Town Hall Southwold, on Thursday last [21st December 1865] for the purpose of constructing a line from Southwold to Halesworth, through the Valley of the Blyth. The

BLYTH VALLEY RAILWAY

HALESWORTH TO SOUTHWOLD.

THE Parliamentary Plans for this Line having been deposited, and the Notices served, a

PUBLIC MEETING,

In furtherance of the project, will be held in the

TOWN HALL SOUTHWOLD,

on THURSDAY, 21st Inst., at which several influential county gentlemen have promised to attend. The Chair will be taken at 2.30. for 3. p.m. precisely.

Fig 8: Advertisement of public meeting in Town Hall, Southwold.

meeting was well attended, and so far as popular feeling went there could be no doubt that the line now projected was greatly desired.

'The meeting was well attended by the inhabitants of Southwold and the neighbourhood. The Mayor, A. Lillington Esq, was called to the chair and among those present were:

- Sir John R. Blois Bart
- A.R. Johnston Esq
- Frederick Cross Esq, Halesworth
- W.F. Bruff Esq, Civil Engineer
- Robert Wake Esq
- J. Read Esq
- G. Fenn Esq
- J. Farrow Esq
- R.J. Gooding Esq (Town Clerk)
- Rev H.W. L. Ewen
- Thos. Freeman
- Rev William Hay Chapman
- Dr E. Blackett
- W.R. Bruston Esq
- S.H. Fitch Esq
- Messrs William Sewell, Chilvers, F.J.T. Cobb, Prestwidge, Jillings, Worsden Moore, of Beccles &c.

'Mayor: … all [must] be aware of the great importance of railway communication to any town to which the railway ran; how much it increased the trade of a place and the value of property, and they must, therefore, be fully convinced of the desirability of getting a line made from Southwold. But at the same time it must be remembered that without the assistance of the inhabitants of the town of the various classes, they could have no hope of carrying out the project which was now brought under their notice. He hoped the project would, therefore, meet with the unanimous support of all classes in Southwold, whether on behalf of their own private interest or for the public benefit. He called on Sir John Blois to move the resolution.

'Sir John Blois Bart: moved the following resolution: "That in the opinion of this Meeting the proposed Blyth Valley Railway will be of great advantage to the Borough of Southwold and the district through which it passes.

'"It was a well-known fact that whenever there was a railway it benefited the population. The line would

cost from £60,000 to £80,000. Of course the gentlemen who proposed to make that railway would not do it without certain benefit to themselves, but they proposed that the inhabitants of Southwold should have some of the benefit if they came forward and took up the shares. They would, therefore, not only share in the profit of the Company but they would reap the benefit of it in the good it would do to the trade and property of the town. They could not expect that the gentlemen who had taken this up would make the line without a certain amount of assistance. They expected that at least £10,000 would be raised in the neighbourhood. It might seem a rather large sum but if everybody would take a certain number of shares, according to his means, that amount might be raised amongst them.

'"The question of the opening of the railway was closely connected with the improvement of the harbour. It did not follow that if they got a railway the harbour would be opened, but he was satisfied that if the railway was not made the harbour would not be opened. It was quite certain that the railway would do them much more good if the harbour should be afterwards opened. It would cost a large sum of money to open the harbour, but Sir Morton Peto came forward and did much for Lowestoft and why should not another Sir Morton Peto do the same the same for Southwold?

'"For when men had acquired wealth, the next thing to acquire was renown, and he did not see why somebody should not come down to Southwold and make them a harbour. Some men when they had acquired wealth spent their money in building churches and hospitals, and at any rate the opening of their harbour would do them as much good as churches and hospitals. He had much pleasure in proposing the resolution which he had read."(*Applause*).

'Mr W. Bruff: …had great pleasure in appearing before the meeting to endeavour to rescue that fine old town and harbour from the present position. … he thought that they would all agree with him … that the town and harbour of Southwold were not in the position in which they ought to be. (*Hear! Hear!*)… There was plenty of ground for building upon, and nature had provided them with a splendid harbour, which beyond all doubts, might be made an excellent harbour for shipping once they got railway communication with the interior of the country. But it was quite useless to attempt to improve the harbour until they got a railway. It was no use getting colliers and others to bring their cargoes into Southwold when they had no means of rendering those cargoes available except by carting, which was so expensive as to be quite out of the [question] in the present day.

'As to the country through which the line would run anyone who knew the district must be perfectly aware that, in engineering phraseology, it seemed made for a railway. . . and these were the days of railways. It was a level piece of country and easy gradients and [the railway] could be made, without difficulty, to follow the course of the river. It would not be an expensive line, and no obstacle whatever stood in the way of the undertaking. He had seen most of the landowners over whose property the line was proposed to run, and they were all favourable to the project. Of course every man ought to be paid the value of his land, and a little more, if he were compelled to give it up for the purpose of a railway; for if a man's land were cut up, it was often spoiled for the uses to which he might wish to put it to. But if a man got a fair price for his land, and a fair compensation for the compulsory sale, he ought not to stand in the way of the public good.

'...the watering places on the coast which had advantage of railway communication had increased in importance. [For instance] some thought that no one would ever go to Hunstanton, but the promoters were sanguine and they carried the project through to a successful issue. The line was made, principally by means of small subscriptions, and when it was opened building companies were started, and now Hunstanton was quite a large town, and always full of visitors, and the last dividend paid to the shareholders was 5%. . . and land in Hunstanton had gone up to quite fabulous prices.

'Then there was Cromer, which was an aristocratic place, and opposed railways for a time, but now there were 3 companies proposing lines to Cromer, and they would soon have a railway.

'They all knew the effects of the railway on the prosperity of Lowestoft, and there was no earthly reason why Southwold should not become a second Lowestoft. They were better placed than Lowestoft, and had a better natural harbour, if it were opened for shipping, and there was nothing to prevent Southwold from becoming a very important port, having as it had an easy access to the coast of Holland.

'... he believed [the Southwold line] could be made for £60,000. He had put it down . . . [to] Parliament . . . at £75,000, because it was necessary to have a margin, to prevent the necessity of going to Parliament with a second Bill. The list of Directors was a sufficient guarantee that everything would be done that was possible for carrying the Bill properly through Parliament.

'With regard to the shares, they had been placed at the lowest amount to ensure the co-operation of classes. They had fixed the shares at £10. They did not ask for money, they only asked that the subscribers should give in their names, subscribing to pay only on condition of the Act being obtained; no call would be more than £2 per share, so that the shareholder could not be called upon to pay up the full amount of his shares under 2 years. Under those circumstances he thought anyone at all interested in the prosperity of Southwold would come forward and put down his name for one or more shares [and] they might look for a fair dividend, say 4% or 5%.

'Upon the capital. He was very sanguine about it himself, as promoters always were, but he saw no earthly reason why a line running from Halesworth, a town of 3,000 inhabitants, to Southwold, a Corporate town of similar extent, a watering place, with plenty of building land, should not be profitable.

'There would be a station at Wenhaston, and one at Blythburgh, from which he looked for large results.

'The fishing trade would of course be vastly increased by the opening of the line. No doubt an immense number of Southwold fishing boats now went to Lowestoft to disembark their fish, and there was no reason why they should not bring the fish home to Southwold, and many other boats besides . . . (*Applause*)

'The resolution was carried unanimously.

'Mr Gooding, the Town Clerk, of Southwold, and Secretary to the [Blyth Valley Railway] Company . . . hoped the harbour would receive some consideration. At present it lay under the old disadvantage described by the poet when he said:

"To Dunwich, Sole and Walberswick
We go in at a lousy crick'" (*Laughter*)

'Bearing in mind the great energy and ability of Mr. Bruff, [Mr Gooding] hoped that by and by the authorities would entrust Mr. Bruff with the commission to improve the harbour (*Hear! Hear!*) so that the shipping could deposit their merchandise at Southwold at all seasons.

'Mr. Jillings, fish merchant, said he would come forward and do as much as he could, and he hoped his neighbours would do the same.

'Mr. T. Freeman, Agent to the Earl of Stradbroke, said the Noble Earl was very favourably disposed towards the project. The line had, however, been originally projected over a portion of his Lordship's property which it would be inconvenient for him to dispose of. Mr. Bruff said that was so at first, but the necessary alterations had been made to meet his Lordship's wishes, and his Lordship had assured him that he was pleased at the project, and quite satisfied with the plan.

'Sir John Blois said he would put his name down for 40 shares. (*Applause*).

'The share list was opened. Several gentlemen put their names down for shares, ranging from 40 shares to a single share, and it is expected that in a few days a considerable amount of stock will be subscribed for. About £2,000 was subscribed.

During the year 1866 a number of people, often using *nom de plumes*, wrote to the *Halesworth Times* expressing a variety of views, such as this on 9 January 1866 from INTEREST:

'Sir, I think it is most generally felt in the neighbourhood that the construction of a railway from Southwold to Halesworth would be most advantageous to both towns.

'You might travel along the whole Eastern Coast and not find a spot where nature has done so much – a port and a harbour of refuge being made to hand, only requiring a moderate outlay to make it all that could be desired.

'Such however appears to be the apathy in taking shares that unless more strenuous efforts are made a railway will be still in the dim distance. This town is crushed with a lot of obstructives who for their own selfish purposes throw cold water upon the project – the well-being of fishermen and the inhabitants generally being a secondary consideration.

'At least £10,000 are required from the neighbourhood to start with, and at present little more than £3,000 has been subscribed. Every man should endeavour to get a subscriber – the money laid out in shares will pay the investor, if not directly then certainly in an indirect manner. Now or never!

'Our old town has let slip one grand opportunity, let it see to it that the second – and it may be the last – shall not be allowed to pass . . . Faithfully yours, INTEREST.'

16 January 1866 from SUDWALDUS:

'Dear Sir, At length it appears a settled matter that this delightful watering place is to have communication with the outside world by rail. The plans for the Blyth Valley Railway are deposited, the Bill prepared, and the required 8% paid. Great praise is due to Mr. Bruff the Promoter and Engineer for his perseverance and urbanity in thus far effecting so great a desideratum.

'It has even been a source of wonderment to those who know Southwold that it was so long overlooked by men of capital. Travel the wide world round you could not find another place possessing so many natural advantages, an abundance of magnificent building sites commanding the most extensive and uninterrupted view of the "old ocean" – a harbour requiring only the extension of the piers to make it The Best on the East Coast of England, there being no rocks, sands, shoals, or other ocean impediment outside till you reach the coast of Holland; within the harbour a large amount of dock room ready formed by "Dame Nature."

'The town standing on an eminence, with a gentle slope all round, is favored [sic] with admirable non-artificial drainage, causing its inhabitants to inhale the purest air – thus accounting for their proverbial longevity, and freedom from disease. As Southwold far exceeds all other places in Suffolk, Norfolk, and Essex in position so will her natural facilities for trade and commerce (when the rail is completed and the piers lengthened) point her out as The Place most advantageous for continental traffic.

'Better even than this, our gallant tars who are now compelled to ride out the storm and tempest in Yarmouth and Lowestoft roads will find Southwold a good and safe harbour into which they may run and be at peace; thus preventing immense loss both in life and property.

'It has often been said "those who purchase railway shares burn their fingers" – it's a true aphorism – and may in the general be true. The Blyth Valley Railway will be The Exception and it must, necessarily be a great success.

'Heartily wishing the Bill a safe and speedy passage through both Houses of Parliament, I am Dear Sir, Faithfully yours, SUDWALDUS.'

During the summer, the *Halesworth Times* reported a good number of visitors to Southwold but remarked that the coming of the railway would bring even greater numbers.

The Parliamentary Bill was presented in the Autumn of 1866 but failed to gain parliament's approval with the result a meeting was held at Southwold, Sir John Blois presiding, on 24 October 1866. The *Halesworth Times* of 30 October 1866 reported:

'**Blyth Valley Railway** – A meeting of the provisional directors of this railway was held at the Town Hall, on Wednesday last, Sir John Blois Bart in the chair, to take steps for making another application to Parliament in this Session.

'The canvass for shares up to this short period has been more successful than on any previous occasion, which leads the promoters to anticipate a successful issue . . . '

The *Suffolk Mercury* did mention that there had been some apathy about subscribing for shares.

On the 4 December 1866 the *Halesworth Times* reported:

'**The Railway to Halesworth**. Hopes are again entertained that the projected line from Southwold to Halesworth will ere long be an accomplished fact. Railway Surveyors have been busy within the last fortnight, but whether the pecuniary means will be forthcoming is still a matter of uncertainty. The promoters of the line are very sanguine as to the advantages that would be derived from its

formation – no pleasanter a spot to spend a summer visit to could be found on the whole eastern coast.'

Further plans were lodged with the Clerk of the Peace for Suffolk dated 30 November 1866 and application made for an Act. A notice appeared in the *Halesworth Times* of 4 December 1866:

'BLYTH VALLEY RAILWAY
The Parliamentary Plans &c, for this proposed Railway having been deposited, a PUCLIC (sic) MEETING in the furtherance of it will be held (by the Kind permission of the Mayor) in the Town Hall, SOUTHWOLD
on MONDAY, the 10th of December 1866.
The Chair will be taken at 3 p.m. precisely.'

There appears to have been no report of this meeting, and it is to be assumed, in spite of SUDWALDUS's fine words and Bruff's endeavours, that the Act was not passed by parliament.

And there was already some competition for any proposed railway. Morris & Co.'s *Suffolk and Yarmouth Directory* of 1869 lists two omnibus services running from Southwold to Darsham. That of Mrs Jane Catton, proprietress of the Swan Hotel, left Southwold at 10.00 am and returned from Darsham following the arrival of the 1.16pm train. (**Fig 9**)

The omnibus of James Jillings, proprietor of the Crown Hotel, Southwold, left Southwold at 5.00pm and returned on arrival of the 3.30pm train at Darsham. These services did not operate on Sundays.

In January 1868, a report in the *Halesworth Times* referred to the bankruptcy of Sir Samuel Morton Peto, Bart; however, the notion for a railway connection to Southwold persisted and a letter signed with a *nom-de-plume* was printed in the *Halesworth Times* of 12 May 1868.

'**A Railway to Southwold**. Sir, This heading will attract the attention of many of your numerous readers. I am not going into the merits of the scheme, or the defects, if any such there be. Those who are acquainted with Southwold know that Nature herself commands that this beautiful little seaport, so admirably adapted for commercial enterprise, should at once be placed at the service of others than the present townspeople, by

CATTON, "SWAN" HOTEL, SOUTHWOLD.

POSTING IN ALL ITS BRANCHES.

PRIVATE OMNIBUSES, CARRIAGES, AND CAREFUL DRIVERS,

Supplied on the Shortest Notice.

A PUBLIC OMNIBUS

LEAVES THE ABOVE HOTEL

DAILY,

FOR DARSHAM STATION,

At 10 in the Morning, and Returns at 1.20 in the Afternoon.

Fig 9: Advertisement for private omnibus services running from Southwold to Darsham by Mrs Jane Catton, proprietress of the Swan Hotel, Southwold.

efficient means of communication with the leading commercial cities and towns of this kingdom.

Will you allow me to ask your readers one question? – viz: Why do we hear nothing about the construction of the Railway, the starting of which caused not a little satisfaction and pleasure to the people of East Suffolk?

I am, Sir, your obedient servant, J O S.'

A reply to J O S's letter appeared a week later:

'**A Railway to Southwold**. Sir, Having been for several years past endeavouring to promote the above, perhaps you will permit me to reply to a letter under this heading signed "J O S."

'In 1865, acting for some influential men in London, I surveyed a line from Darsham to Southwold, and another from Halesworth to Southwold, and also inserted the requisite Parliamentary notices in the newspapers. The landowners being more in favour of the proposed line from Halesworth to Southwold than of the other, my plans were deposited for that line, the usual formalities of Parliament gone through, public meetings held and the district canvassed, and the result being that about £3,500 was promised to be subscribed, if an Act were obtained.

'The deposit to be made to the Court of Chancery amounted to £4,800; and the promoters in London, after expending so much of their time and money, did not consider it desirable to lock up such a sum on the promise of so limited an amount of support. The Bill of 1865 was therefore withdrawn.

In 1866, acting for some other railway men, I again surveyed a line by a different route. The usual Parliamentary notices were inserted in newspapers, my plans and other documents deposited, public meetings held, and district canvassed, the result being a promised subscription of about £4,500 if an Act were obtained, and a promised deposit of 10% down to partly defray the expenses of endeavouring to obtain such Act, but none of this deposit was ever paid.

'Notwithstanding this the promoters in London were perfectly willing to lodge the Parliamentary deposit of £3,000 in the Court of Chancery, provided the provisional directors named in the Bill (all local men), and who would have the entire control of such deposit, became sureties to the promoters for it. Some of them refused, and as it was too late to withdraw their names and substitute others who would become sureties, the Bill of 1866 was obliged to be withdrawn. In 1867, acting for the same men as in 1866, I again surveyed the line, revising it in several places to better accommodate the landowners, and also inserted the usual Parliamentary notices in the newspaper, but although arrangements had been made for finishing the line by the summer of 1869, if an Act were obtained, a private canvas of the district showed such a falling-off from former promised subscriptions, that, coupled with the railway panic, the hope of commencing work even until a considerable time after the Act was obtained, was so remote as for the third consecutive time to compel this much-needed railway to be postponed.

'In conclusion I would add that, from having all the plans, estimates, &c, prepared, and also from an intimate acquaintance with the details of the work required, I can afford 'J.O.S.' and other well-wishers to the line every requisite information, and, if necessary, introduce capital, I shall also *con amore* – be happy – to meet him, or them, either in London or the district, with a view to carry out the project.

'Remaining Sir your obedient servant,
'WILLIAM F. Bruff C E, Associate, Institute of Civil Engineers.
5 Charing Cross, London, May 14 1868.'

Bruff had a personal interest in the Blyth Valley Railway, but his explanation of the project to the Public Meeting in Southwold Town Hall and, above, his account of what happened subsequently is very balanced and fair-minded. But a London engineer, who closes his letter with an Italian phrase – with a helpful gloss for those not familiar with the phrase – is socially, and educationally, different from simple Suffolk folk.

The *Halesworth Times* of 22 February 1870 printed a letter about developments in Southwold and the difficult sea approach to Lowestoft Harbour because of shifting sands. The letter concluded with the paragraph: 'Harbour and rail [projects in Southwold] will soon meet if one is but begun and the hungry strife for building land, on common, beach, and field, prove beneficial to the Corporation and . . . to us natives. PS We also say with them may it come quickly!'

Further news of the Blyth Valley Railway appeared in a report in the *Halesworth Times* (and in the *Suffolk Mercury* of 14 October 1871):

'The Blyth Valley Railway: The Blyth Valley Railway to connect Southwold with Halesworth, of which Mr W.F. Bruff CE of London is the Engineer, is now being revived under influential London auspices, and there is every prospect of this much-wanted and long talked-of project at last being carried out.

'Mr Bruff has had all the necessary plans prepared for deposit this November, and the promoters intend shortly visiting the district, with a view to obtain local co-operation. It is to be hoped that no fractious opposition will prevent the promoters from urging on the Bill this ensuing session as, from its natural advantages, Southwold can hold its own with any seaside place of resort, were it but developed by connection with the railway system of England.'

There appears to have been no follow-ups of this report. The *Halesworth Times* of 25 August 1874 reported:

'[Southwold has] not for many years had such an influx of visitors

'The question of a railway [is still in the air] but the inhabitants have been so bitten that, although they fervently desire greater travelling facilities, they manifest no intention of investing money in a concern which after all may come to naught.

'If ever a railroad should be constructed to Southwold, the means for doing so will have to come from without, and not within the Borough.'

Research evidence shows that Southwold needed a railway for goods transport as well as for seasonal visitors. In an account of travels in Suffolk in 1875, Mrs E.B. Scott tells of riding on a coach from Darsham to Southwold, which was also carrying 'Her Majesty's Mail'. She also remarked about Southwold having a small Gas Works for which the coal supply, from Pelaw Main Colliery, C° Durham, had to be carted across the Common (from the Harbour). Bedingfield was a carter whose business was between Halesworth and Southwold, so he may have carted the Gas Works coal from Halesworth Station or from Southwold Harbour. However, neither the East Suffolk Railway nor its successors, the Eastern Counties Railway and the Great Eastern Railway, had shown any inclination to construct a branch line to Southwold. Locally promoted schemes had also met with no success. Southwold was still isolated.

The Blyth Valley Railway Company (BVR) made a third attempt in 1875 to promote their scheme. It was its intention to apply for an Act to build a line to Southwold:

'Commencing in the Parish of Halesworth, by a junction with the GER near Halesworth Station at or near the south end of the bridge carrying the said railway over the public road leading from Halesworth to Holton …'

This application was dated 30 November 1875 and was to be deposited at the House of Commons before Christmas that year, but it does not appear to have been proceeded with. As was the custom at that time, a copy of the Plans was deposited with the local Clerk of the Peace and they are now in the Suffolk Records Office.

At much the same time as the BVR was promoting its third attempt, the promoters of the SOUTHWOLD RAILWAY were busy enlisting support for their basically similar scheme at public meetings held in Halesworth and Southwold. The Halesworth meeting was presided over by Mr Charles Easton of Holton Hall and that at Southwold presided over by the Earl of Stradbroke of Henham Hall. Both of these gentlemen were prominent landowners in the area.

A principal speaker was Arthur C. Pain, a civil engineer with an extensive experience in railways, who recommended that the railway be built to a gauge of 2ft 6in as being cheaper to build than a Standard Gauge line. Another leading promoter and speaker was Richard C. Rapier of Messrs Ransomes and Rapier, the well-known Ipswich engineering firm, who supported Pain with stories of the prowess of a 2ft 6in gauge locomotive built at his works and sent to China. These speakers were met with loud applause. At both gatherings the following Resolution was passed:

'This meeting, having heard the description of the proposed railway from Halesworth to Southwold, is of the opinion that the 2 towns and the intervening district will be greatly benefited by it, and the meeting warmly approves the proposal.'

The enthusiasm engendered at these meetings, coupled with the active support of a number of influential local people, led to the formation of the Southwold Railway Company. Colonel Heneage Bagot-Chester of Henstead Hall was appointed Chairman with Arthur C. Pain and James B. Walton as Engineers and H.P. Allen, a local Solicitor, as Secretary. The office was at Halesworth and all but one of the Directors were Halesworth men. Statutory Notices appeared in the press during November 1875, plans were deposited with the Clerk of the Peace and a Bill was presented to parliament.

The Southwold Railway was incorporated by Act of Parliament dated 24 July 1876, (39 & 40 Victoria, Cap clxxxix) which authorised the construction of a main line of 8 miles 63.5 chains from Halesworth through Wenhaston and Blythburgh to Southwold within 5 years. Branches to the River Blyth Navigation at Halesworth Quay of 3 furlongs 84 chains and to Blackshore Quay at Southwold of 2 furlongs 30 links were also authorized. The Authorised Capital was made up of £40,000 in £10 Ordinary Shares, with borrowing powers for £13,000 in Debentures. The gauge was to be not less than 2ft. 6ins. and in accordance with the Regulations of Railways Act of 1868 the Board of Trade permitted light earthworks and simple signalling provided speeds were less than 25 mph and loads were limited. In practical terms this meant a journey time of 30 minutes with a maximum of 100 passengers.

The first meeting of the Directors after the passing of the Act was held on 10 August 1876 with Colonel H.C. Bagot-Chester in the chair and the following appointments of Officers were confirmed:

- Engineer Arthur C. Pain
- Solicitor W.H. Stephens
- Bankers Messrs Gurneys & Co.
- Secretary H.R. Allen (Solicitor, Halesworth)

C.J. Wall, formerly manager of the Bristol & Exeter Railway, made a report on the traffic expectations of the proposed railway (**Fig 10**).

Mr Wall's report was very encouraging – although he makes the valid point that the working expenses for the transfer at Halesworth '… will be a comparatively heavy item'. Wall's general conclusions helped the Board of Directors to adopt a gauge of 3ft. because they believed that the extra carrying capacity would offset the slight increase in constructional costs. Wall's report was included in a Prospectus, issued on 3 November 1877 with the blessings of the Earl of Stradbroke, Lord Mahon and Lord Rendlesham, which stated that provisional contracts had been entered into with contractor Charles Chambers of Westminster for the construction of the line, stations, etc., at a cost of £30,000, and with the Bristol Wagon & Carriage Works Co Ltd for the supply of '… engines, carriages, wagons and brake vans …' for £4,000.

The Secretary, meanwhile, had been asked by a number of local landowners to act for them in a

REPORT OF MR. J. C. WALL, OF BRISTOL.

(26 Years Manager of the Bristol and Exeter Railway.)

SOUTHWOLD RAILWAY.

BRISTOL, *November 25th,* 1876.

SIR,

In obedience to your request on the 24th ultimo, I went over the proposed Railway on the 17th and 18th instant. In my opinion there is not the least difficulty in stating with confidence that the receipts, on the opening of the Line, will amount at the commencement to at least £12 per mile per week. The present traffic from Southwold alone to Halesworth and Lowestoft amounts to about £100 per week; between Southwold and Lowestoft there is a purely Railway traffic, which would be at once diverted to Halesworth, and the present road route of 16 miles changed to a railway route of about 9 miles. To this must be supplemented the traffic from Halesworth to Southwold, as well as the local traffic from the Termini to Blythburgh, Wenhaston and other places in the contiguity of the proposed Line; and also there must be added the summer pleasure traffic, which cannot now be enjoyed by any place, however attractive, that is without a railway, when in competition with other watering places which have the advantage of railway communication. I have had 26 years of practical railway management, and I feel confident that in less than 3 years the traffic on the Southwold Railway will reach £20 per mile per week. The fact of the existing traffic being so good does not to my mind leave the matter at all speculative, for if it were not increased (a case which up to the present time has been unknown) the present income is sufficient to pay a good interest on the expenses of construction, if your Engineer's estimate is at all within the mark, whilst the Line would undoubtedly be of immense service to the District. With the class of traffic which will be conveyed on the railway, the working expenses ought to be under 50 per cent. The transfer at Halesworth will be a comparatively heavy item, but this will be met by the increased mileage always allowed by the rules of the Clearing House to the Company providing the necessary station accommodation and performing the transfer.

H. R. ALLEN, ESQ.,
    Halesworth,
        Suffolk.

I am, Sir,
    Your obedient Servant,
        (Signed) J. C. WALL.

Fig 10: Copy of Report by C.J. Wall, formerly manager of the Bristol & Exeter Railway, on the traffic expectations of the proposed Southwold railway.

professional capacity in negotiations with the Railway Company so he therefore resigned as Secretary to the Company on 29 August 1877 and was replaced by T.H. Jellicoe, Solicitor of Southwold.

By this time the Board had been enlarged to include J.E. Grubbe, Mayor of Southwold, and Richard C. Rapier of London and Ipswich, but they found difficulty in raising sufficient funds. Chambers refused to enter into a definite contract until assured that the necessary land could be acquired. The Board therefore resigned *en bloc* on 5 November 1877 and were replaced by an entirely new Board apart from Col Bagot-Chester, who remained as Chairman, and Richard C. Rapier. Henceforward, Board Meetings were held in Rapier's London office and Rapier himself took over the Chairmanship from 20 December 1877. Col Bagot-Chester finally resigned from the Board on 29 January 1879.

Rapier managed to get matters moving so that by May 1878 construction had started and a Report to the shareholders in July 1878 gave a favourable account of progress (**Fig 11**).

Progress was maintained with most of the work completed for inspection by the Board of Trade on Friday 19 September 1879. The official opening of the Southwold Railway was on the following Wednesday, 24 September 1879. At that time, Wenhaston was the only intermediate station completed.

SOUTHWOLD RAILWAY COMPANY

———

SECRETARY'S OFFICE,

SOUTHWOLD,

SUFFOLK,

July 22nd, 1878.

SIR,

I am instructed by my Directors to inform you that on the 3rd of May last the works for the construction of this line were commenced by Mr. Chambers, the Contractor.

The Company have now acquired all the land for 5 miles through the parishes of Southwold, Walberswick, and Blythburgh, also about $1\frac{1}{2}$ miles through the parishes of Halesworth and Holton St. Peter, and negotiations are in progress for the early acquisition of the remaining $2\frac{1}{2}$ miles.

The Contractor has ordered the whole of the sleepers, fencing, rails, and fastenings 18,000 sleepers have been delivered at Blackshore Quay, and the remainder are being shipped. A considerable length of fencing has been erected, and a quantity more has been delivered, and is in course of erection. The whole of the rails have been rolled by the Tredegar Iron Company, in South Wales the first shipload has been delivered, and the remainder are lying at Newport waiting shipment.

Two bridges have been erected and the earthworks for a mile and a quarter of the railway at the Halesworth end are completed, and ready for the permanent way. The Southwold station-yard, and nearly half a mile of line at Southwold are in a similarly forward condition. The cutting through the Southwold Common and the embankment across the marshes are proceeding as rapidly as possible.

The Great Eastern Railway Company have agreed to subscribe towards the cost of the Halesworth Station works, which will effect a saving to this Company.

My Directors are anxious to have the line opened in time for the winter fishing season, which they feel confident can be done if the works are pushed forward energetically.

Fig 11: First page of Secretary Jellicoe's Report to Shareholders.

PART 2

TELLING THE TALE

CHAPTER 3

CONSTRUCTION, INSPECTION BY THE BOARD OF TRADE AND GALA OPENING

Before starting construction of the line, Chief Engineer Pain conferred with the Board of Trade (BoT) in a letter dated 28 March 1878. He attached to his letter a tracing setting out in detail the complete specification, with drawings to full size, of all necessary components for the plain track to seek approval from the Board. The BoT referred the matter to the Railway Inspecting Officer Colonel Holland, who met Pain and suggested some alterations. A modified tracing was sent to the BoT on 12 April 1878 which Col. Holland termed 'Plan B' which can be consulted at the National Archives.

The Act of Parliament authorising formation of the Railway Company and construction of the Southwold Railway had been passed in July 1876 but there were initial difficulties in raising the necessary finance.

Land acquisition was often a contentious problem for railway developers and although there was no strong opposition to the proposed Railway, which only required a total of 39 acres, acquisition was mainly in small lots which took time to negotiate and complete. 31 freehold owners were involved and in some instances, compensation had to be paid:

24 sold less than 2 acres
4 sold up to a total of 13 acres
3 leased land for rent.

The leased land comprised 5 acres in Southwold Parish at £52.10.0 pa; Walberswick Common Lands Trustees for 1 acre at £10.0.0 pa and Holton Parish, also for 1 acre at £20.0.0 which total of £82.10.0 had to be covered by operating revenue each year from the opening of the Railway (figures from Southwold Museum). Another route-planning matter was time-consuming to resolve. In some cases, it was capital-costly and invariably required careful negotiation with land-owners and local authorities to provide access over, across or under the Railway. The Southwold, including the under and over bridges, and the Swing Bridge, had over 50 accommodation and occupation crossings as well as one public road level crossing adjoining Wenhaston Station.

The Secretary, then T.H. Jellicoe, advised the Directors that, following a call by letter to shareholders for £4.00 per share, the contract with Chambers could be signed and construction could start at both Halesworth and Southwold.

Work started on 3 May 1878. Material arriving by sea at Southwold Harbour, including timber from Norway, was recorded in the Southwold Port Book:

Date	SHIP	Port of Registry	From	Cargo	Draught
25 June 1878	IDA GEZINA	SAPPEMEER	GOTHENBURG	Timber	6' 6'
5 July 1878	IBESSTINA	BLUMENTHAL	BLUMENTHAL	Timber	9' 6'
30 July 1878	HARRIET	GOOLE	NEWPORT	Railway iron	9' 11'
7 February 1879	ELIZA	IPSWICH	IPSWICH	Iron Rails	6' 2'
7 February 1879	VICTORIA	IPSWICH	IPSWICH	Iron Rails	6' 3'
7 February 1879	TERTINS	IPSWICH	IPSWICH	Iron Rails	6' 4'

Information about construction material arriving by land transport at either Halesworth or Southwold has not been traced.

In a further letter to shareholders (**Fig 11**) the Secretary reported that construction of the Railway was in hand and progressing well. The letter concluded with a request to shareholders for immediate application for 550 shares at £10 each.

The Great Eastern Railway had agreed to subscribe towards the cost of the Halesworth Station works, including the connecting footbridge, for which the GER Locomotive, Way and Works Committee had agreed a tender submitted by Messrs Stanley Hall & Company.

In March 1879 the Chairman (Richard Rapier) assured a crowded meeting in Southwold Town Hall that work was proceeding satisfactorily and that: 'in a very few months you will actually see the iron horse marching triumphantly into the town.' (*The Southwold Railway. Eric S. Tonks. Published by the author. 1950.*)

Further details of the construction period have not survived in either the Chambers' family papers or in the local press, neither is there any knowledge of the motive power used during construction. Contractor Charles Chambers encountered, so far as is known, no difficulties or need for major work in crossing the gently undulating terrain which the line's formation followed. The only earth works of any size were List's Bank and List's Cutting (both 12 feet high/deep respectively) and the cutting through Southwold Common 20 feet deep. Other cuttings and embankments were quite shallow. However, completing the track-laying was delayed because Ransome & Rapier of Ipswich, the sub-contractor for the component parts of the siding points at stations, could not make them available until late June 1879.

It seems likely that the required 30lb rail for fabricating the Southwold Railway points was what R&R had originally supplied for the 'Woosung Road', China's first railway from Shanghai to Woosung, early in 1878. Through no fault of R&R, this 2ft 6ins gauge railway failed. (*Woosung Road – the story of China's first railway*. Peter Crush. The Railway Tavern, Hong Kong. 1999.) The rail was returned to the UK but did not arrive until June 1879. A note in R&R Order Book for job number 291 reads, 'The following iron rails have come home and must be cut.'

The order for C. Chambers, dated 21 June 1879, gave precise details for 19 sets of points and crossings and two 'elbow crossings.' Fabrication started on 27 June 1879

and was probably completed by 19 August 1879. The components were installed at Halesworth, Wenhaston and Southwold by 19 September 1879.

On 3 September 1879, the Company advised the Board of Trade that the line was sufficiently completed for conveying passengers safely by 12 September and ready for inspection during the following ten days. Official inspection for the Board of Trade was by Major General C.S. Hutchinson RE on Friday 19 September 1879 who also investigated complaints which had been received from the following with requests that they be investigated:

- Charles E. Easton of Holton Hall about cracks in the concrete abutment of the over line bridge in Holton and fencing
- Suffolk County Council Surveyor was concerned about the decking of the bridge at Blythburgh under the Yarmouth turnpike road
- Messrs Cross Ram, Solicitors, Halesworth, representing their clients (J.E. Ewen owner, W.S. Kett tenant and miller), expressed concerns about occupation level crossing to Kett's Mill (at lm. 72.25c).

Hutchinson's principal Inspection Report, dated 19 September 1879, stated:

- General satisfaction with permanent way being laid to specifications agreed, to the three completed stations' accommodation and the station platform height of only 9 inches which was adequate as carriages had steps to their end platforms. Arrangements for signals and points interlocking similar, for instance, to those on other light railways was in order but the low permitted speed of 16MPH on the Southwold meant that distant signals could be dispensed with and working the Railway with one engine in steam was considered satisfactory.
- Bridges over and under the line were mostly satisfactory including observations on Mells Road Bridge which, despite the cracks in the concrete abutments, was considered to be adequate. The Yarmouth Turnpike road (now A12) bridge at Blythburgh was a cause for concern because the construction was unusual for a turnpike road. The decking was barely

suitable to take the weight of a traction engine and additional deck planking was required. The River Blyth Swing Bridge, described in great detail, was very infrequently opened and train safety arrangements were acceptable. It was recommended that supports to bearings at the ends of the bridge girders required attention.

- At the level crossing at Kett's (or Wenhaston) Mill it was suggested that gates should be provided and a crossing keeper employed, but both Hutchinson and the BoT advised there were no powers to enforce either suggestions, though they were commendable.
- Fencing in some locations was not considered satisfactory and required replacement by post and rail fencing within six weeks.
- The engines and rolling stock to work the line were satisfactory.

Hutchinson, subject to attention to his requirements, had no hesitation in recommending that the BoT would have no objection to the line being brought into use.

The Railway Company, advised by Engineer Pain, argued that the decking of the Blythburgh bridge was adequate for the road traffic it carried but they were over-ruled because both the BoT and the Clerk of Peace to Suffolk County Council required that Hutchinson's recommendations must be completed without delay.

Following the opening, Charles Easton of Holton Hall, wrote to the BoT on 25 September 1879 pointing out that ballast had been washed away during flooding, the sleepers had been covered with water and the train service had been interrupted on the opening day. He was also concerned that the water level at Wenhaston Mill head-race was above that in the surrounding meadows. He suggested that the Railway should be on a piled bridge because flooding was considered to be a permanent feature in that area. In fact, the Railway was already on a timber viaduct so there is no evidence of any further action here.

Major General Hutchinson made a second Inspection in February 1880 and noted that Blythburgh Station, with accommodation similar to Wenhaston, was inspected and '[should] not, I submit, be objected to by the BoT.' (NA) He also recorded that when built, the line had been equipped with mile posts on the right hand side from Halesworth and gradient posts on the left hand side.

THE OPENING OF THE SOUTHWOLD RAILWAY (Fig 12)

One day before the Gala Opening Day, on Tuesday 23 September 1879, there was a private view of the Railway for an invited party of engineers, promoters interested in the potential for narrow gauge railways as feeders to a standard gauge main line, and other guests. They travelled to Halesworth in a saloon carriage 'placed at their disposal' by the Great Eastern Railway. Unfortunately, it rained heavily most of the day.

The private view, and the subsequent Gala Opening festivities, were very fully recorded in the *Ipswich Journal* – and the following paragraphs, partially rewritten by Rob Shorland-Ball retaining the original style, draw on this record. (from: British Newspaper Archive):

'The invited party arrived at Halesworth at about 1.00pm and were met by the Vicar of Southwold, Rev Cautley, the Secretary of the Southwold Railway

Fig 12: Poster advertising Southwold Railway Opening Day – Wednesday 24 September 1879.

The Ipswich Journal,

SUFFOLK, NORFOLK, ESSEX AND CAMBRIDGESHIRE ADVERTISER

(ESTABLISHED 1725.)

| No. 7,774.] | [Registered for Transmission Abroad.] | SATURDAY, SEPTEMBER 27, 1879. | [TWO EDITIONS WEEKLY]... |

Fig 13: The *Ipswich Journal* header.

Company, Mr Jellicoe, and several other Southwold gentlemen. Their Southwold train was waiting, the engine …blowing off steam, as if eager to show that it had perfect mastery over the long row of handsome carriages to which it was attached.

'The remarkable steadiness of the carriages was a subject of general remark and congratulation. The sides of the carriages are composed of glass half way down and in consequence the traveller has an uninterrupted view of the surrounding country, and as the different churches and other noticeable buildings came in turn to view, the Southwold gentlemen, familiar with the district, very courteously volunteered all the information in their power thus making the journey additionally enjoyable and pleasant.'

The train stopped briefly at Wenhaston Station where: 'A number of villagers were at the level crossing anxiously awaiting the arrival of the train.' Blythburgh Station was not yet complete but, not surprisingly, the party were particularly interested in the line's principal engineering feature, the swing bridge over the River Blyth. They 'dismounted' there to hear from Richard Rapier, Chairman of the Railway Company, how the opening arrangements were so secure that it was impossible for the bridge to be opened without the Annetts key which was 'part of the furniture of the engine.'

The party 'remounted' and travelled to Southwold Station where they were met by the Mayor and transport provided by Mrs Catton, Landlady of the Swan Hotel, was '. . . in readiness to convey the party to that most hospitable hotel where an elegant luncheon was in readiness.' Perhaps the rain had eased, or temporarily ceased, while the party was inspecting the swing bridge but it continued for much of the day so the transport to the Swan was very welcome and several speakers at the luncheon referred to the inclement weather.

The *Journal* provides a very useful account of all the toasts and speeches at the luncheon – '(*Hear, hear*)' and '(*Cheers*)' – but what is especially relevant to this book is Chairman Rapier's several references to the value of the Southwold Railway as an exemplar of a narrow gauge line which was a feeder to a main line railway. (*Remunerative Railways for New Countries with some account of the first railway in China (1878)*. Richard C. Rapier. London: E.F. & N. Spon.1878.)

The Contractor, Mr Chambers, took up the same point in responding to a toast to his work (*Cheers*): 'The presence of so many gentlemen from a distance on this inclement day led him to believe that there was indeed a hearty and widespread interest felt in light railways. The Chairman and other Directors, and Mr. Pain the Engineer, had entered heartily into the question of providing railways with 3ft. gauge, and he [Mr Chambers] thought that there were hundreds of towns in the United Kingdom that might advantageously be supplied with a railway such as that which had just been laid down between Halesworth and Southwold. (*Cheers*) Such railways could be made at a far cheaper rate, and worked at a far less percentage of the gross receipts. (*Hear, Hear*)'

Another speaker, railway engineer, Mr John Dixon, responding to the toast 'The Visitors', added to the praise for narrow gauge feeder lines: 'He was very glad of the opportunity of seeing a fair example of a narrow gauge railway and what it was capable of doing. There was, on the one hand, great opposition in some quarters to such railways but, on the other hand, there were many warm advocates of the light railways who were not slow to point out the advantages which the little gauge would confer. The interest that the Chairman took in undertakings of this kind was very great. He [Mr Dixon] had been a colleague of that gentleman in the far distant land of China, (**Fig 14**) which, there was no doubt, would be productive of great results. (*Cheers*)

It is an interesting irony, in the hindsight we can exercise today, that it was the Woosung Road, to which Mr Dixon referred. For that project, he had secretly invested £8,000 to enhance Ransome & Rapier's original tender which proved to be under-priced. When he was speaking, he must have known that the Woosung Road Company Ltd's assets had all been seized by the ruling Mandarins, that the railway had been dismantled and only the earthworks of the trackbed had been retained as a road for wheelbarrows.

'Mr Dixon concluded with some perceptive comments on the Southwold Railway: [I have] … had some experience of the way in which country towns supported enterprises of this kind. They were never the leaders in those matters which were likely to be of great and lasting benefit to them. The benefits had to be thrust upon them! He had no doubt that the gentlemen of Southwold would have to acknowledge that the gentlemen from Ipswich, London, and elsewhere, who had imposed this narrow gauge railway, had conferred a real benefit on the town. (*Cheers*)'

After one more toast – 'received with three times three' – the luncheon party ended and *The Journal* account moves on:

'The weather on Tuesday was excessively wet and the downpour increased in intensity so that on Wednesday morning the low lands in the neighbourhood of the new line were flooded, and this greatly interfered with the arrangements which had been made for the running of the trains on Wednesday. In fact, on the arrival of the second train from Southwold at Wenhaston the water had risen so rapidly that Mr. Pain, the Engineer, had thought it prudent not to continue the journey [to Halesworth]. There was,

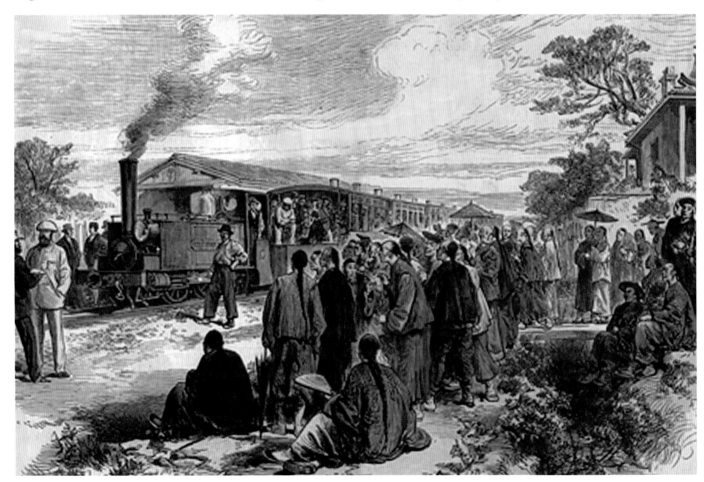

Fig 14: The opening of the Woosung Railway in China. (*Illustrated London News 1876*) The gauge was 2ft 6ins but there are similarities to the 3ft gauge Southwold Railway and some of these similarities are explored later in this book.

however, nothing in the nature of an accident, nor was there at any time any danger.'

The Journal also reported at length on the Gala events promised in the Gala Opening poster (**Fig 13**):

'The proceedings really commenced with a perambulation round the town to see the decorations [and concluded in the evening with a torchlight procession through Southwold, accompanied by two bands, and including a visit to the Station Yard]

for end of interpolated description … where three cheers were given for the Directors and Promoters of the Southwold Railway … The weather [now] … was all that could be wished and the memorable day was brought to a happy close by public appreciation and applause. The floods subsided so that the regular train service commenced on Thursday.'

So Southwold was no longer isolated. The Railway was open and operating, for the next 50 years.

CHAPTER 4

HISTORY OF THE RAILWAY UP TO THE FIRST WORLD WAR – 1880 TO 1914

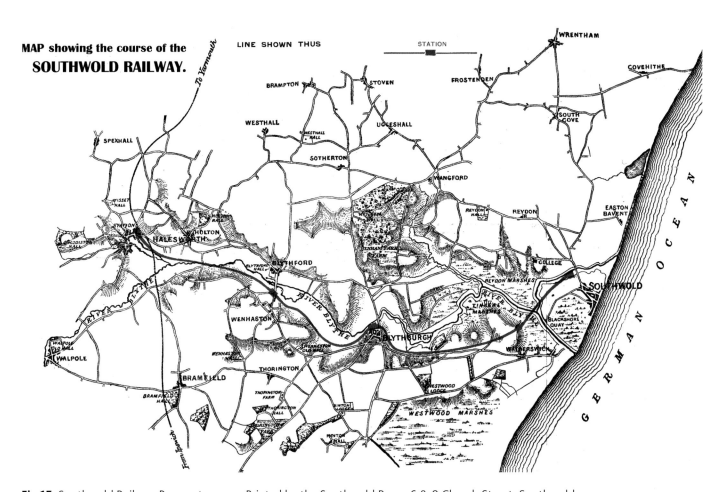

Fig 15: Southwold Railway Prospectus map. Printed by the Southwold Press, 6 & 8 Church Street, Southwold.

Unlike many light and narrow-gauge systems, the Southwold did not suffer overburdening financial difficulties and was never under Receivership during its working life, but the Company never had any large capital resources so expenditure had to be watched. The cost of the line, originally estimated at £30,000, proved to be nearly £90,000, partly due to the wider gauge (3ft 0in instead of 2ft 6in); partly because the River Blyth had been made a navigable water way so a swing bridge was required to sustain access for keels and wherries (**Fig 16**); and the rest to over-optimism in the original estimate.

Under the 1876 Act, the authorised capital was £40,000 in £10 shares and £13,000 in debentures. Authority for extra capital was sought from the BoT in 1880 which put the railway in a slightly better position, but it was still largely a hand-to-mouth existence. For instance, two thirds of the price of the locomotives had been paid in the form of debentures but from 1883, the locos and rolling

Fig 16: Pencil sketch of keels on the Blyth. H. Davy c 1824.

stock were hired from the makers. In 1888, therefore, the Southwold Railway (Additional Capital) Certificate was obtained in order to raise £12,000 in 4% Preference stock to pay off arrears of debentures interest and to pay for the locos and rolling stock, which was achieved by 1890.

When the Southwold Railway was incorporated by Parliamentary Act of 1876, the Act made reference to provisions in several previous railway Acts by which the Southwold must abide. Unfortunately, reference was not made to the Regulation of Railways Act 1868, which would have authorised the line to have Light Railway status and a speed limit of 25mph. Engineer Pain had advocated previous lines with which he was associated to be constructed as Light Railways for economic reasons, but for some reason this status was not sought for the Southwold Railway in their Act. In consequence, even though the BoT Licence refers to the 'Southwold Railway As A Light Railway …' the BoT could not agree to the Southwold being licensed as a Light Railway. When the BoT Licence was issued dated, 11 March 1880, it specified a 16mph speed limit (**Fig 18**).

Initially the speed limit did not seem to be a problem but as motor road transport began to develop it was.

Motor lorries could collect and deliver goods to a customer's door and motor buses from Halesworth, or Lowestoft, terminated at the Market Place in the centre of Southwold, saving a half-mile slightly uphill walk. The history of the railway over the period of this chapter is the chronicle of a leisurely but initially – within the requirements of the time and place – efficient transport service between Southwold and the outside railway world. The Company relied on the passenger traffic for a substantial proportion of its revenue, but the conveyance of goods provided, as usual, a useful source of income (**Fig 17**). Fish from Southwold, milk and other agricultural products from Blythburgh and Wenhaston stations and miscellaneous parcels formed the bulk of the received goods traffic. Coal and general goods and parcels were carried to Southwold but the manual transhipment at Halesworth was always a deterrent.

The 1890s showed a steady overall rise in all classes of traffic; by 1900, the railway carried over 100,000 passengers, over 9,000 tons of minerals and over 6,000 tons of goods of which a substantial portion was directly attributable to Southwold's development and rising popularity as a watering place. The Directors'

Fig: 16	1880	1890	1900	1910	1913
Passengers	65,749	78,655	103,539	104,197	108,677
Parcels	9,354	21,952	32,603	38,506	41,462
Goods (tons)	1,960	2,907	6,608	6,566	7,334
Fuel (tons)	3,502	5,712	9,313	6,258	6,474

Fig 17: Table illustrating tonnages of goods traffic on the Southwold Railway, 1880 to 1913.

reports for the closing years of the nineteenth century show a generally satisfactory state of affairs in spite of sometimes rather heavy maintenance expenses, especially caused by floods, and the net receipts had risen almost steadily from £100 in 1880 to £1,872 in 1900. It is not surprising, therefore, to learn that possibilities of expansion were entertained and passing of the Light Railways Act in 1896, which was designed to enable lines to be constructed and worked with modified conditions resulting in much reduced costs than hitherto, gave the impetus to local enterprise in this field.

There were two schemes, both put forward by the Southwold Railway Company. The first was a proposal to build a 12 mile standard gauge line from Southwold to Lowestoft at a cost of £74,734 13s, which was submitted to the Light Railway Commissioners in May 1899. It was withdrawn because of opposition by Southwold Corporation and the GER, before reaching even the stage of a Local Enquiry. With our benefit of hindsight, it is difficult to see how a standard gauge branch from Lowestoft to Southwold Station could work efficiently if the Southwold Railway remained 3ft gauge.

CONDITIONS AND REGULATIONS

MADE BY

The Board of Trade and referred to in the License issued by them, and dated the 11th day of March, 1880, for the maintenance and working of the

SOUTHWOLD RAILWAY

As a light Railway 8 miles 63.5 chains in length.

1. As regards the permanent way, the description and dimensions of the sleepers, the nature, description, and weight of the rails, chairs, and fastenings, used in its construction and maintenance, shall be such as were approved of by the Board of Trade on the 17th of April, 1878, namely :—wrought iron flat-bottomed rails, weighing 30 lbs. to the yard, 21 feet long, and fished at the joints, the rails resting on rectangular sleepers measuring 6 feet long by 3 inches deep, and 6 inches broad, laid at central intervals of 2 feet 4 inches, a sleeper being laid under each joint of the rails, the rail secured at the joints, and at two intermediate sleepers in the length of the rails by a clip fastened by two fang bolts, the remainder of the fastenings being dog spikes.

2. In working the Railway, only one Engine in steam or two or more Engines coupled together, shall be upon the single line at one and the same time, and this mode of working shall be combined with the train staff. The opening bridge over the River Blyth, when in position, to be locked by means of Annett's Key attached to the train staff, which the engine working the traffic must always carry.

3. The speed of the trains running upon the Railway shall not exceed 16 miles an hour.

4. The greatest weight on the wheel of any engine or vehicle used on the Railway shall not exceed two tons.

5. These Conditions and Regulations may be varied or amended by the Board of Trade from time to time.

Signed by order of the Board of Trade this 11th day of March, 1880.

C. CECIL TREVOR,

An Assistant Secretary of the said Board.

Fig 18: BoT Licence for the maintenance and working of the Southwold Railway 'as a light railway' with a speed limit of 16MPH but less than the 25MPH speed limit permitted on Light Railways defined in the Regulation of Railways Act 1868.

There would need to be transhipment at Southwold and at Halesworth and no possibility for through working of GER stock from Lowestoft to Halesworth via Southwold.

The Southwold to Lowestoft Railway proposal was replaced by an amended scheme in May 1900 for a standard gauge extension to Kessingland (**Fig 19**). This modified application was a direct result of the realisation that both the proposed new railway and the existing narrow gauge railway must be all to the same standard gauge. The Light Railway Order was referred to by the title *Southwold Light Railway Order 1902* and provided for the building of a nine-mile standard gauge line between Southwold and Kessingland at an estimated cost of £48,583 and the re-laying of the existing Southwold Railway to standard gauge at a cost of £35,666. By stopping short at Kessingland (four miles south of Lowestoft), the Southwold Railway Company obviated opposition by the GER, who were themselves contemplating a branch from Lowestoft to Kessingland. A local enquiry held in Southwold on 18 December

1900 enabled the Light Railway Commissioners to approve the application and an Order was submitted to the Board of Trade on 23 July 1901 and approved by them in 1902, the work to be completed by April 1907.

So far, so good; the SR then set about raising the money. Rightly, they considered that the widening of their existing line to standard gauge should have priority so holders of 5% debentures were asked to surrender these and accept the equivalent of 4% debenture and ordinary shares. The majority of the holders – albeit tardily – agreed to this and the task of widening went slowly ahead, commencing with the swing bridge. The new bridge proved, however, to be practically a white elephant. It was last turned for navigational purposes in 1914 and thereafter once yearly only to test the mechanism.

A number of minor bridges were also widened, including three in 1906/7 – No 1 over Holton Road (B1123), No 4 the Mells Road over-bridge near Corner Farm and No 11 Yarmouth Turnpike (A12) over-bridge

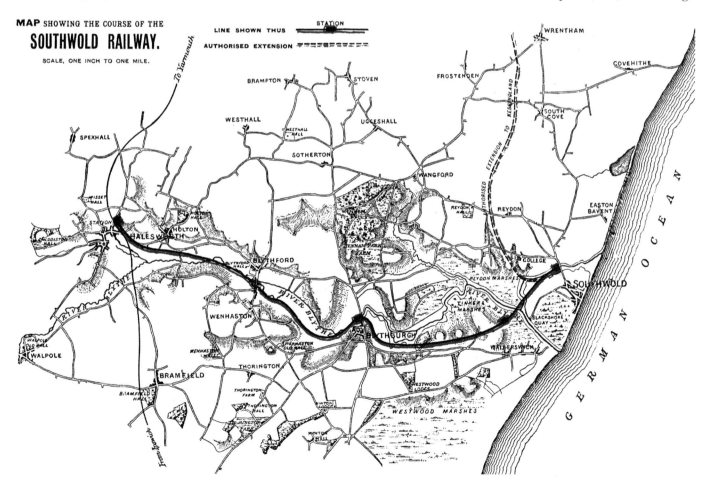

Fig 19: A standard gauge extension from Southwold to Kessingland proposed by the Southwold Railway Company.

at Blythburgh station. By then, the time allowed for completing the work under the Order had almost expired and a fresh Order was obtained. *The Southwold Light Railway (Borrowing Powers Extension) Order 1907* confirmed by the BoT on 27 September 1907 – extending the time limit to April 1909 'or as the BoT approve' and authorising the Company to raise a further £10,000 by borrowing. No 2 bridge by Halesworth Ballast Pit was widened in 1908 – a concrete underline bridge over an accommodation road.

In the following year a well was sunk at the Bird's Folly Ballast Pit Engine Shed near Halesworth. It was fitted with a chain pump, so that locomotives could take water there instead of at the Water Mill during widening and ballast operations, which were prosecuted in desultory fashion for another 18 months. Ditches on the Up side were filled and new fences erected, from Halesworth to Wenhaston Mill, and on Southwold Common; and that was all.

There was no progress on the extension to Kessingland, even on paper. It was clear that the raising of the capital required for this entirely new venture would be a hard job, though the presence of brickworks at Frostenden (**Fig 19**) on the proposed route promised some useful basic traffic. The promoters therefore approached the Gooch Trustees (the principal landowners) in the summer of 1901, to see if they would be prepared to finance the line, to be worked by the SR. It was suggested that when Sir Thomas Gooch came of age, he would be invited to become a Director. But, in a letter to the SR dated 30 September 1903, the Baronet declined, though promised to let the Company have the land on favourable terms.

So vanished the Southwold Railway's hopes of extension, for it would have been useless without conversion of the existing line to standard gauge which the Company found itself unable to carry out, though they had set considerable store by this task. At a Board Meeting on 27 August 1903, when Arthur Pain was elected Chairman, the future of the railway was discussed. Even this early, it was realised that the railway was antiquated, the narrow gauge offered substandard comfort to passengers and delayed freight by transhipment. But new money was not forthcoming; to the casual observer, the railway can hardly have appeared an attractive investment and the SR at no time received much encouragement or help from wealthy landowners, Southwold Corporation, businesses in the town or from the GER. An indication of the economic realities the Railway had to face was that Southwold Gas Works, near enough to the Railway to permit a short branch, found it cheaper to bring in coal by sea and to use horse cartage from the Harbour to the Works.

At this period too, began the long-drawn-out wrangle over the proposed Harbour Branch with the Southwold Harbour Company (see in Chapter 7). The SR were naturally unwilling to see a 3ft gauge branch laid when there was still a hope of gauge conversion and, as a last resort, in 1910 they appealed to the GER with the suggestion that the latter provide standard gauge permanent way (including a Harbour Branch) and rolling stock on loan secured by 5% debentures. The GER refused, as an offer by them to purchase the SR in 1893 had been turned down by the Southwold Company as not sufficiently attractive.

Nevertheless, the opening years of the twentieth century might be termed the heyday of this railway. **Fig 20** shows Southwold station crowded with long-skirted and high-bonneted young ladies, together with young men in straw hats. The station yard was filled with horse buses for the Swan, Crown, Grand, Centre Cliff and other hotels, private carriages and up to three carriers' carts. Passenger traffic continued to improve up to the outbreak of the First World War but by then goods traffic showed a tendency to diminish. The net receipts were at the £2,000 mark, and for the years 1911-13 the Company paid a 2% dividend on ordinary shares for the first time.

It must be remembered too, that operating difficulties were not unknown; in particular, the Railway was constantly liable to flooding from the swollen river Blyth and the railway banks by the river had been washed away several times by 1897. In readiness for such an emergency, it was the practice to keep one locomotive and rolling stock at Halesworth in the winter to maintain a service. If a through run to Southwold was impracticable, passengers were brought across the river by rowing boat. Severe NE gales took their toll in winter also, in 1881 blowing off part of the engine shed roof. There were no serious accidents, apart from the death of the lad in charge at Walberswick who was killed on 14 November 1883 when trying to board a train in motion.

There were several changes in management: at the beginning of 1879, R.C. Rapier was Chairman:

Fig 20: Southwold was a popular holiday resort in the early 1900s.

T.H. Jellicoe Secretary; and Arthur Pain Engineer. The last-named was undoubtedly the guiding power and his promotion was rapid; he became Manager on 30 August 1879, just before the railway was opened for traffic and combined this with the office of Secretary from 30 August 1880 on the resignation of Jellicoe. On 3 September 1884, Pain was elected to the Board as Managing Director, from which time H. Carne was appointed Secretary, but died in 1900 and was replaced by H. Ward (of the GNR but formerly a Southwold Railway employee). Ward became Manager and Secretary from 22 March 1910 and remained so throughout the rest of the railway's lifetime.

Rapier retained the Chairmanship until his death in 1897, when he was succeeded by Charles Chambers, who had been an enthusiastic supporter of the line during its promotion and was elected to the Board in 1889. On Chambers death in 1903, Pain became Chairman,

a position he retained until the end as well as the post of Engineer which he finally relinquished on 27 August 1903, when his son Claude was appointed to the post.

By the outbreak of the First World War, the Southwold Railway was very much as it was on opening and was already an anachronism. The Company had tried to modernise and extend but failed so had decided to make do with what they had, which was successful enough in its limited way. A branch to the Harbour was being constructed but some Directors were uneasy about this development. (see Chapter 7).

An unusual incident for the SR took place in the early summer of 1912. A small circus paid a two-day visit to Southwold Common; a young lion arrived by rail in a cage and was duly loaded on Walter Doy's lorry with instructions for the collection of £8.00 carriage charges. When the circus failed to pay, the lion was returned to the station and placed in the waiting room. Aldis,

THE SOUTHWOLD 'EXPRESS'   A SLIGHT ENGINE TROUBLE CAUSES A DELAY – BUT IS SOON REMEDIED.

Fig 21 (top): Reg Carter (Southwold artist) keeps up-to-date on English affairs so subsequently . . .

Fig 21 (bottom): . . . has to air-brushe out 'Votes for Women,' the suffragette, and the branch on which she was sitting!

THE SOUTHWOLD 'EXPRESS'   A SLIGHT ENGINE TROUBLE CAUSES A DELAY – BUT IS SOON REMEDIED.

a porter (usually known as Old Fogey) was put in charge and sent to the butcher for a shillings-worth of cheap meat, which he fixed to the end of a long pole and gingerly pushed through the bars of the cage. The waiting room served as a booking office so a short time before the departure of each train, a tarpaulin was placed over the cage to screen it from passengers. At other times, the waiting room was locked but Stedman, the Goods Department clerk, had access to the key and was able to put on a private show for his pals when the rest of the staff were at lunch. The circus had a good first night and was able to pay the combined carriage and feeding charges, so the lion was collected but for some time afterwards, Aldis was somewhat disgruntled; he felt he was entitled to danger money.

In 1914, the local artist Reg Carter published a series of postcard-sized cartoons about the Railway under the heading 'Sorrows of Southwold' which were very popular. A second series appeared in 1921 and reproductions are still available today. A notable card showed a suffragette sitting in a tree and throwing bombs at the train with the slogan 'Votes for Women' (**Fig 21 top**).

After the war women won a partial suffrage so the woman, the bomb and the slogan were deleted from the scene, leaving an awkwardly shaped tree. Post card collectors treasure the original version which is quite rare (**Fig 21 bottom**).

CHAPTER 5

PROPOSALS FOR TAKING OVER THE SOUTHWOLD RAILWAY COMPANY

In the absence of the Southwold Railway Company's Minutes, there is little information about how the Southwold responded to, or perhaps resisted, at least five of the proposals known to have been made to take over the Southwold Railway. Nevertheless, proposals were made and they are relevant to this book because they give an indication of the context for Southwold, and particularly the supposed potential of Southwold Harbour, with entrepreneurs exploring new ventures in Suffolk and beyond. It seems, however, that most proposals envisaged a take-over of the Southwold Railway rather than a partnership with the Southwold Company.

A Railway from Cambridge to Southwold, 1893

'**Proposed Route:** It is proposed to construct a line traversing in a direct manner to the Centre of the County of Suffolk thus supplying a demand which has become almost imperative and opening up a district which contains much of the most fertile land in Suffolk. The line would start from Cambridge – at which place centre the London and North Western, Midland, Great Northern and Great Eastern Railways – and would proceed either by means of running powers over the present Great Eastern Line or by a new line traversing a somewhat similar route to Bury St. Edmunds. From which place a line would be constructed across a new country to Mellis, the junction of the Great Eastern and the Mellis and Eye Railway. Running powers would be applied for over the latter line to the Town of Eye and from thence a new line would be constructed through an entirely unserved and highly productive neighbourhood to Halesworth where the Great Eastern main line and the Southwold Railway connect. The latter Company

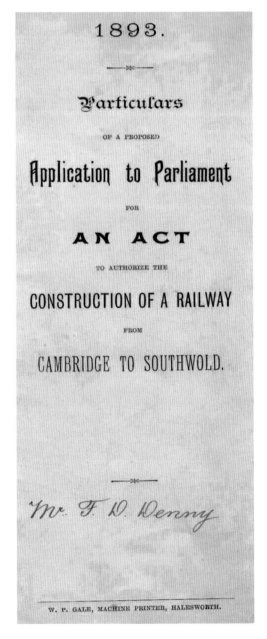

Fig 22: 'Particulars of a proposed Application to Parliament for an Act to authorize the construction of a Railway from Cambridge to Southwold'.

[is] not in a very flourishing condition and it is believed that the undertaking might be acquired on favourable terms, the line reconstructed and the railway from Cambridge carried through to the sea coast at Southwold which is rapidly extending and bids fair to become a very popular seaside resort.'

This Proposal estimates that the route outlined above will serve a number of Suffolk towns and villages '… none of which are at present within reasonable distance of any railway station'. The aggregate population so served would be between 7,000 and 8,000. It would be interesting to know what, in 1893, constituted a 'reasonable distance' because Southwold Station was downhill from the heart of the town and nearly a mile from the seaside in what the promoters envisaged would be a very popular seaside resort.

Passengers to Southwold on the proposed railway would be one source of income, but the best-earning business for most railways is goods traffic and it was the benefits from an enhanced Southwold Harbour which this proposal addresses:

'**Southwold Harbour:** Some years ago there was a small but efficient harbour at Southwold with a considerable coasting trade and although it has now much fallen into disuse and the works into decay, there is no doubt that with a comparatively moderate expenditure a harbour as good as that at Lowestoft could be constructed and maintained at Southwold. And the offing being clear of sand banks, and having a good depth of water, and there being unlimited low-lying land available for docks, it is probable that a harbour there would be extensively used especially with the advantage of a direct railway route to the Midlands. The Harbour is in the hands of the Corporation of Southwold who, it is believed, are prepared to hand it over to any Company who will undertake to open and maintain the harbour. The Corporation have granted to the Committee promoting this scheme a 3-years option of purchase of about three-quarters-of-a-mile of the north bank of the river extending from the harbour's mouth to the present Quay at Blackshore, reserving only a roadway for the use of the public, at a price to be fixed at the present value of the land, which is very small.

'This Committee will transfer this option to the Company to be formed by the Act of Parliament and it cannot fail to be seen what an immense advantage is thus secured to the Scheme. The north bank would become invaluable to any Company developing the harbour for the construction of wharves, warehouses and [railway] sidings.'

Support for this scheme, the Application explained, had already been approved by major local landowners – Lord Henniker, Lord Huntingfield, Sir Ralph Blois – a number of other wealthy men, and the Mayors of Eye and Southwold. Perhaps many of these potential supporters were attracted by the promoters' suggestion that this should be a 'Landowners Line' and that the cost of the Application to Parliament should be subscribed by those '… along the route affected'. The sum required, the Proposal assured readers '… will not exceed £5,000' but sufficient support was not forthcoming and this proposal never reached parliament. It is, however, a proposal that contributes to our knowledge of Southwold, and Suffolk, in the late nineteenth century and emphasises the potential of Cambridge as a rail entrepôt. (See *Cambridge Station – its development and operation as a rail centre*. Rob Shorland-Ball. P&S Transport. 2017.)

Takeover approaches by the Great Eastern Railway (GER):

The Great Eastern Railway Company was incorporated by the Great Eastern Railway Act of 7 August 1862. The purpose of the Act was: 'To amalgamate the Eastern Counties, the East Anglian, the Newmarket & Chesterford, the Eastern Union and the Norfolk Railway Companies, and for other purposes'.

The Eastern Counties Railway had previously leased and absorbed the constituent companies which morphed into the GER in 1862 but the ECR was never financially stable and lacked holistic management. The GER Act was an expression of Parliamentary good sense in bringing together in one company a diverse miscellany of management and operational practices.

By the late 1870s, GER Board Minutes indicate that the Company was taking an interest in the Southwold Railway – for instance by assisting in an extension to the main line footbridge towards the Southwold platform and a rearrangement of GER sidings to facilitate transhipment to and from standard to narrow gauge goods vehicles (**Fig 23**). The GER derived £11,000 per year from traffic exchanged with the Southwold Railway.

Negotiations on a possible takeover are recorded in the GER Board Traffic Committee Minutes. At a meeting on 1 August 1893, it was noted that Richard Rapier, Chairman of the SR Board, had approached the GER General Manager in November 1892 suggesting that the GER should purchase the Southwold Company or assist that Company by giving a rebate on rates for conveyance of their traffic. The General Manager responded that he was unable to 'see his way into the matter', suggesting that a submission be made in the summer of 1893. Rapier's submission was discussed by the GER Traffic Committee on 15 May 1894 and the response was a 5% discount on rates and an option to purchase the Southwold line within 21 years. The GER directors were aware of the proposed Cambridge to Southwold Railway and the prospect of another railway company obtaining access to Southwold Harbour alarmed them so a Southwold take-over by the GER

seemed wise. Rapier felt that a 21 year option was too long and suggested 10 years and a 5% discount on traffic rates. The GER proposed that this revised offer should be subject to a survey, report and valuation by the GER Engineer and Locomotive Superintendent.

The GER Valuation was based on a survey in 1892 and was subsequently updated in pencil in 1894. The First Cost Estimate is a fascinating summary of the civil engineering which had been necessary to create the Southwold Railway (**Fig 24**).

Research has not revealed any further meetings or discussions between the GER and the Southwold Company between 1894 and 1900. At a GER Board meeting on 30 October 1900, the proposed purchase of the Southwold Railway was discussed at a total valuation, including all rolling stock, of £60,000. By 1900, the Southwold was in a very run-down condition so the offer was a surprisingly generous one but it may have reflected the GER interest in acquring a right-of-way to Southwold and the Harbour. We know from the GER Minutes that the GER General Manager requested

Fig 23: Halesworth GER Station and the transhipment facilities from standard gauge to narrow gauge for the Southwold Railway in the 1880s. The GER was using heavy horses for shunting which was helpful but slow when one of the problems between the two companies was emptying and releasing the standard gauge wagons.

| | THE FIRST COST OF THE WORKS [ESTIMATED] AS FOLLOWS | | |
| | as per details: | | (Fig 24) |
Numerals	Category	Works	£ s d
2,756	Linear yards	One rail fencing	137 16 0
4,537	Linear yards	Two rail fencing	283 11 4
19,611	Linear yards	Four rail fencing	1,715 19 3
2,364	Linear yards	Quickset hedge	33 8 0
2	Number of –	Wickets in Station yards	5 0 0
70,000	Cubic yards	Excavation to form banks	4,083 17 2
4,847	Square yards	Road making in Station yards and approaches	363 10 6
130	Square yards	Gravel to footpath	3 5 0
11	Number of –	Underline bridges	2,767 0 0
2	Number of –	Overline bridges	644 0 0
—		Culverts – bricks or concrete	nil
—		Pipe culverts	54 5 0
51	Number of –	Occupation Crossings, complete	510 0 0
1	Number of –	Level Crossing over public road (Wenhaston)	20 0 0
14	Number of –	Lamp post	14 0 0
—	—	Telegraph	nil
—	—	Station and other buildings at Halesworth	982 18 2
—	—	Station and other buildings at Wenhaston	186 3 10
—	—	Station and other buildings at Blythburgh	187 11 6
—	—	Station and other buildings at Walberswick	122 0 11
—	—	Station and other buildings at Southwold	639 10 6
8¾	Miles	Permanent way and ballast complete (Running Road)	7,178 15 0
1,416	Linear yards	Permanent way and ballast complete (Sidings)	660 16 0
21	Number of –	Points and Crossings	147 0 0
10	Number of –	Buffer Stops and Scotches	10 0 0
—	—	Signals	90 0 0
—	—	Exchange Footbridge at Halesworth – proportion paid by Southwold Company	242 0 0
42	Acres	Land at, say, £100 per acre	4,200 0 0
Total estimated first cost of works and land			**£25,288 8 2**
Plus 3 locomotives, 6 carriages and 17 Wagons @ **£2,033 0 0**			**£27,321 8 2**

Fig 24: The GER's First Cost Estimate of the civil engineering which had been necessary to create the Southwold Railway.

his Engineer and Locomotive Superintendent to inspect the Southwold again and ascertain the cost of rebuilding the line to standard gauge with sufficient land purchase to allow for double track at some time in the future. The Engineer was also ordered to ascertain the cost of building a new standard gauge line from Southwold to Saxmundham or to Leiston.

The Minutes for the GER Board meeting of 7 November 1900 indicated that Southwold Railway Engineer Pain had virtually accepted £60,000 for the line when he stated that '... his Board ... would be willing to sell the line at a fair and reasonable price to be agreed upon or, in the event of disagreement, to be settled by an arbitrator'.

The GER Engineer & Locomotive Superintendent duly reported to his Board that rebuilding the Southwold Railway as a single standard gauge line would be £98,887 plus £60,000 for purchase totalling £158,887. A new standard gauge line, but not to 'Express line' standard, from Southwold to Saxmundham would cost £145,445.

'Proposed Saxmundham to Southwold GER line: the proposed route would have "served" even more sparsely populated territory than the Southwold Railway hinterland along the Blyth valley. The route started about 57 chains north of Saxmundham Junction Signal Box which controlled the Leiston and Aldeburgh branch. Proposed stations were Westleton, Dunwich and Walberswick and then one of two possible sites on the outskirts of Southwold; a total length of just over 10 miles. Since the route would be across the lie of the land there would have been extensive cutting and filling and most gradients would be at 1 in 100.'

Despite the apparent saving in the Southwold to Saxmundham project, the Engineer did not recommend this outlay probably because the GER was already committed to considerable civil engineering works in the London District and at several other stations. After consideration by the GER Board '... it was resolved that no steps be taken at present'.

When their limited capital funds permitted, the Southwold Railway continued with gauge-widening works until 1910 then a further approach was made to the GER Board. The SR Board suggested the GER should provide standard gauge track, including for the Harbour Branch, and rolling stock on loan all secured by an issue of 5% debentures. Debenture share issues would have been backed only by the general creditworthiness and reputation of the issuer and were often used to secure capital for the issuer.

Not surprisingly, the GER Board refused this suggestion, not least because their earlier and relatively generous offer to purchase the SR had been refused. The GER General Manager had visited and inspected the Southwold Railway with Engineer Pain, including the Harbour which did not impress him. He did not believe Southwold Harbour could rival Lowestoft or Great Yarmouth – both of which had GER rail connections – without considerable expenditure. The GER General Manager presented a Report, dated 3 January 1911, to the GER Board meeting on 6 January which recommended that '... under the circumstances [no action] be taken in the matter'. The GER Board then resolved that: '... the General Manager's recommendation be approved'.

The Mid-Suffolk Light Railway from Haughley Junction to Halesworth and thence to Southwold:

The **Fig 25** map shows the ambitions of the Mid-Suffolk Light Railway Company (MSLR). The principal route was a meandering line purporting to serve a rich agricultural area with a number of stations for the villages north and south of the railway. A spur from the main line was south from Kenton to Debenham and Ipswich. This Prospectus map looked convincing, crossing a large area in Suffolk which had no railways and seeming to serve more than 50 named settlements. The fact that many were small villages, quite distant from the proposed railway, and with little business to generate income was the sort of *caveat emptor* that potential shareholders needed to investigate before investing. The 1896 Light Railways Act was a useful stimulus to the MSLR promoters because, in return for a 25mph speed limit, their railway needed less demanding operating standards and it could be approved by the President of the Board of Trade – advised by the Light Railway Commissioners – so avoiding the expensive and time-consuming procedure of an Act of Parliament. On 5 April 1900, the BoT granted a Light Railway Order and the MSLR began to raise capital to build and operate their railway.

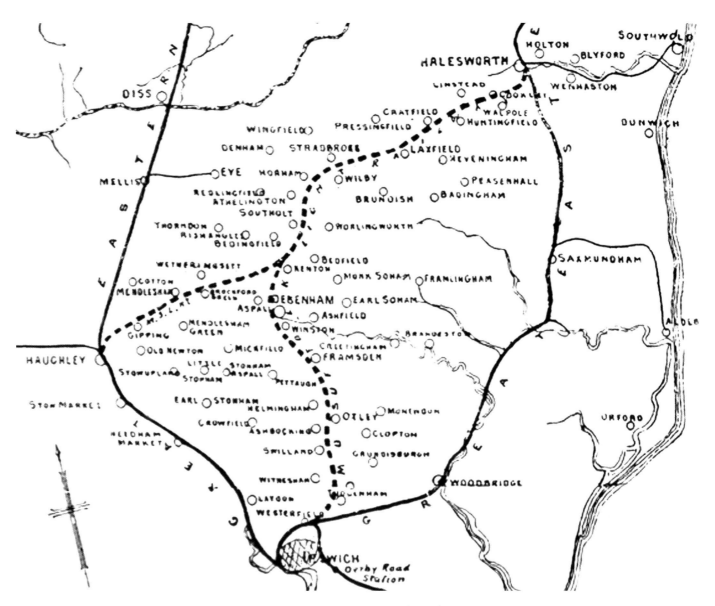

Fig 25: Map shows the ambitions of the Mid-Suffolk Light Railway Company (MSLR). It is an edited extract from a 1901 MAP SHEWING [sic] ROUTE which was issued with an MSLR Company Prospectus.

The 1901 Prospectus wrote of the Haughley-Halesworth line as '… giving a direct route from Cambridge and the Midlands to the numerous popular seaside resorts of the East Coast'. Construction started from Haughley Junction and slowly progressed north eastward, but it became apparent from surveys and inspection on the ground that the original route through Halesworth and to a junction with the GER was not practicable. A deviation of the LRO – an expensive and time-consuming process – was necessary and provisions for compulsory purchase of land had to be made. Meanwhile, the line was opened to goods traffic from Haughley Junction to Laxfield in 1904, but public

passenger traffic was forbidden although the AGM on 24 September 1905 was advised that the Company had an optimistic future. In truth, the lack of capital and the relatively small revenue from goods traffic did not bode well for the extension to Halesworth or for an extension to Southwold.

A public enquiry into the Halesworth Deviation and the proposed connection with the Southwold Railway was held in the Corn Exchange, Halesworth, on Tuesday 26 February 1907 with Engineer Pain representing the SR and E.R. Cooper the Southwold Harbour Company. It was acknowledged that the SR had powers within their Act to change their gauge from 3ft to standard gauge which would greatly benefit the MSLR, SR, and Southwold Harbour's anticipated fish trade. The GER, however, saw this development as harmful to their business because no longer would the MSLR and SR be feeders to the GER but would create dangerous competition. After the hearing the Light Railway Commissioners announced that, in their opinion, there was insuffcient evidence of commercial justification for the deviation so could not consent to the proposed alterations.

The MSLR finally opened to passenger traffic on Tuesday 29 September 1908 but only, as the timetable advised, 'The section of the [Railway] between Haughley and Laxfield'. The MSLR Board made application to the Light Railway Commissioners in May 1909 for a revival of the powers authorised in their earlier Orders of 1900 and 1905 and on 4 December 1909 *The Mid-Suffolk Light Railway (Amendment) Order 1909* was authorised including a 3 year extension of time for construction towards Halesworth and Southwold. Alas, in August 1912 the MSLR Board finally accepted that their grandiose plans could not be achieved, that receipts from goods and passenger traffic were diminishing and that their railway was still in the hands of the Official Receiver. Halesworth, let alone Southwold Harbour, were no longer realistic ambitions – if, indeed, they really ever were.

The Southwold Railway was also experiencing financial difficulties so the dream of a through railway from Cambridge to Southwold via the MSLR, with which this chapter began, remains a dream.

Fig 26: The MSLR was a standard gauge 'country railway' still operating in the 1950s and very like the Southwold Railway was 30 years earlier. At a level crossing the fireman has opened the gates; he then returns to the footplate and the guard, at the back of the train, closes them.

CHAPTER 6

A VIRTUAL JOURNEY FROM HALESWORTH TO SOUTHWOLD

Another **Preambulation by Rob Shorland-Ball** is a preliminary statement about the intentions of this chapter so another 'walk in front.' I have, since the 1950s, explored on foot the whole length of the SR trackbed from Halesworth, via Blythburgh, to Southwold on a number of occasions.

This chapter is a virtual journey along the SR from Halesworth down to Southwold – and here 'down' is the railway term for direction of travel. 'Up' trains took the running [single] line towards London as far as Halesworth where change of gauge meant a change of train for passengers and goods. The SR as described in this chapter is from 1879 to its closure as an operating company in 1929.

The Railway remained in dereliction until dismantled in early 1941. Most of the track bed still remains so Chapters 17 and 18 take the story forward to the present day.

Halesworth

The first station, to the north of the present station, was opened in Halesworth in 1854 by the Haddiscoe, Beccles and Halesworth Railway. This line, subsumed by the East Suffolk Railway, was extended south to Woodbridge and there, at an end-on junction, met the Eastern Counties Railway from Ipswich. In 1859, the present Halesworth Station was opened by what, through subsequent amalgamations, became the Great Eastern Railway [GER].

This was the nearest standard gauge railway to Southwold, 8.5 miles east of Halesworth and, although there was some local interest in building a branch line to link the two towns, there was concern, too, that the Blyth Navigation's traffic from Halesworth to Southwold Harbour would be threatened by a railway. However, the promoters of the railway were enthusiastic and very determined so succeeded with a 3ft gauge feeder line. Southwold Railway [SR] Station was squeezed into a rather cramped site adjoining the main line Station up platform. Because of the change-of-gauge no inter-connection was possible and a transhipment platform adjoining a small goods shed was built. Passengers could reach the SR by a footbridge, extended from the existing GER footbridge and paid for by that railway **(Figs 27 and 30).**

On the Southwold platform was a flat-roofed wooden building that included a small office for the SR Station Master and a covered waiting area with bench seats. The office, 10ft long and 6ft wide, with a door at the north end contained a heating stove and a desk for the Station Master's clerical work. He did not issue tickets which was undertaken by the GER Booking Office on their down platform on an agency basis. The 239ft long Southwold Railway platform was lit by gas lights and served by one line on the eastern side. The other side was fenced off from the loco run-round loop.

HALESWORTH STATION (1884)

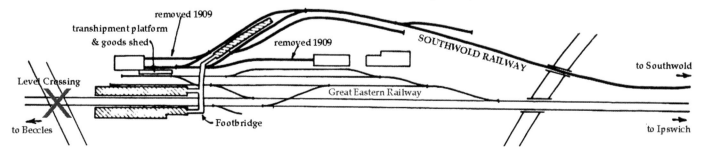

Fig 27: Layout at Halesworth Station, GER and SR, 1884.

Fig 28: A mixed up train arriving at SR's Halesworth Station c1920.

A mixed up train arriving at Halesworth in **Fig 28** shows the Southwold platform, the busy standard gauge goods sidings in the background and the steeply rising ground on the left (the east side) which accounts for the cramped SR Station site.

A barrow crossing formed from old sleepers and under the footbridge facilitated passenger-rated traffic and luggage between the SR and GER but any heavier goods and parcels traffic went via the Goods Shed and the transhipment platform. This platform was constructed so that the floors of standard gauge and narrow gauge wagons were level on either side and everything was open to the elements. It was never an easy station to work so some changes to try and improve operation are shown in the final layout (**Fig 29**):

HALESWORTH STATION (Final layout)

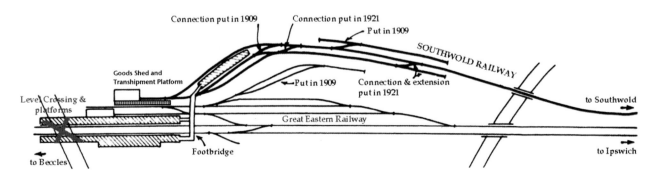

Fig 29: Final layout at Halesworth Station, GER and SR, 1922.

Road access for goods traffic to the SR Station was between the two bridges over the Holton road but all passenger access was via the GER Station.

The principal sources of complaint between the SR and GER and, after 1922, the SR and LNER were the delays caused by goods transhipment, particularly coal which was needed in Southwold. The coal had to be shovelled from standard gauge to narrow gauge wagons which was slow and hard work for the SR's one transhipment porter. Various small changes to track layout were made over the years but the transhipment problem remained; the Southwold Railway should have been made a standard gauge branch allowing through working of goods and passenger stock from Halesworth to Southwold. **Fig 30**, looking north under the Station footbridge, illustrates the cramped site of the transhipment facilities.

Passengers could tranship themselves so were less of a problem, but after the Southwold Railway opened in 1879, the GER enjoyed a continuous growth of passenger traffic for Southwold which overloaded the relatively short platforms at the north end of their standard gauge station. **Fig 31** illustrates the lengthened platforms which were created in 1886 by the GER Chief Engineer; he designed and patented two level crossing gates to which a length of platform was attached. Each gate and platform, mounted on roller-wheels, was manually closed to road traffic – providing a lengthened platform. The original construction was by Ransome & Rapier, Ipswich, replaced for the LNER in 1922 by like-for-like gates by Boulton & Paul, Norwich. They remain today but no longer in use for level crossing gates after a road by-pass was built in the 1950s.

The Southwold Railway line left Halesworth on a falling gradient of 1 in 66 and parallel to the GER lines before an easterly curve shown on the OS 1904 map extract in **Fig 32**.

The SR's first bridge is across the Holton road and almost parallel to the main line bridge. A revealing picture (**Fig 33**) is that of the bridge being dismantled in the 1960s. It shows the substantial abutments, which remain in part today, and the main line bridge in the background behind and above the crane.

The OS map extract (**Fig 32**) shows both bridges and the Southwold Railway curving away to the east past an old gravel pit called Bird's Folly. In 1904, in order to meet a continuing need for ballast, the SR Company purchased the site and laid in a ballast siding, facing towards Southwold, inspected and approved by General Hutchinson for the BoT in February 1907.

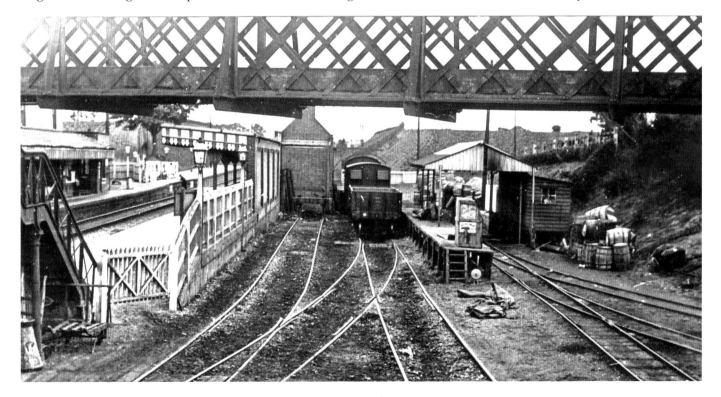

Fig 30: The SR transhipment platform and goods shed on the right and the GER Halesworth Station platforms on the left.

Fig 31: Halesworth Station level crossing gates which also include a platform section, on wheels, to provide a lengthened platform for the greater number of passengers travelling to and from Southwold.

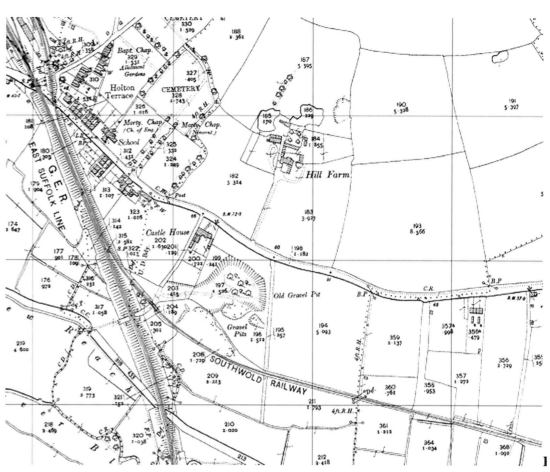

Fig 32: 1 – 2,500 OS map extract 1904.

Fig 33: Dismantling SR Bridge No 1 over Holton road, Halesworth, in 1962.

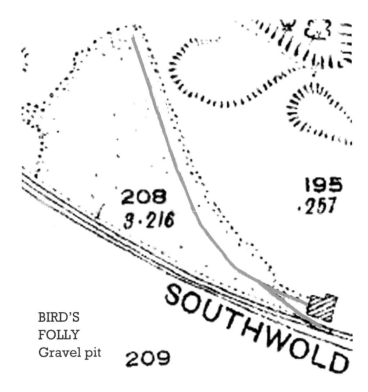

BIRD'S
FOLLY
Gravel pit

208
3·216

209

195
·257

Fig 34: Bird's Folly gravel pit: 1 – 2,500 OS 1904 map extract shows both the siding to the pit and the subsequent addition of an engine shed which was required in 1914 to accommodate an additional locomotive.

Fig 35: Foundations and inspection pit of the SR Halesworth Engine Shed uncovered and stabilised by a Southwold Railway Trust working party.

Fig 34 OS map extract shows both the siding and the subsequent addition of an engine shed which was required in 1914 to accommodate an additional locomotive. The engine shed was wood framed and clad with asbestos sheeting on a brick plinth and inside an inspection pit and space for a workbench. A well was sunk outside and a chain-driven pump installed to provide water for the locomotives.

It is a measure of the relatively primitive nature of operational facilities for the Railway that there was no room for an engine shed at Halesworth Station and quite limited workshop and shed space at Southwold. The Bird's Folly site was over half a mile from Halesworth and the shed was a bleak work place, especially in winter.

The site of the Bird's Folly engine shed – usually referred to as Halesworth Shed – has survived and is now being rehabilitated by the Southwold Railway Trust which, in time, hopes to be using the shed again for its original purpose. Meanwhile **Fig 35** shows the uncovered inspection pit and the brick footings.

A little beyond the engine shed was the first of the Railway's many accommodation crossings which were necessary because the line divided a number of agricultural holdings, especially in the first four miles of the line to Blythburgh. David Lee estimates that there were approximately 60 such crossings, a public

road level crossing at Wenhaston and two unprotected level crossings on the Harbour Branch. The BoT's requirement for a 16mph speed limit may be their response to the potential dangers along the line from these many crossings and the likelihood of animals and farm machinery needing to move back and forth.

From the Bird's Folly quarry and engine shed, the line continued in a southerly and easterly direction, following the River Blyth and through a jigsaw pattern of fields, water meadows, small streams and drainage channels. The *Ipswich Journal* for 27 September 1879, reporting the opening of the railway, states that 'Most of the country is somewhat flat and the views which present themselves at different points stretch away for miles; the commanding towers of the beautiful churches of the district are prominent objects in the landscape.'

A surviving over-bridge is on a public road, the unclassified road which joins what is now the B1123 at Corner Farm (formerly Holton Farm) and leads to the hamlet of Mells. It is a substantial structure which still stands and carries traffic today. To local people it was known as 'Ball's Bridge' after an adjacent land tenant.

Fig 37 is from a 1985 photograph which shows that there was still walking passage along the trackbed but the vegetation on the cutting sides and on much of the former trackbed is growing vigorously. Today it is completely choked with growth, very wet underfoot and the parapet brickwork of the bridge – structurally weak in 1985 – has been renewed, but the concrete arch and abutments and much of the brickwork are original and still serving their purpose. Mr Contractor Chambers did a good job.

The next significant structure near the railway is Wenhaston Water Mill, also known as Kett's Mill, but reaching that meant crossing the River Blyth, the New Cut which was the Blyth Navigation, and then the Mill Pond as shown in the bridge's elevation **Fig 38**, photograph **Fig 39**, and the edited OS map extract **Fig 40**.

Wenhaston Water Mill, (**Figs 41** and **43**) like most wind or watermills which ground wheat to flour for our daily bread, has a long recorded history. Originally it had an undershot waterwheel, but in the 1770s it is recorded as 'lately new built' and had a breast shot

Fig 36: an up mixed train passing a typical accommodation crossing on the way from Southwold in the early 1900s. The railway fences are sound, the crossing gates painted white and the track well-ballasted and weed-free so, it seems, this was a railway proud of its standards, maintenance and appearance.

Fig 37: SR Bridge No 4, Mells Bridge, under an unclassified road near Corner Farm on what is now the B1123 – photographed in 1994.

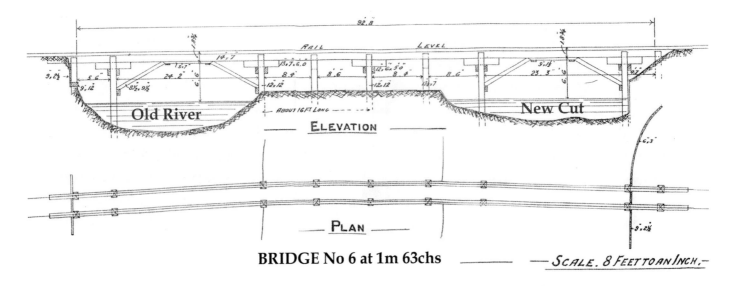

Fig 38: Elevation of SR Bridge No 6 near Wenhaston Mill.

Fig 39: Steel RSJs and timber baulks supporting the SR track on Wenhaston Mill bridge.

Fig 40: Edited map extract from 1904 1 – 2,500 OS map.

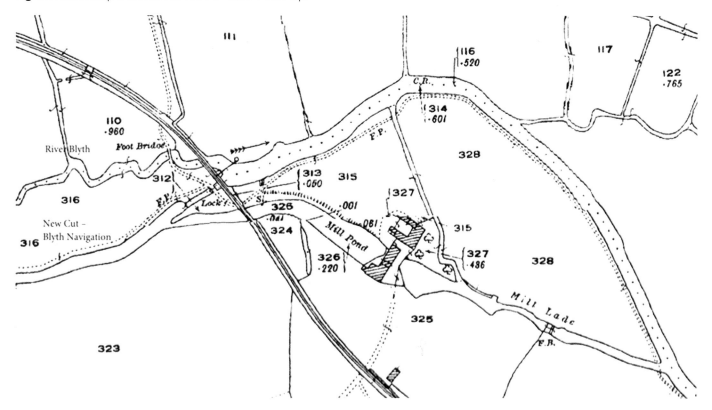

Fig 41: SR Bridge across the Mill Pond and Wenhaston Water Mill in the background.

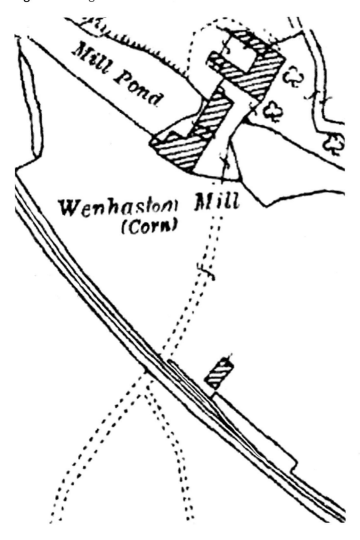

wheel which would provide more power for turning the millstones. The Kett family acquired the mill about 1865 when they were already well-established millers in the area with windmills at Mells and at Wrentham. By 1883, Wenhaston was advertised as a wind, water and steam mill so seemingly a prosperous venture and justifying the private siding which is marked on **Fig 40** OS map extract, dated 1904 and, in a little more detail, in **Fig 42,** extracted from another 1 to 2,500 OS map surveyed in 1927.

A photograph (**Fig 43**) is dated to the 1920s and, as in the picture of the bridge over the Mill Pond (**Fig 41**), suggests a busy and prosperous mill though there is unfortunately no evidence in this picture, or on the OS map extracts, of the chimney which a steam-powered mill would require adjoining its boiler house. However, the SR private siding can be dated from 1880 when the SR Board sought authority from the BoT for connection to their running line which was granted after inspection. The connection faced towards Southwold so suggests that grain may have come from ships into Southwold Harbour – because there were two windmills in Southwold and a steam-powered roller flour mill. It seems likely, however,

Fig 42: Edited map extract from 1927 1 – 2,500 OS map.

Fig 43: Wenhaston Water Mill and house, 1920s.

that these mills would have supplied the demand for flour in Southwold so perhaps Miller Kett and his successors looked to the Halesworth area for their market. Kelly's *Directory for Suffolk 1896* lists James Long as miller at Wenhaston who was also a coal and corn merchant so perhaps he was diversifying as many millstone millers did when steam-powered roller flour mills took their business.

As the **Fig 40** and **42** map extracts show, Wenhaston Mill was reached by a private road so an occupation crossing over the railway was required and Miller Kett claimed that the number of horse-drawn wagons to and from his mill required a gate keeper for the crossing. When approached, the BoT ruled that the crossing was a good idea but the requirement for a crossing keeper was outside their jurisdiction.

Wenhaston

At 2m 75ch from Halesworth Station, the SR crossed a public road on a level crossing which adjoined Wenhaston Station serving the nearby village of Wenhaston. **Fig 44** is an 1880s photograph.

On 26 September 1879, the station was carefully described in the *Halesworth Times, Southwold and General Advertiser* as '… a pretty station which is a happy combination of cheapness and convenience and it is, at the same time, a model of what good architectural taste can do with very circumscribed materials.'

The corrugated iron roof was not especially 'pretty' but very serviceable. The station, seen in **Fig 44** looking south into the beginnings of the village, has Southwold to the left and Halesworth to the right. The building was timber-framed with brick infilling to create what was described by the Railway Company as a 'Tudoresque period effect'. It consisted of a booking hall, accessed off the platform through the double doors in the centre with a ticket window and Station Master's office to the right and a Ladies Waiting Room plus WC to the left. The lean-to roof on the road side of the building covered a lamp room and there was a brick-built Gentleman's urinal and WC to the left. The platform was about 240ft long with a gravelled surface and timber decking in front of the building.

Fig 44: Wenhaston Station and adjoining level crossing – 1880s.

The level crossing over Blyford lane, open to road traffic in **Fig 44**, was the only public road crossing on the whole length of the railway and was conveniently near the station for observation and operation.

Fig 45 below shows the final track and buildings layout in 1921. A Goods Shed was added in 1881 and, later, a Coal Shed for coal merchants who were delivering locally by horse and cart and subsequently by lorry. The final connection put in, as shown in **Fig 45,** in 1921 made it possible, if necessary, for trains to pass each other at Wenhaston and especially facilitated the working of goods trains which could be clear of the single main line for loading and unloading. The main tonnage carried was coal, then cattle-cake, milk in churns and, from 1927 onwards, sugar beet was a principal outward traffic.

Wenhaston Station served a small but busy village with 157 pupils attending the Elementary School, built and opened in 1882. Twelve farmers are recorded as living in the village and there were some retailers, victuallers and artisans including shoemakers and

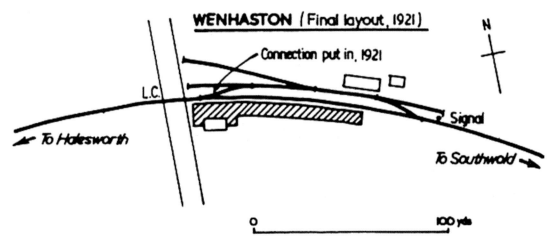

Fig 45: Final layout of Wenhaston Station, 1921.

Fig 46: undated but probably taken in the 1920s and a useful contrast to **Fig 44** from the 1880s. One addition is the telegraph pole which carries telephone wires to the all-stations circuit that was installed in 1899, enabling the Station Masters to communicate with each other for safe working and for dealing with any emergencies which might arise.

Fig 47: An up mixed train arriving at Wenhaston in 1902 to pick up a number of passengers or, perhaps some villagers meeting friends returning from Blythburgh, Walberswick or Southwold.

a blacksmith, millwright and wheelwright listed in William White's *History, Gazette and Directory of Suffolk* in 1885.

Onwards to Southwold, this virtual journey continues towards Blythburgh through low-lying water meadows and some arable land passing Low Farm and Beaumur (now Laurel) Farm. The farmland required about ten accommodation and occupation level crossings for footpaths and for farm labourers, some machinery, and sometimes stock to move between fields divided by the Railway, so illustrated the problems to landowners and tenants.

Soon after the opening of the Railway in September 1879, an Inquiry was held at the Angel Hotel, Halesworth, on Friday 27 February 1880. It was chaired by Arthur Garrard Esquire, Arbitrator, of Whitehall Place, London. The Inquiry was to consider a claim for compensation by Mr Ewen, 'A gentleman living in Southwold' for 'damages alleged to have been sustained by him in consequence of the [Southwold] Railway passing through some property of his'. Mr Simms Reeve appeared for Mr Ewen and, in opening his case, he explained that 'the Southwold Railway passed through Mr. Ewen's estate, cutting through the pastures, or best part of it, passing through no less than nine different pieces, and thereby causing much injury and inconvenience. The estate … was, in fact, severed into two parts. In addition to this, the line was not properly fenced.'

A long account of the Inquiry proceedings was immediately published in the *Ipswich Journal* of Saturday 28 February 1880 and another relevant passage was from two witnesses for the executors of another part of Mr Ewen's estate. William Lines, farm bailiff, said: '… he thought the cutting up of the farm was a great inconvenience, and it took a man and two boys to drive sheep and lambs across the line, whilst a boy could have driven them from place to place before, and it therefore cost more for labour. A good deal of trouble was also caused in keeping lambs from getting through the fence onto the line, and expense was caused in doing up the fence.' Solomon Fisk, head horseman, corroborated, adding that some sheep got upon the line and on one occasion '… the train had to pull up in consequence'. Typical SR track-side fencing is in several pictures (**Figs 36 & 49**).

Mr Eaton Turner, for the Railway Company, and Engineer Arthur Pain, acknowledged that there were

sometimes problems – like the lambs through the fences – but they maintained that there were a number of accommodation crossings and that some were hardly ever used. They attested, 'The gateway . . . was but very little used, as evidenced by its grown-up condition'. Perhaps to the relief of the Railway Company, 'the Arbitrator reserved his decision' but it is apparent that not everyone welcomed the new railway.

Fig 48 is an edited OS map extract from a 1-2,500 map of 1904 and shows the Railway in a sweeping curve around Blythburgh village, through Blythburgh Station and under what is now the A12 and was then the Yarmouth Turnpike. Passengers on our virtual down train, had they looked out to the right, would have seen the magnificent Holy Trinity Church, dating from 1412, rebuilt in the late sixteenth century after serious storm damage and restored in the late twentieth century to its present glory. It justifies its local name as the Cathedral of the Marshes.

At the time of the Norman Conquest in 1066, Blythburgh was part of the royal estate and one of Suffolk's twelve market towns. Its church was especially rich, worth ten times the average for Suffolk which was one of the wealthiest counties in England. However, time and events made Blythburgh much poorer by the time the Railway came. In 1881 the Bishop of Norwich deemed the fabric of the church to be unsafe and ordered it to be closed. Fortunately, the church was saved – but its rescue involved a bitter twenty-five year long dispute between Blythburgh vicars and committees, and William Morris and the Society for the Protection of Ancient Buildings, who feared that the medieval fabric would be over-restored and the historic character of the building lost forever.

When news of the closure of the church was published in London's daily newspaper, the *Morning Post*, Southwold Railway Engineer Arthur Pain wrote to the paper proposing the formation of a committee to raise the '… necessary funds to render the edifice safe and fit for public worship.' This reference and the details of the long battle about conservation or restoration of the church is told in Alan Mackley (Editor), (*The Restoration of Blythburgh Church 1881 – 1906*, Suffolk Records Society, The Boydell Press, 2017.) Perhaps Engineer Pain was not only concerned to save the church but to promote the use of the Southwold Railway? Certainly Alan Mackley's book records several references to the

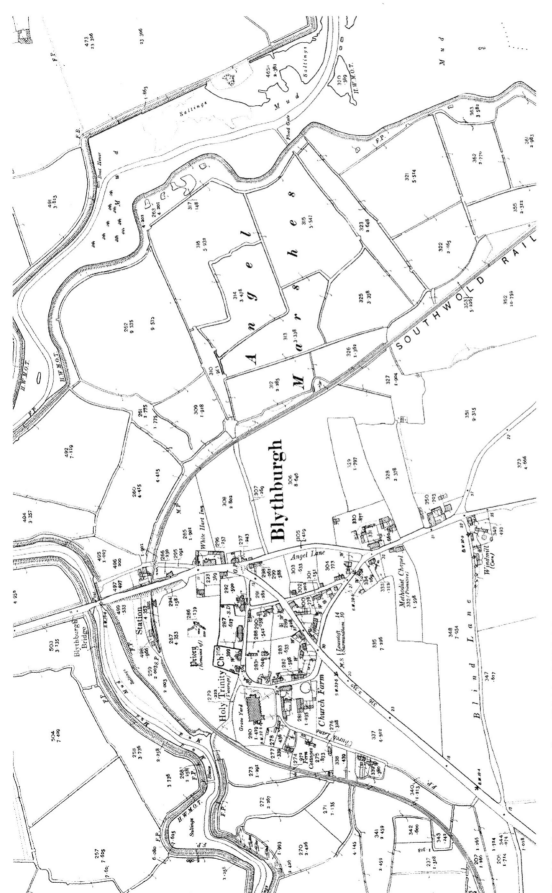

Fig 48: Edited map extract from 1904 1 – 2,500 OS map.

Fig 49: (from Southwold Museum collections) Blythburgh church in 1898. In the middle foreground is an accommodation crossing and Southwold Railway fencing – which is clearly not lamb-proof!

'convenient little railway'. A lengthy account of a fund-raising Bazaar from the *Ipswich Journal* on 12 August 1882 mentions the size of the 'sacred edifice' which is 'especially noticeable in the journey to Southwold by the model little railway opened within the last two years'.

So the plight of Blythburgh church did generate some traffic and the Railway helped in another way because a corner of a field owned by the church was conveyed to the Railway in the late 1870s for payment of a permanent annual rent charge of £2.

The village is in a rich agricultural area and Blythburgh road bridge is the lowest crossing on the river Blyth. The village had a quay over which some river traffic was loaded or landed and in the 1920s the White Hart coaching inn was still in business as were a post office, a general store, a shoe maker, a shoe-repairer, a dairy, and a carpenter/wheelwright/decorator/undertaker but there was little business for the Southwold Railway, especially as motor cars, lorries

and buses were now offering serious competition to a 3ft gauge railway and the necessary transhipment at Halesworth.

Blythburgh Station

Situated at 4m 70c from Halesworth, this station did not open until December 1879 because the building was only completed then. The building was very similar to Wenhaston Station except that the accommodation and the adjoining external structures were opposite hand to those at Wenhaston. The only access to the Station building was across the 225ft platform, timbered in front of the building and otherwise gravelled.

The plan (**Fig 50**) shows the goods provision which was relatively generous for a small village but perhaps reflecting that this was a mid-point of the Railway, so the eventual track layout provided a passing loop as well as a loading stage adjoining the loop, a separate shed built and owned by Odams Manure Co. and the

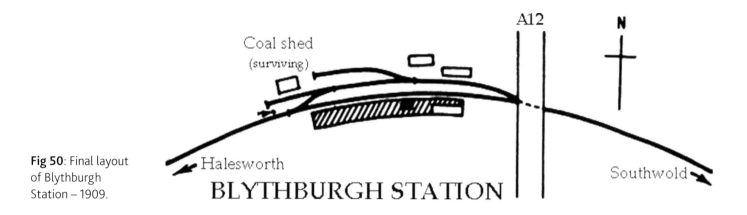

Fig 50: Final layout of Blythburgh Station – 1909.

Fig 51: View of Blythburgh Station looking towards Southwold and illustrating some of the details on the Station plan (**Fig 50** - above).

coal shed which was let to coal merchants and, albeit almost covered with vegetation, survives today.

On from Blythburgh towards Southwold, the Railway travelled through very different country from that between the eastern end of the Blythburgh map (**Fig 49**) and Southwold so it has been possible to illustrate the whole distance in one OS map extract in **Fig 56**. The names on the map – Blythburgh Covert, Deadman's Covert, Tinker's Covert, Walberswick Common, Squireshill Marshes, Busscreek Marshes, Woodsend Marshes and Southwold Common speak for themselves. Coverts are thickets where game can hide so they suggest shooting country and the marshes by the river imply an area which may be flooded, as it sometimes is because

the Blyth is tidal as far inland as Blyford bridge, near Wenhaston. **Fig 57** is a down train in Tinker's Covert and was used by the Railway Company for advertising their Railway and the Suffolk country.

Fig 56 is an edited OS map extract from a 1-10,560 (or 1 inch) map dated 1938 but still showing the Southwold Railway, and the Harbour Branch, which had been disused since 1927. However, it serves our purpose well, indicating the sort of slightly undulating and rougher land through which the Railway passed to Southwold.

As on the Halesworth-Blythburgh section of the Railway, the Blythburgh-Southwold section passes through land owned by several very wealthy landowners such as Ewen of Reydon Hall, Gooch of

Fig 52 : Blythburgh Station photographed after 1908 because the brick abutments of the Railway bridge carrying the Yarmouth Turnpike road have replaced the timber props (in **Fig 51**) which were the Company's first response to concerns expressed about the carrying capacity of the bridge as heavy motorised road traffic replaced the horse-drawn traffic of the later nineteenth century.

Fig 53: Blythburgh Station: the photographer is further back from the road bridge than **Fig 51** and has captured an up mixed train on the platform road, the passing loop empty, the Coal Shed, and 4 sheeted wagons on the goods siding to the north of the Coal Shed; note that there was no rail connection into the Shed. The churns on the platform, like the single churn in **Fig 52**, show the milk traffic which was probably in both directions and a timbered barrow crossing which would make moving full churns a little easier.

Fig 54: Blythburgh Station, viewed from the road bridge, shows the carriages of a Southwold bound down train and Odam's shed. This view (**Fig 54**) must date from before September 1908 when the passing loop shown in the Station plan was completed and inspected by the BoT. Here it is a siding for Odam's shed and unloading platform. The functional simplicity of the buffer-stop at the end of the siding is typical of the Southwold Railway and can also be found in an illustration of the Harbour Branch.

Fig 55: Blythburgh Station, viewed from the road bridge and after 1908 when Odam's Manure Co. had sold their shed to the Railway Company. A down mixed train and a crowded platform, perhaps in the 1910s.

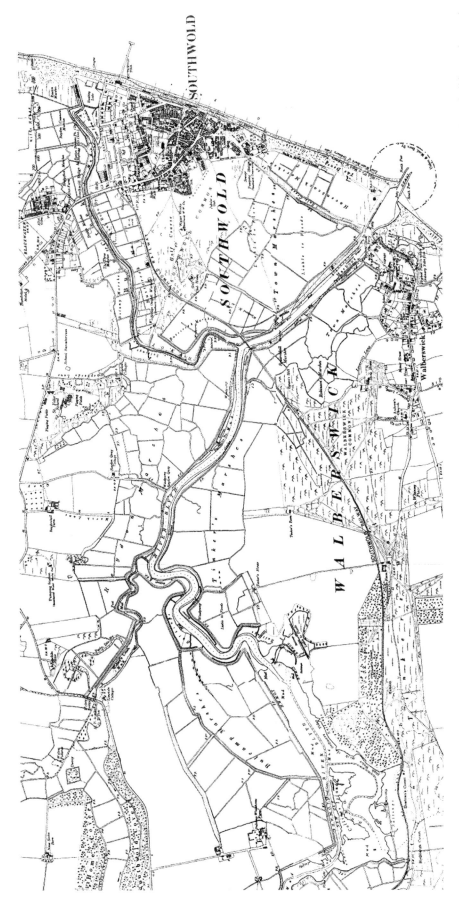

Fig 56: Edited OS map extract from a 1-10,560 (or 1 inch) map dated 1938 but still showing the Southwold Railway, and the Harbour Branch, which had all been disused since 1929.

Benacre, Barnes of Sotterley, Vaneck of Heveningham, Rous of Henham, and Blois of Cockfield Hall, Yoxford. They generally did not oppose the development of the Southwold Railway, nor did they encourage the use of it because a number of them were Harbour Commissioners. Their interest was in making their land near the river Blyth productive and encouraging trade to the Harbour and on the river. As Chapter 7 on Southwold Harbour and the SR Harbour Branch explains, the Commissioners' interest in making the marshes useful as arable and grazing land – shown by the field boundaries on the 1938 **Fig 56** map – was at odds with their concern for the Harbour. However, the Southwold Railway avoided disturbing the agriculture by taking a route through slightly higher land with soils more suited for woodland coverts for shooting and commons for grazing, but there were still several gated occupation and accommodation crossings to provide and maintain. **Fig 58** is such a crossing in Tinker's Covert looking east towards Southwold and including a gradient post. This section of the Railway is slightly more undulating requiring

some shallow cuttings and embankments as can be seen in **Figs 58** and **59**.

Much of the Blythburgh-Southwold section is today an attractive footpath and, for walkers who have an enthusiasm for railway memories, a driver's eye view can be imagined.

East of the wooded coverts, the line crossed Walberswick Common on a low embankment, pierced by bridge 12, at 7m 18ch from Halesworth providing what was generally known as the 'Cattle Creep.' (**Fig 184**.) Any animals grazing on the common – and there were often sheep as well as cattle – could use the creep for access to pasture on either side of the Railway. Like the embankments and cuttings in Tinker's Walks, the Walberswick Common embankment remains as do the concrete abutments of the bridge.

Walberswick Station, at 7m 45c (**Fig 61**), is now only the concrete base of the enhanced station building shown in **Fig 62**. Originally, a station was not planned on this site because it was over half a mile from the village – which was anyway very small with only 289 inhabitants recorded in the 1881 census. However, the Common was a popular

Fig 57: A mixed down train passing through Deadman's Covert between Blythburgh and Walberswick Stations – 1900s.

Fig 58: Accommodation crossing and adjoining gradient post in Tinker's Covert looking towards Southwold.

Fig 59 (above): List's embankment, 2015.

Fig 60 (right): List's cutting, 2015.

venue for walking and picnic parties. Engineer and Chairman Pain recalled to the 1923 AGM of the Railway Company that:

> 'When the railway line was laid it was not thought worthwhile to make a station. But visitors to Southwold found advantages in the breezy stretch of common and gorse-land, and spent afternoons there, with the result that a small platform and siding was put down by arrangement with the Common Lands Charity Commissioner. Later the comfort of visitors was improved by the addition of a shelter.' *Halesworth Times* 18 April 1923.

The land on which the Station was built belonged to the Walberswick Common Lands Charity and was leased to the Railway Company for £2 7s 6d per annum. The original building was a small wooden structure 12ft x 6ft and there was an adjoining urinal on the Southwold side. The one room was a combined booking office, waiting room and the clerk-in-charge's office. The 9ins

Fig 61: The original Walberswick Station – 1890s.

high platform, as elsewhere on the Railway, was a gravel surface with a timber edge towards the trains and 230ft long. The Station was fully opened to traffic from 1 July 1882 from when it was included in public timetables.

In 1899, a petition from local inhabitants was presented to the Railway Company complaining about the lack of facilities at Walberswick Station including difficulty with booking tickets and the unlit and very rutted footpath to the village. This access track was a continuing problem because the village was not willing to spend any money on improving access and as late as the 1923 AGM, Engineer and Chairman Pain expressed his concern and impatience:

'... all the Company's efforts to get the local people to make a road ... from the Station to the church, or in the other direction, have been unsuccessful. [The local's] can get nothing done, although the Company has offered to assist ... by bringing gravel ... suitable for the construction of the roadway. Today what traffic does come across the Common is confronted with a more or less dangerous route owing to the darkness and ruts ... Any traffic coming by railway has great difficulty in being conveyed to the village

whether it is for the building trade or anything else ... It might have been unwise, perhaps, to have put the Station there without binding the local people to make their own road.'

Despite the continuing access problem there must have been sufficient potential – and a petition to improve – to encourage the Company to much enlarge the Station in 1902 (**Fig 62**). A 42ft x 10ft wooden framed and corrugated iron clad building was provided on a concrete base – which is all that remains today. There was now a booking/clerk's office, a large parcels office, a waiting room and toilet facilities.

Two sidings were laid behind the Station building with a small goods platform and a coal storage shed which was leased to coal merchants. Mr Etheridge was succeeded by the Lowestoft Coaling Company but both, in turn, terminated their leases because of the state of the access track.

The cartage agent who worked for the Railway Company terminated his agreement for the same reason so traffic to and from Walberswick Station became very light. During the First World War the Station was closed from February 1917, ostensibly to release an unspecified member of staff for war service, and it did not open again

Fig 62: Walberswich Station enlarged in 1902.

WALBERSWICK STATION – final layout

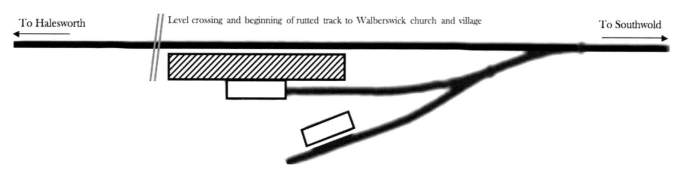

Fig 63: Final layout Walberswick Station 1902.

until July 1919 when it reappeared in the timetable. It probably had so little effect on business that it was not until 18 December 1919 that the GER Commercial Superintendent at Liverpool Street issued a notice advising that 'The issue of passenger tickets to and from Walberswick will be resumed from 1 January 1920'.

Although Station business was slow, Walberswick in the late nineteenth and early twentieth centuries was becoming an attractive venue for artists and the Railway did provide an access for them. Nevertheless, some were worried and a notice in the 1881 edition of *The Etcher* declared '… that the silting of the River Blyth and the arrival of the railway had finished off this easterly outpost as a fertile sketching ground', *Making Waves – Artists on Southwold,* Ian Collins, Black Dog Books, 2005. Fortunately, a number of well-known artists ignored this notice and it may be that some, like Henry Moore, Charles Rennie Mackintosh, Walter Sickert and Sir Muirhead Bone, used the enlarged Walberswick Station and trudged along the rutted track to their sources of inspiration from the river, beach and fishermen of the village.

From Walberswick, the Railway continued in a north easterly direction past Squires Hill and across Squires Hill marshes to the line's principal engineering feature, the Swing Bridge across the River Blyth. (**Fig 64**)

The Blyth was a navigable waterway between Halesworth and Southwold Harbour, so the Railway was required to provide access for vessels which could only be done, without excessive embanking to create greater height over the river, by building a moveable bridge. The details of the bridge are explained and further illustrated in Chapter 10, so it is sufficient here to add that the bridge was rebuilt, and widened for possible standard gauge track, in 1907. It is apparent in **Fig 64** that this was not a swing bridge with its own steam-powered mechanism to open it, or a cabin on the top of the swinging span

to control operations. Perhaps characteristically, the Southwold Railway arranged for the bridge to be opened, and closed, using a rope attached to the river-side end of the swing section and to a rowing boat manned by at least one railwayman; the bridge turned on a large wheel-race mounted on the substantial caisson in the middle of the navigable channel, but it was rarely required because traffic on the River had almost ceased by 1884 only five years after the Railway opened.

To cross the bridge, the railway line ascended and descended for 100 yards at gradients of 1 in 66 and then continued on a low level embankment across Woods End marshes, past the 1914 junction to the Harbour Branch, described in Chapter 6, and along a curving cutting about 20ft deep through Southwold Common. The cutting was crossed by a footbridge erected in 1903 and built at the expense of Southwold Golf Club to give their members access when the course was extended to 18 holes. Readers who play golf may be amused to learn that – to avoid too many lost balls – the Club also paid for nets to cover the dykes draining Woods End marshes which adjoined their course. The Railway built a sturdy but cost-saving bridge using brick and concrete for the two bases and the approach steps and scrap rails for the bridge itself. (**Fig 65**).

The Golf Club's course, on Southwold Common was, and is, accessible to walkers and it may be that the three ladies in **Fig 65**, photographed in the 1920s, were enjoying the sunshine and the view over the marshes and the River Blyth valley to the left of the photograph. Since the bridge was freely accessible stories are told of children attempting to drop small stones down the funnel of passing engines. Drivers and firemen, who could see if any children were on the bridge, discouraged them with a shovel-full of gritty small coal on the fire and turning on the engine blower as they passed beneath.

Fig 64: Original swing bridge across the River Blyth – 1879 to 1907.

Fig 65: Footbridge across Southwold Cutting for members of Southwold Golf Club – and used by folk enjoying the sunshine.

Fig 66: Original layout for Southwold Station – 1879.

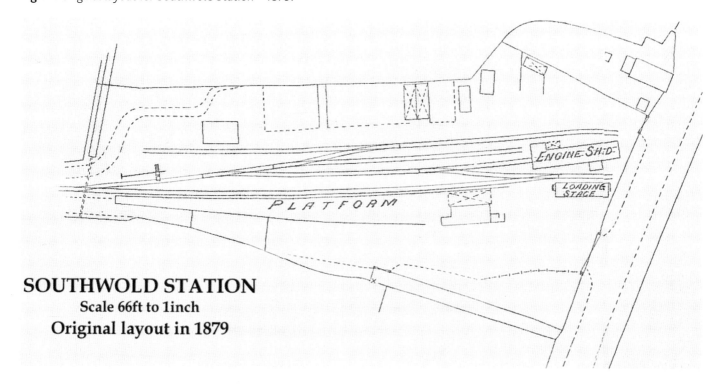

SOUTHWOLD STATION
Scale 66ft to 1inch
Original layout in 1879

The Railway entered Southwold Station on a slight curve along the single face gravel-surfaced platform which was approximately 300yds long. The line terminated alongside an open goods loading stage and just short of Station Road at 8m 63ch from Halesworth. The plan, **Fig 66**, shows the Engine Shed and the sidings to the NW which provided a goods yard for coal merchants and for consignees to unload their own goods. The final layout (**Fig 67**) was a little more comprehensive including a carriage siding which, eventually, was partly covered with a Carriage Shed of corrugated iron sheets fixed to the frame which was made of scrap rails in typical Southwold Railway pragmatic frugality.

The single storey station building was originally 28ft x 12ft 6ins and was internally similar to Wenhaston Station. Heating of the booking office area was with an open coal fire (**Fig 68**).

In 1900, the East Coast Development Corporation built Pier Avenue from Station Road to Southwold Pier which was a landing stage for Belle Steamers. The Corporation also built Pier Avenue Hotel opposite Southwold Station and on the corner of Pier Avenue, in anticipation of holiday-makers visiting or staying in Southwold. (**Figs 69** and **70**).

From the early 1900s, the hotels in Southwold – unless they were in walking distance like the Pier Avenue Hotel – sent their own horse-drawn bus to meet all the trains and Walter Doy had a cab-stand in the Station forecourt. But, from 1904, the GER began to operate their own three motor buses from Lowestoft to Southwold (**Fig 71**). On 5 April 1928 Eastern Counties Road Car Co began to operate Service 30 between Halesworth, Walpole and Southwold and the buses, though calling at the Station, terminated in Southwold Market Place, in the centre of the town within a 5-minute walk of the seashore.

Competition, though unwelcome to the Southwold Railway, was to be expected but the Railway Company did not help itself by distancing its administration from the operating railway in Suffolk. From the 1880s, the Head Office was in Victoria Street, London,

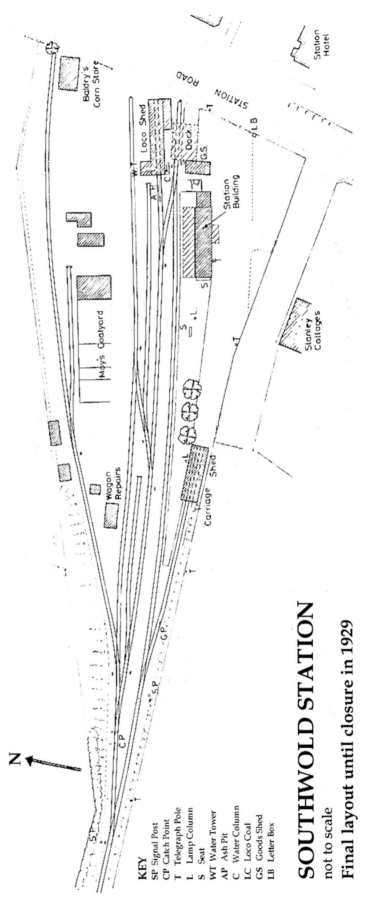

KEY
SP Signal Post
CP Catch Point
T Telegraph Pole
L Lamp Column
S Seat
WT Water Tower
AP Ash Pit
C Water Column
LC Loco Coal
GS Goods Shed
LB Letter Box

SOUTHWOLD STATION
not to scale
Final layout until closure in 1929

Fig 67: Final layout for Southwold Station until closure in 1929.

SOUTHWOLD STATION BUILDING

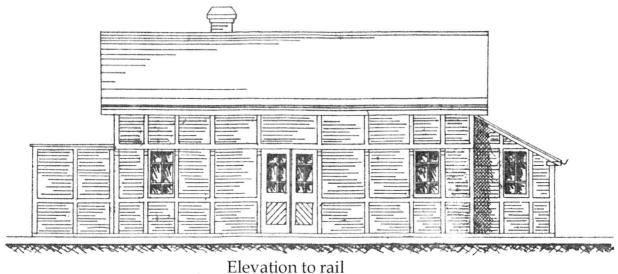

Elevation to rail

Plan of Booking Office etc

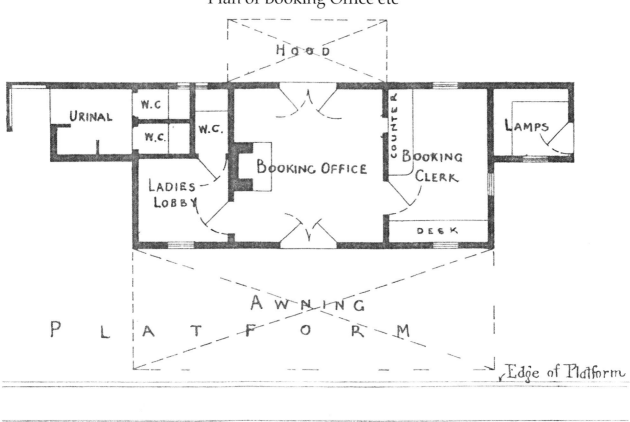

Fig 68: Elevation and Plan of Southwold Station building from GER Valuation of 1892 & 1894.

Fig 69 (above) and **Fig 70 (below)**: panoramic view of the Station approach and, in the background, Pier Avenue Hotel in the early twentieth century. The busy platform and the well-dressed passengers in **Fig 70** show the relative prosperity of Southwold, and of the Railway, in the early 1900s. However, the problems brought by the First World War and the growing competition from motor buses – and from motor lorries – did not bode well for the Railway's long-term sustainability.

Fig 71: GER motor bus from and to Lowestoft outside Swan Hotel, Southwold Market Place.

and although Southwold Station was the centre of day to day operation, there was no telephone connection to the Head Office and even an internal station-to-station telephone link was not in place until 1899. Contact with London was by letter and the Halesworth Station Master's Wet Copy Letter Book illustrates the volume of correspondence. The Company Secretary, also based in London, periodically visited Suffolk to check the books at each station.

Relations with Southwold Corporation were never very amicable because there was no direct contact with the Officers of the Corporation and the Railway Company; Southwold Station was a half-mile walk from the Town Hall.

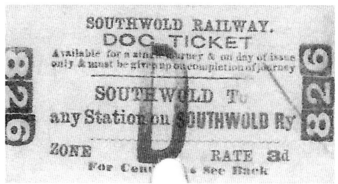

Fig 72: SR Edmundson card tickets, for bicycles and dogs accompanying passengers.

CHAPTER 7

RIVER BLYTH, SOUTHWOLD HARBOUR AND THE HARBOUR BRANCH

'Southwold Harbour is the only reasonably accessible haven between Harwich and Lowestoft and is increasingly frequented by fishing and other small craft ... It is considered, that the closing of the Harbour would cause considerable hardship to small craft on the East Coast.'

Memo from the Cruising Association to the Ministry of Agriculture and Fisheries, 1949.

Quoted from: *Southwold Harbour and the Blyth Marshes*. Mackesey P.J. Privately printed.

Early details of the River Blyth valley, and of Southwold Harbour, must be pieced together from rather fragmentary evidence. It is known that the present mouth of the river – which constitutes Southwold Harbour – dates only from 1590. Prior to this, the Blyth turned south and flowed parallel to the coast, hemmed in by a spit which periodically choked the mouth entirely. Southwold lacked a harbour, but Dunwich prospered until coastal erosion became increasingly serious. Thomas Gardner in his *History of Dunwich*, (published by the author, 1745) quoting with apparent veracity from 'several ancient Records, Manuscripts, etc. which were never before made public' (and unfortunately not specified further by Gardner), shows the increasing decay of Dunwich: '... antiently a city, now a Borough and the rise of Southwold, once a village, now a town Corporate'.

Fig 73 is based on a map in Gardner's book and shows the coastal changes engendered by erosion which have almost obliterated Dunwich and given Southwold its present sea-scape.

The relevance of this earlier history to the Southwold Railway story is to give a context to the significance of Southwold Harbour in the minds of nineteenth century entrepreneurs and for Southwold Corporation. The letter below is from E.R. Cooper, Town Clerk and solicitor in Southwold, addressed to the Mayors of several nearby towns:

'Ernest E. Cooper, Esq.,
'Solicitor, Southwold.   21 April, 1893

PROPOSED TRANS-EAST-ANGLIAN RAILWAY

'Sir,—A scheme has been put forward in this Borough with the object of promoting a Trans-East Anglian Railway, originating from the Midland system at Cambridge, and terminating at this place, which is considered to be eminently adaptable to the formation of a commodious seaport . . . and by the acquisition and re-modelling of the Southwold Railway.

'The Midland Railway Directors have already been approached by our Corporation upon the subject, and although their reply was necessarily somewhat guarded, it is confidently believed, from information acquired indirectly, that the Midland Railway are anxious to secure a port on the East Coast, and the promoters of this scheme have every reason to believe that, if the necessary powers can be obtained, the line will be constructed, and the harbour at this place developed, to the incalculable advantage of the whole of Mid-Suffolk.

'Tabled at: SOUTHWOLD HARBOUR IMPROVEMENT COMMITTEE MEETING ... 23rd AUGUST 1893.'

The letter is also interesting in suggesting that the Midland Railway were 'anxious to secure a port on the East Coast' and we know today, 'from information acquired indirectly' that the local railway companies which became the GER were developing Lowestoft and Yarmouth Harbours so would not welcome a rival railway company crossing 'their' territory to Southwold Harbour.

The Trans-East-Anglian Railway was never built, not least because sufficient money could not be raised to finance it. However, Southwold Corporation persisted in a belief that the Harbour was an important element in the town's prosperity and a Harbour Branch off the Southwold Railway was built but the Harbour, and therefore the Harbour Branch, were ultimately unsuccessful and a little more history explains why.

Southwold obtained an Act of Parliament in 1746, 'To open, cleanse, scour, widen, deepen, repair and improve our Haven' and a body of Harbour Commissioners was appointed with powers to levy charges on vessels using the Harbour. The necessary improvements were set in hand but, at first, with little understanding of the natural conditions involved. The Blyth was originally tidal to Halesworth and flowed over the lower part of its course through a large area of mud flats which flooded at high tide.

These flats acted as a reservoir greatly augmenting the normal flow of the river on every ebb tide and thus providing a considerable scour over the Harbour bar. By 1761, work had been completed to make the Blyth a Navigation from Southwold to Halesworth for the mutual benefit of both towns. Four locks were necessary and the tidal extent of the Blyth was reduced by more than half. Furthermore, local landowners, noting the fertility of the tidal mud flats, began to enclose them with embankments. By 1845, 2,704 acres had been so enclosed and the scour of approximately 950,500,000 gallons of water was lost on every ebb tide.

The irony of the situation was that most of the landowners – the wealthy local gentry – had been made Harbour Commissioners under the 1746 Act. Their original enclosures of the tidal flats had doubtless been made in ignorance of their possible effects on the Harbour, but their ignorance was short-lived. Rapid and serious silting occurred and it soon became obvious to the Commissioners that their interests in their land and in the Harbour they administered were directly at variance. To ensure that their interests in the land were not

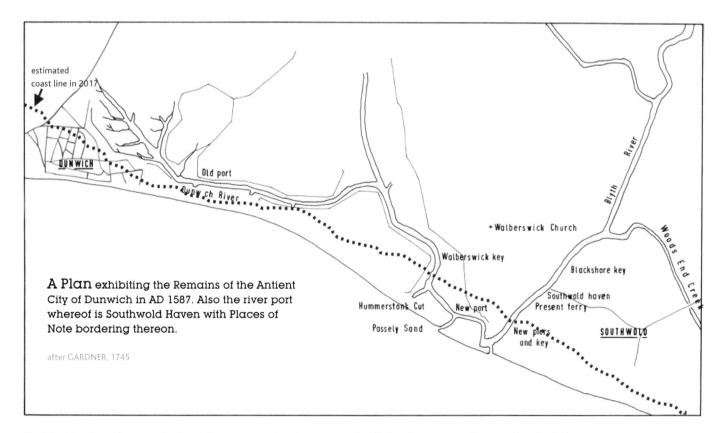

A Plan exhibiting the Remains of the Antient City of Dunwich in AD 1587. Also the river port whereof is Southwold Haven with Places of Note bordering thereon.

after GARDNER, 1745

Fig 73: Map based on and edited from a map in Thomas Gardner's book, *History of Dunwich*, which shows the coastal changes engendered by erosion that have almost obliterated Dunwich and given Southwold its present sea-scape.

endangered, they succeeded in maintaining the Board of Commissioners as almost wholly gentry and landowners under four further Harbour Acts (of 1756, 1789, 1809, l830). Attempts were made to improve the Harbour by dredging but the Commissioners were as nicely on the horns of a dilemma as any men could be and inevitably their actions met with little lasting success.

The Tidal Harbours Commission – 'appointed by Your Majesty to inquire into the state and condition of the Tidal and other Harbours … of Great Britain and Ireland …' – gave an unbiased assessment of their findings in 1845. On Southwold they stated:

'Commissioners have manifested great want of vigilant control and the landed, and fishing, and Corporation interests have often been preferred to the rights of the merchants and ship-owners and to the general interests of navigation. These interests having been so powerful as to occasion a dry bar, a deserted port and all but ruin of the ship owner and merchant.

'It appears in evidence that, with the exception of two, the Southwold Harbour Trustees are self-elected; they consist of land proprietors, merchants, etc., but only a single Southwold representative.'

The 'dry bar' to which the Tidal Harbour Commissioners referred was already well known to Southwold folk and merchants trying to use the Harbour. In 1839, a bar had formed across the Harbour mouth wide enough and dry enough to drive a carriage across and a number of vessels were trapped in the harbour. Many of these belonged to a wealthy Halesworth Maltster, Patrick Stead, and he called for:

'… a better Harbour and a new Bill. Unless a new Act of Parliament be obtained so as not to exclude from the Commission practical and nautical men, I submit that the confidence of the public and parties interested cannot be supported.'

Application was made for a new Bill but the Commissioners attempted to introduce clauses making legal their claims to the lands they had embanked. In 1845, however, the passing of the General Enclosure Act gave them all they required; they abandoned the new Harbour Bill and virtually abandoned the Harbour. It rapidly decayed as shown in the account of a visit made in 1882:

'The piers are tumbling to pieces and the great worn capstans which are used for hauling vessels through the shingle [and over the bar] looked almost past use. All around are speaking evidences of its decay as a port: rotting barges, disused smacks and desolate wharves.'

The last wherry worked up the Blyth Navigation in 1908. A short-lived attempt was made to cleanse and overhaul the whole Navigation passage but failed, largely because the Southwold Railway was operating an efficient through service to Halesworth.

In 1891 the Harbour Commissioners attempted to have the Harbour taken over by a public organisation with a view to improvements being made. An approach was to be made to the General Manager of the GER at a meeting on the 5 June 1891, but it was subsequently reported that the GER had declined to take on the Harbour because they claimed not have powers to raise funds.

Nevertheless, development of the harbour was important to Southwold Corporation so in 1898 they successfully dissolved the Harbour Commission by Act of Parliament. At this time, Lowestoft and Great Yarmouth were thriving fishing ports and were packed to capacity suggesting an opportunity to transform Southwold Harbour into a commercial undertaking.

The Corporation now owned their Harbour and evolved an improvement scheme with the BoT and a London contractor, W. Fasey & Son of Leytonstone. Fasey had done work for the GER at Lowestoft to develop a fishery harbour to relieve the congestion at Great Yarmouth and Lowestoft. Southwold Harbour Company was created and a BoT-approved scheme gained a Government grant of £21,500 subject to the Harbour and several acres of adjoining land being freely conveyed to Messrs Fasey.

Work started in 1906 and was completed by late October 1907 but too late for that year's herring season. **Figs 74** and **75** are map extracts edited from OS County Series 1- 2,500 for 1904 and 1927 respectively; they illustrate the changes made to the Harbour. Both maps (**Figs 74** and **75**) include the ferry which was steam-powered from 1899. The 1927 map (**Fig 75**) illustrates the substantial changes which were made and shows the eastern end of the Harbour Branch railway.

Fasey rebuilt the Harbour piers with a SE sweep giving sheltered water in the Harbour even during

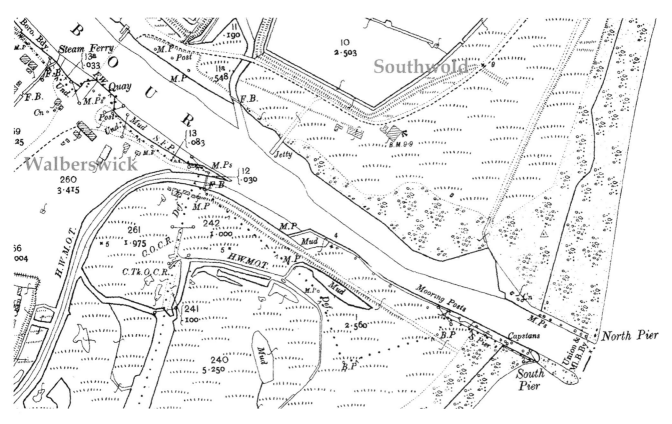

Fig 74: Southwold Harbour on map extract edited from OS County Series 1- 2,500 for 1904.

Fig 75: Southwold Harbour on map extract edited from OS County Series 1- 2,500 for 1927.

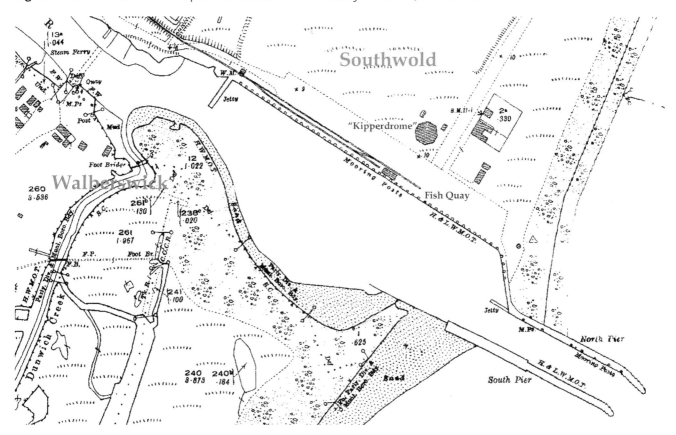

onshore gales. A 1,200ft fish quay was constructed on dry land on the Southwold bank of the river, then the sand on the waterside was removed by the Dutch dredger *Zealand* which also dredged the Harbour bottom to give a maximum high water depth of 18ft. 6ins. **(Fig 76)**

Gutting areas – staffed by many Scottish women who travelled to Southwold for the autumn herring season – curing houses, a fish-market locally known as the *Kipperdrome*, and a multi-gauge weighbridge were erected. On the Walberswick side, a spending beach absorbed waves which travelled up the Harbour.

And the ferry continued to be busy. **(Fig 77)**

The first commercial cargo landed in the 'new' Harbour was 272 tons of granite in April 1908 off the SS *Commandant* from Guernsey. The peak year for fish landings and general cargo was 1909, including a visit by two RN torpedo boats, but business declined gradually year by year to 1913; in 1914 the outbreak of the First World War ended all commercial shipping until 1919.

The *Kipperdrome* survived into the 1920s, but the fishing trade never recovered in Southwold as Lowestoft and Yarmouth developed and there was no standard gauge railway from Southwold. The 1927 map does show the seaward end of the Harbour Branch but it, like the Harbour it was intended to serve, did not last long and it seems likely that the 1927 map is based on earlier surveys which had not been updated. Another important factor in the herring industry which the SR Directors seemed never to have considered is that, before the First World War, more than 80% of the herrings landed were then exported to Germany, Russia and Norway. Some were first gutted, cured or salted but, once ice was readily available, many went as fresh fish to Northern Europe. Some business for Southwold Harbour but very little for the Southwold Railway.

The Harbour Branch

In July 1910, the Harbour Grants Committee of the Board of Trade, '… expressed the opinion that

Fig 76: Southwold Harbour Fish Quay and the Kipperdrome with several Scottish steam drifters alongside and the ferry continued to be busy.

Fig 77: Blyth steam-powered chain ferry lands on the Southwold shore in 1904.

[a Southwold Harbour Branch] line is all important for the development of the fishing industry and in fact is the key to the situation'. **Fig 78** is an aerial view of the inner harbour area in the 1980s showing the highlighted ground-shadow of the SR main line and the Harbour Branch.

The meeting of the Southwold Railway's directors in September 1910 includes their first reference to a Harbour Branch following a proposal from W. Fasey & Co that they could build the railway and have it ready by the autumn if the Southwold Railway Company supplied the rails. The Company made a counter proposal, that they would build and maintain the branch and allow Fasey one penny per ton on all traffic but that proposal was declined. Nothing was done, even though the Harbour works were finished and there was extensive fish traffic being landed and, as we now know, being exported.

SR Engineer and Chairman Arthur Pain believed that a Harbour Branch could have potential so made application for a Free Grant, under the Light Railways Act, 1896, to construct the branch as a Light Railway. In

October 1911, a meeting of the Light Railways (Grants) Committee recommended a grant with condition that it was paid by HM Treasury. During November 1911 Fasey finally agreed to the Southwold Railway constructing and operating a harbour branch and signed an Agreement dated 30 November 1911. In the same month the Light Railway Commissioners held a public enquiry at Southwold Town Hall into the Southwold Harbour Light Railway application which had been made by Fasey:

'Light Railway Commission, November, 1911.

'SOUTHWOLD HARBOUR LIGHT RAILWAY

NOTICE is hereby given, that application … is intended to be made in the present month of November to the Light Railway Commissioners by William Robert Fasey, carrying on business under the style of the Southwold Harbour Company at 1 Market Place, Southwold, (hereinafter referred to as 'The Company'), for an Order under the Light Railways

SOUTHWOLD STATION

Harbour Branch junction

Former swing bridge

Approximate line of
Blackshore Quay spur

Along Fish Quay to
"Kippermarket"

Highlighted ground shadow of Harbour Branch

Fig 78: Aerial view of the inner Southwold Harbour area in the 1980s showing the highlighted ground-shadow of the SR main line and the Harbour Branch.

Act, 1896, to authorize the Company to make and maintain the light railways hereinafter described with all necessary stations, buildings, sidings, junctions, approaches, wharves, works, appliances and conveniences connected therewith that is to say:

'A Railway (No. 1) 7 furlongs 5 chains or thereabouts in length, wholly situate in the parish and borough of Southwold, in the county of Suffolk, commencing by a junction with the Southwold Railway at a point thereon 9 chains or thereabouts, measured in a north-easterly direction from the eastern end of the Swing Bridge by which that railway is carried over the River Blyth, proceeding thence in a south-easterly direction across the marsh lands adjoining, and on the east side and along the bank of the said river and Southwold Harbour to, along, and terminating on the New Quay at Southwold.

'A Railway (No. 2), 10 chains or thereabouts in length ... commencing by a junction with **Railway (No.1)**, hereinbefore described, at a point thereon 125 yards or thereabouts measured in a south-easterly direction from the south-west corner of Blackshore Quay and passing thence in a north-westerly direction to, along and terminating on that quay at or near the northern end thereof.'

Progress was still very slow but finally, after another two years of negotiating with Fasey's Harbour Company and Southwold Corporation, the Southwold Harbour Light Railway Order 1913 was authorised by the Board of Trade on 25 September 1913, to construct and operate the proposed branch on a gauge of three foot, with authority to convert the line to four feet eight and a half inches. David Lee's researches have also uncovered some concern amongst the directors of the Southwold

Railway Company in a letter to W.C. Chambers from H.W. Chambers:

'Then there is the rotten branch to the Harbour (which won't pay for years) which Pain is very keen about going on with at once now that the Order and legal preliminaries are all settled with the Harbour Company and Southwold Corporation.'

Before any work started, the question of funding had to be resolved because Pain, at the meeting of the directors on 20 March 1914, stated that it was necessary to raise about £2,000. The directors decided to approach the Ordinary share and Debenture stock holders but that resulted in insufficient funds being raised so a bank loan was negotiated and the free grant from HM Treasury was also available.

Messrs Howard Farrow of Brixton were appointed to construct the branch in a contract dated 12 August 1914 (**Fig 79**). During that month, 602 tons of railway material was landed for construction and the work was completed by November 1914. E.R. Cooper, Secretary of the Harbour Company, reported the Branch as being ready for traffic with a newspaper notice on 18 November. The line was passed by the BoT for goods and mineral traffic in 1915 although it had already carried at least one load of fish. E.R. Cooper recorded in his diary that on Sunday 6 December 1914, '…the first fish train ran from the Quay with 11 tons of sprats; on the 7 December 17 tons went from the Quay by train.'

There were great expectations that the branch would enable the fish landed during the herring season to be more conveniently transported by train – even to a greater advantage should the gauge be altered to standard – but it was probably not appreciated at the time that the majority of fish landed would be exported to Northern Europe from the Harbour. Business for the Harbour but not for the Railway.

Unfortunately, because planning and construction of the Harbour Branch had been so protracted, the 1914 herring season was over before the BoT passed the line. Shortly after completion of the Light Railway the SR was faced with further expense following erosion of the river bank during 1915 near the weigh bridge and on 13 January 1916 severe gales caused more damage there and considerable further damage to the whole Harbour Light Railway. An appeal was made to the Southwold

Fig 79: Farrow of Brixton were the contractors who laid the Harbour Branch – using this temporary railway on the line of the Branch (see embankment in background).

Corporation to share the costs but they 'could not see their way to make any grant towards the cost of the work'.

In 1917, the Railway Company considered having the Harbour Light Railway approved permanently by the BoT for conveyance of passengers. The line was again inspected and passed in 1917, the only requirements being that the line should only be used in daylight, the turnout to Blackshore Quay siding be padlocked, and the line worked by one engine in steam.

The final costs for the SR of the construction of the Harbour Branch was £3,920 4s.6d, of which half (£1,960 2s.3d) was received as the free grant from HM Treasury. The Company finances were hard pressed to cover this debt burden, particularly as insufficient funds were not raised on appeal to existing shareholders and a bank loan had to be financed and repaid.

Figs 74,75 and **78** show the course of the Branch which was built as a Light Railway so reasonably sturdy but functional. However, the preceding Figures have not shown the complexity of the Harbour Branch Junction which is sketched in **Fig 80**. To avoid interfering with traffic on the main line, the Branch has a short loop which can be approached from either down trains from Halesworth or up trains from Southwold. There was also a head shunt at either end of the loop for shunting manoeuvres or to stable the 'Ballast Engine' referred to in the working instructions below. Such a junction suggests that the Harbour Branch might be handling a lot of traffic; alas that was not so, although it was used for military traffic during the First World War but after the war, traffic rapidly declined.

The SR worked the Branch although the Company did not own it. To facilitate working, the block section Southwold/Blythburgh was divided into two sections as described in Chapter 12. Before opening the Branch, instructions were issued for the working of the line by a 'Ballast Engine' which was presumably used for construction trains:

- The Ballast Engine was to leave Southwold Station at 6.20am with the Train Staff.
- On arrival at the junction the Fireman was to let the Engine onto the Light Railway and walk back with the Train Staff to Southwold station.
- At 11.00am the Engine was to return to the junction where the Walberswick Station Master let the engine onto the running line to proceed with the Train Staff to Southwold where the Engine was to take water.
- In the meantime the Walberswick Station Master was to remain at the junction for the return of the engine, let it onto the Branch and then return to his station with the Train Staff.
- On conclusion of the day's work at 6.00pm (7.00pm Saturdays) the Walberswick Station Master again walked to the junction with the Train Staff and a Train Staff Ticket, to let the Engine on to the running line.

**SKETCH PLAN (from OS maps)
of HARBOUR BRANCH JUNCTION**

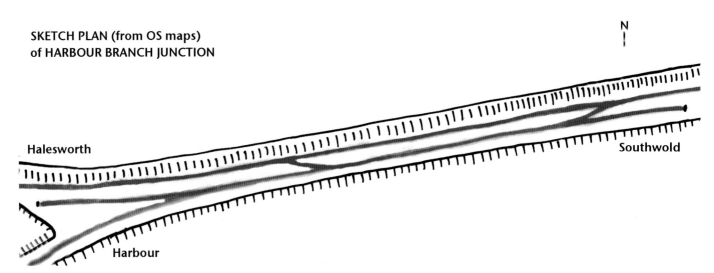

Fig 80: Sketch plan, from OS maps, of the Southwold Harbour Branch junction.

- The Driver was shown the Train Staff, given the Train Staff Ticket, and returned to Southwold while the Station Master returned on foot to Walberswick with the Train Staff.

After the construction period finished, no further instructions were issued – or have survived – so there is no record of how the branch was worked. Between 1920 and 1927 (no statistics for 1919), tonnage carried on the Branch dropped from a total of 455 tons to under 20 tons in 1927, giving a total for the eight years of 1,594 tons. During the early 1920s, the traffic was

mainly material for improving the county's roads and some coal for the Southwold Gas Works. With the decrease in traffic, the Railway Company, who still worked the branch, ceased to use it from 1927. As early as 1922, one platelayer/general labourer was discharged from No 2, Southwold length which included the Branch. Coincidentally, Fasey went bankrupt but the Southwold Corporation declined to have any interest in the Harbour. In 1929 there were discussions about the possibility of the Harbour being taken back by the Corporation; it was finally re-purchased in 1931 for £2.0.0.

Fig 81: Southwold Railway Harbour Branch multi gauge weighbridge on the Fish Quay – early 1920s but already boarded up.

Fig 82: Southwold Railway Harbour Branch track to the Fish Quay – mid-1920s. The fence to the left is beside the Ferry path.

Fig 83: Remains of Blackshore Quay siding and a timber buffer-stop similar to the one shown at Blythburgh in **Fig.54**.

CHAPTER 8

SOUTHWOLD RAILWAY DURING THE FIRST WORLD WAR – 1914-1918

The First World War broke out on 4 August 1914 when the Government, having formed the Railway Executive Committee in 1912 to run the railways in times of emergency, immediately took over running of most railway companies, including the Southwold Railway. From 1914 until the summer of 1916, the Southwold Company continued to operate the same train service and then reduced it to only four trains each way with an extra on Saturday evenings. From September 1914, special constables were recruited to guard certain UK railway installations including the Southwold Railway at Blythburgh.

When Southwold became active with military personnel, the Railway ran special trains for troop movements and two contingents of volunteers left by train. On 15 October 1914, the Ostend-registered fishing smack *Anna William* 028 brought into the Harbour some Belgian refugees who went to London by train via Halesworth on the following day. *Anna William* left Southwold for Lowestoft on 19 October. The Harbour Branch's purpose was reversed by conveyance of military traffic and coal for Royal Navy (RN) patrol craft and mine sweepers. The RN used the Harbour as a coaling station, replacing all export and import of civil traffic. The total tonnage of coal, for bunkering RN Patrol Boats and Minesweepers, was 4,663, all of which must have been manually transhipped at Halesworth Station –

Year	Tons
1914	66
1915	1,072
1916	1,510
1917	1,446
1918	569
Total	**4,663**

The Southwold Harbour Light Railway became available for traffic on 18 November 1914. Early in 1915, the swing bridge was operated on at least 17 occasions to pass 25 Lowestoft steam and sail drifters for laying up in the River Blyth. It was not long, however, before these vessels were commandeered by the Admiralty to become Patrol Boats; all had sailed by early February 1915.

On 14 April 1915, the town sustained its first attack by Zeppelin (L5 commanded by Kaptain-Leutnant der Reserve Alois Bocker) which flew over Southwold, on to Halesworth and then over Henham Hall where some bombs were dropped with minimal damage. The airship flew on to Wolsey Bridge, at the head of Wolsey Creek, where one bomb resulted in slight damage, then returned over Southwold and dropped a bomb in the Station yard damaging six-wheeled wagon 31 and the Carpenter's shop causing a small fire. The airship then set course for Lowestoft where bombing caused some more damage.

In early June, barbed wire entanglements were erected on the top of the cliffs in front of the town for which five and a half tons of wire were brought from Halesworth by train to Southwold Station. About the same date, the swing bridge was close-boarded between the rails and for three feet on either side of the track, to make it a suitable walkway for evacuation in case of a threatened invasion.

In October, General Manager Ward informed the Southwold Station Master and the Locomotive Foreman that Special Trains were required by the Military Authorities on Sundays to Halesworth, but there was not sufficient time to advise all concerned by notice from the London Office, the Southwold/Walberswick train staff would operate throughout the three Block Sections to Halesworth. As the signals would be at 'danger', drivers were cautioned to proceed at 5mph past them; Wenhaston station would be open for operation of the level crossing gates.

Locomotive Foreman W.G. Jackson retired aged 65 because his work for the Railway, and the strain he suffered, became too much for him. Guard A.E. Wright had retired in October 1914. The successor to Jackson, George Belcher, was reminded by letter that an engine should be ready on week days at 7.00am for shunting.

Southwold was bombarded from the sea on 26 January 1917 when about 70 shells caused damage to at least three properties, but not to the Railway apart from a broken carriage window in the Station yard caused by a splinter from a shell which damaged the nearby Police Station in High Street.

On 30 April 1917, probably the most outstanding wartime activity of the Railway and the Harbour Light Railway was their part in repatriating a number of neutral Dutch nationals. They were stranded seamen from torpedoed or mined ships, and civilians, who were conveyed from London to Flushing via Southwold. The steamer SS *Zealand* (850 tons), of the Zealand Steamship Company, anchored off the Harbour about noon to embark these people and convey them home. This route was used because the German Government would only assure safe passage from Southwold Harbour. About 100 passengers with their baggage arrived at Southwold station by the 1.42pm train; they walked across the Common to the Harbour where they were conveyed in three RN Patrol Boats, provided by the Admiralty, to SS *Zealand*. Meanwhile, their baggage was moved by 'special' engine and a short goods train along the Harbour Branch to the Harbour and the baggage was ferried by the same Patrol Boats to the ship which left at 6.00pm. It is understood that a further 580 Dutch nationals were similarly conveyed on 7 occasions.

The incident caused some public interest and enquiries if this was a new steam service from Holland to Southwold! General Manager Ward suggested that in future it might be possible at Halesworth Junction to hear Porters calling 'change here for Flushing'. The Southwold Harbour Light Railway was passed by the BoT for conveying passengers with restrictions, as mentioned in Chapter 6.

From 2 April 1917, arrangements were made for Walberswick station to close entirely on account of lack of traffic and to enable one man to join up. In fact, W.J.V. Nicholls, Walberswick Station Master, moved to Southwold station as a clerk, but it is not known who was released for the armed forces. In all probability, two men actually joined up, one being Arthur Pain's son, Claude.

The Southwold Railway's contribution to wartime manpower is referred to in *The Railway Workers 1840 – 1970*, Frank McKenna, Faber & Faber, 1980, but incorrectly: 'The Easingwold and Avonmouth Light [Railways] sent two men each and the Southwold Railway one man from its staff of ten.' The Southwold Railway was employing nearly 30 men by 1918 but the surviving records do not show any temporary replacements which, on other railways, were often women. There is no record of any women being employed at any time on the Southwold Railway.

CHAPTER 9

HISTORY OF THE RAILWAY TO CLOSURE – FROM 1919 TO 1929

The First World War was the turning point in the career of the Southwold Railway, which up till then had enjoyed a sustained increase in traffic, but which afterwards was to suffer a rapid recession of fortune. The war years themselves brought great changes to the line; gone were the crowds of holidaymakers upon whom the railway had relied so much for revenue (**Fig 84**) and in their place were movements of troops. The fishery traffic for which the harbour branch was then being constructed also vanished, though the line proved very useful in the transport of materials for construction of sea-shore defence works. At the outbreak of hostilities, the railway was taken over by the Government 'for the duration' and was virtually handed over to the War Department. Large numbers of troops were stationed in the district because of its vulnerability as a possible invasion target.

By the end of the war, the Southwold Railway Company had abandoned all hope of extension, conversion to standard gauge, or even replacement of existing stock, at any rate by their own efforts. The

Fig 84: Wealthy passengers and 'quality' luggage at Southwold c1900.

Company concentrated their dwindling resources on keeping their existing equipment going as long as possible. A healthy step in this direction was the rebuilding of the coaches.

Government control continued until midnight on 15 August 1921. Traffic in the war years had been heavy and dividends continued for a few years. 1% was paid on ordinary shares for each of the years 1915 -1921 and 2% in 1922, but then ceased, as did payment on 5% preference shares, as there loomed the menace of road competition. In April 1921, Southwold Corporation suggested that the Railway Company's Chairman meet them to discuss improvements to the railway, including gauge conversion, but Chairman Pain declined, with the plea that there 'would be no advantage in such a discussion at the present time'. Possibly the Corporation thought the archaic and run-down railway was making the town look ridiculous; the Corporation's sudden interest seems inexplicable otherwise, as they had never shown the railway a helping hand while the management remained in London, nor did they ever again.

In 1921, the Railway Act, often known as the Grouping Act, was initiated by the Government and passed by Parliament – (**Fig 85**).

The Southwold Railway was not included in the provisions of the Act and remained independent of the LNER, but the Company was not much more successful in negotiating good working arrangements at Halesworth, or in general, with the LNER than they had been with the GER.

Nevertheless, road competition did not have any immediately ruinous effect on the railway, which continued through the early 1920s to carry a substantial traffic of all classes, averaging around 85,000 passengers and 15,000 tons of freight annually. These were, respectively, lower and higher than the pre-war figures of 105,000 and 13,000. Though the receipts were insufficient to permit the replacement of rolling stock, they were enough to keep things moving and to provide a net balance in the order of £250. The Southwold Railway, it should be remembered, was not to be classed with such chronically hard-up systems as the Shropshire & Montgomeryshire or the Bishop's Castle Railways, which never really had sufficient traffic to pay their way. On the contrary, the Southwold Railway had a solid local patronage, built up over 40 years of

faithful if unspectacular service. There were still plenty of holidaymakers too, adding their quota to the revenue and to many the trip over the Southwold Railway for the last lap of the journey was a happy anticipatory climax to the holiday. As the LNER train left Halesworth station and the passengers crossed over the footbridge to the Southwold Railway, the bustle of the twentieth century fell away and gave place to a world of earlier tempo. The porters loaded the luggage, everyone boarded the train and with a shrill squeak from the engine, the train moved off for its journey. The 'regulars' would foregather in the guard's compartment to chat about local affairs, the familiar landscape forgotten; but to the holiday passengers the rocking carriage brought many unexpected sights of nature which pressed closely on the Railway (**Fig 57**).

To the visitors, the best part of the trip was between Blythburgh and Walberswick, where could be seen herons fishing in the shallows – they still nest at Hill Crest – unfamiliar species of duck as well as the ubiquitous coots and moorhens; and, beyond that, the gorsey expanse of Walberswick Common.

Thus for a few more years the Southwold Railway carried on, as it had done since 1879 and the decline, when it came, was sudden. 1926 was the critical year, with the numbers of passengers more than 10,000 below the 1925 figure, and a net debit of £4. Passenger revenue continued to drop and a principal reason was the improved frequency of the Eastern Counties Road Car Company's bus service from 5 April 1928. In March, Southwold Corporation had granted Eastern Counties a licence to pick up passengers within the town. Service number 30 called at all the Southwold Railway stations except Walberswick and as a result, receipts on the railway were greatly reduced. In order to combat this severe competition from the bus services, it was decided to put into operation from 1 November 1928 special Third Class Day Return tickets, some at pre-war fares, and in conjunction with the LNER.

This was not the first time the Railway had issued tickets at reduced rates; an earlier reduction was in conjunction with the GER in 1912 when members of Southwold Golf Club, travelling to Southwold and presenting their Club membership card, could obtain tickets at a single fare plus one third for same-day returns or, if booked on a Saturday, could return on the following Monday. During the summer months of 1914,

CHAPTER 55.

An Act to provide for the reorganisation and A.D. 1921. further regulation of Railways and the discharge of liabilities arising in connection with the possession of Railways, and otherwise to amend the Law relating to Railways, and to extend the duration of the Rates Advisory Committee. [19th August 1921.]

BE it enacted by the King's most Excellent Majesty, by and with the advice and consent of the Lords Spiritual and Temporal, and Commons, in this present Parliament assembled, and by the authority of the same, as follows :—

PART I.

REORGANISATION OF RAILWAY SYSTEM.

1.—(1) With a view to the reorganisation and more Grouping of railways. efficient and economical working of the railway system of Great Britain railways shall be formed into groups in accordance with the provisions of this Act, and the principal railway companies in each group shall be amalgamated, and other companies absorbed in manner provided by this Act.

(2) The groups to be formed shall be those specified in the first column of the First Schedule to this Act, and as respects the several groups the railway companies to be amalgamated (in this Act referred to as " constituent companies ") shall be those set out in relation to each group in the second column of that schedule, and the companies to be absorbed (in this Act referred to as " subsidiary companies ") shall be those set out in relation to each group in the second column of that Schedule, and the companies to be absorbed (in this Act referred to as "subsidiary companies) shall be those set out in relation to each group in the third column of that Schedule, and the companies constituted by such amalgamations are in this Act referred to as amalgamated companies.

Fig 85: Opening paragraphs of the Railway Act 1921 which, by grouping together most railway companies, created four principal companies – LNER, SR, GWR, LMS.

Fig 86: List's bank and the Heronry on the banks of the River Blyth between Blythburgh and Walberswick Stations.

again in conjunction with the GER, cheap Excursion Tickets were available to Aldeburgh and Ipswich and return the same day.

From 1922 to SR closure in 1929 reduced fare tickets, during summer at pre-war fares, were advertised under a variety of descriptions:-

- Cheap Tickets
- Cheap Day and Half Day Trips
- Cheap Trips
- Cheap Excursion Tickets
- Early Half-Day-Closing Trips
- Half Days to and from Halesworth and Southwold with the intermediate stations but often excluding Walberswick; also to LNER stations.

Some events were specially catered for;

- In 1923 a football match on 2 April – Southwold Town v. Old Nactonians for the Southwold Hospital Cup, when two special trains ran with cheap tickets.
- On 10 October 1924, in conjunction with the LNER, a trip to Wembley for the Exhibition left Southwold at 5.45am and arrived back about 3.45am next day for a fare of 12/- 9d.
- On 24 November 1927 there were Cheap Trains from Halesworth to Southwold for the film 'Ben Hur', with a special late return train.

Following the end of the war in November 1918, the Southwold Railway services were:

- Summer months –   6 trains daily except for Sundays – 4 trains daily
- Spring and autumn – 5 trains daily but no Sunday services.
- Winter –   4 trains daily but no Sunday services.

The bus company ran five journeys, with three extra on Saturdays and five journeys on Sundays. Buses were five minutes swifter than the trains but did not include Walberswick. On Sundays, two additional services were operated by Halesworth & District Blue Bus services from 1925. Despite the Railway's efforts, the bus fares was cheaper at 10d. for the full journey; the Railway charged 1/2d for the whole journey. As a result, payment of interest on 5% debenture stock ceased from December

Fig 87: Unloading goods traffic at Southwold Station – 1920s.

1926 while on 4% preferred debenture stock continued until December 1928. Dividend payment on the Ordinary Shares and Preference Shares had ceased from 1923.

Remarkably, there were short-term improvements for the railway in 1927. Passenger traffic increased and the goods tonnage of 18,460 was the highest since the war; net receipts were £751. But this tide of fortune ebbed even further in 1928 when there were 26,000 fewer passengers in spite of a cut in fares from 2/3d to 1/6d return then a further reduction to 1/- in the summer months. Freight traffic was still heavy (**Figs 87** and **88**) but the Southwold Railway relied largely on passenger traffic and could not survive without it. The direct cause of the fresh decline was the omnibus company giving 'door to door' service including some stops en route as well as at the SR stations. The railway complained bitterly to Southwold Corporation but the latter replied that in changing times, and in the public interest, they could hardly do otherwise than support the bus companies. This last straw, however, merely precipitated the crisis

that was clearly inevitable for there was insufficient traffic for two forms of transport and the railway was in no shape to meet competition; with its dowdy carriages the buses offered better comfort. The SR tightened its belt again and again, but economy was not the answer to its problems and the Board Minutes of these years make pathetic reading.

Wages and salary cuts were accepted by the staff in the autumn of 1921; further cuts were imposed two years later and again in 1925. Some bonuses and pensions to retired employees were reduced, though, to the Company's credit, it must be recorded that they awarded pensions to the newly retired. Examples were a PW ganger who was regarded as 'too feeble to work'; an Operating Staff member who was 'afraid to risk another winter'; and a Fireman. They were all over 60 years of age while the Carpenter was over 70 years. Saddest of all, the Wenhaston Station Master was fatally injured while shunting. Even Walberswick Common Lands Charities had a go at the railway in 1923, ordering them to quit.

Fig 88: Loading goods at Southwold Station – 1920s. Staff, left to right at front of picture are: Porter Stannard; Guard Burley; Porter Fisk.

However, the Solicitors advised the SR to ignore that threat and nothing transpired. On the credit side, the BoT in 1924 released the Company from the statutory requirements of printed returns, except for the annual return, and the LNER in 1928 promised to regard the SR as a Light Railway and afford them protection under their Road Transport Bill.

The tide had turned against the struggling Railway. At the Board meeting in November 1928 it was reported that the following issues needed to be noted or resolved:

- The North British Locomotive Company were pressing for a settlement of the balance of £470.00 due on the new boiler supplied for No 3 *Southwold*
- Mr W. Doy had given up his omnibus standage in Southwold Station yard. It was taken over by Belcher & Son who would supply a taxi to meet all trains
- Messrs Moy (Coal Merchants) were giving up their tenancy at Blythburgh Station. It was taken over by M. Platt.

- Adnams & Co [Southwold Brewery] were giving up the advertising spaces they had on the fixed upper lights of all the carriages
- Lowestoft Coaling Co have given up their tenancy at Walberswick Station because of the bad condition of the cart track between the Station and the village
- The cartage agent at Walberswick Station had given up their tenancy because of the bad condition of the cart track between the Station and the village
- Shell Mex have given up their agency at Halesworth Station
- Eastern Counties Road Car Co started a Southwold – Halesworth motor omnibus service on 5 April 1928.

The above were the Board's main concerns in November, because most of them meant a loss of income, so in December 1928, further cuts in wages were imposed. As a result, several of the staff, no doubt suspecting what lay ahead, left the Company they had served for many years.

In their Report of 31 December 1928, the Directors admitted that the financial position of the Company was causing them considerable anxiety. In their extremity, the Company appealed to Southwold Corporation on 28 February 1929 for help, either in the form of a grant or the imposition of restrictions on the competing bus service. The Corporation, while agreeing that the closing of the line would adversely affect the conveyance of freight and cause hardships to the discharged employees, decided that they had no power to subsidise the railway, nor to interfere with facilities running smoothly in the public service.

At the same time, the SR Chairman and SR Director Walter Chambers approached Mr Wilson, Divisional Manager of the LNER, in the hope that the latter might take over the line.

The normal half-yearly meeting of the Company was held on 22 March 1929. It was reported in the local press the following day that the Chairman:

'feared the end was coming … Southwold Corporation were singularly supine in the matter and had decided there was no way it could assist the Company … matters were now approaching the extreme point in the negotiations and, unless assistance was given, the Southwold line would be closed'.

There is also one other curious item to record from this meeting; Claude Pain was made a Director. Mr Pain stated that this would free his father, Arthur, and Mr W. Chambers from attendance at future Board meetings. He and Mr Herbert Chambers, he said, would form a quorum of two for settling outstanding business, but it was not for another 30 years that this action proved of signal importance.

At their March meeting, the Board, as no reply had been received from the LNER or Southwold Corporation (to whom a further letter had been sent), agreed that it was impossible to continue working and that notice be sent to all servants terminating their employment with effect from 11 April 1929. A letter had been sent to the Ministry of Transport on 27 March 1929 asking for help, but they replied that they had no funds to do so.

The LNER were informed of the Board's decision to close but, as they still had not replied to the SR's appeal by

2 April, a further interview was held with Mr Wilson on 4 April who promised a reply on the following day. It was agreed that, should the reply be unsatisfactory, the Railway would close as agreed. If the LNER did give promise of assistance, notice would be sent to SR staff continuing their employment on a week-to-week basis. The LNER regretted they could not provide financial help and this answer, delivered on 5 April as promised, was telegraphed to the Estates, Works and Repairs Committee of Southwold Corporation, who were meeting that day, in the form: 'Assistance from LNER definitely declined: railway closing 11th instant. Ward, Southwold Railway'.

The ambiguous wording of the first part of the sentence caused a laugh but though the announcement of the impending closure was received with concern – especially for freight traffic – the Southwold Committee concluded that they must adhere to their original decision. On the same day, a notice was sent to all railway companies, the Ministry of Transport, Postmaster General, W.H. Smith & Son, Cartage Agents Day and Belcher, and tenants of Station Yards. Notices were also sent to the *East Anglian Daily Times* and the *Halesworth Times*. The Manager was instructed to 'Go to Southwold and make the necessary arrangements'.

The Company did not incur the expense of a notice informing the public of the closure of the line and it was still possible for the unsuspecting public to purchase tourist tickets (tickets available for a return journey up to six months from the date of issue) until 10 April 1929. It is doubtful, however, whether any other railway closure had such publicity surrounding its demise. Reporters interviewed everyone – Secretary, stationmasters, engine drivers, platelayers – and articles appeared in local papers and in the national press. Enthusiasts came from all over the country for a final trip; and, most spectacular of all, Pathe News made a film of the railway a few weeks before the end and the closure was filmed by Gaumont Pictorial. Arnold Barrett Jenkins also made a local film.

Although the Railway Company, perhaps understandably, did not publicise their plight or their proposed solution, rumours were circulated. The St Edmund's parish magazine, the *Southwold Magazine*, stated in the January 1929 issue:

'The position of the Southwold Railway Co is of vital interest to the Borough. Great has been the fun made of it [but] if it ceased to function the town would certainly be placed in a very difficult position.'

At the meeting of the East Suffolk Finance Committee on 26 March 1929 Mr P.C. Loftus (Southwold) warned the Committee: '[I] would like to warn the Committee … that the Southwold Railway [is] approaching extinction'.

The April issue of the *Southwold Magazine* reported that 'tradespeople were anxious about the position [of the Railway's future] and [asked] what provision would be made to continue transport of goods, especially heavy goods?' On Friday 5 April, articles appeared in several national newspapers, including *The Times*, *Daily Mail* and *Daily News*, outlining the history of the Railway and with some announcing closure on 11 April. On 10 April the *Halesworth Times* carried a front page Notice (**Fig 89**).

The last passenger train from Southwold was the 5.23pm on Thursday 11 April 1929 and was a carnival affair (**Fig 90**).

Despite the bitterly cold weather, several hundred people gathered at Southwold Station to give the well-packed train (there were 150 aboard) a rousing send-off. A wreath of laurels was placed on the coupling hook of the locomotive No 4 *Wenhaston* – in charge of the brothers Stannard – and, the Stationmaster's bell having given official sanction for the journey to begin, the train drew slowly out of the Station, with two extra coaches to deal with the anticipated crowd for the return trip. One passenger at least — Major Debney — had also travelled on the first train nearly 50 years ago (**Fig 91**) but, whatever memories were recalled, the spirit of the last journey was one of gaiety and not of sadness, with everyone storing up yarns to retell later.

Halesworth platform was also thronged, and the LNER engine whistled a farewell to *Wenhaston* whose replying toot showed that she still had a little steam to spare. There were sightseers at each station to see the down last through train which was delayed by the crowds till after dusk but when the guard came along to light the lamps it was discovered that none had wicks! A prolonged whistle as the engine entered the cutting on Southwold Common announced its approach to the crowds at the station, who sang *Auld Lang Syne* as the train drew in. As the coaches were shunted to the bay for the last time, and *Wenhaston* was taken to the Engine Shed, three loud cheers went up and the proceedings were over.

There were still several consignments of coal at Halesworth and other goods at the intermediate stations to be cleared after the last passenger train had run. In order to clear these and afterwards to take the rolling stock up to Halesworth station for storage, No 4 *Wenhaston* was used. According to Mr Ward's instructions, *Wenhaston* was kept at work until the end of the following week, returning to Southwold after the last trip on the morning of Saturday 20 April. According to W.J. Fisk – Goods Porter and Shunter – 'it was a difficult job to get all the stock into the sidings at Halesworth but it was managed, except for Van 14 which remained at Southwold.' Signals were disconnected, stations closed and gates locked; 'The Southwold Railway, ... like an out-of-work actor, was 'resting'.

Mr Girling, the Stationmaster at Southwold, had meantime checked all the books at the other stations and

NOTICE
THE SOUTHWOLD RAILWAY COMPANY hereby give notice that the Railway will be CLOSED for all classes of traffic on the evening of Thursday 11th April 1929

Fig 89: Closure of the Southwold Railway announced in a front page Notice, *Halesworth Times*, Wednesday 10 April 1929.

Fig 90: The 5.23pm ex-Southwold was the last Southwold Railway up passenger train on 11 April 1929.

Fig 91: Major Debney is on the carriage steps; he also travelled on the first train in September 1879.
On the platform is Mr Hurst, Southwold Borough Council Surveyor.

Fig 92: Stationmaster Girling's farewell to his staff at Southwold, April 1929. From left to right: **FRONT ROW** Guard Burley; Fireman Adamson; Station Master Girling; Porter Aldis; Doy's driver Self. **BACK ROW** GPO Telegraph Clerk Marchant; Porter Fisk; and Arnold Barrett Jenkins (with camera).

cleared all outstanding charges. Then he, with the rest of the staff of 30 men, were discharged to find what work there was to be had in a world hit by the depression of the 1920s. Two of them ran garages; the engine crews found work at Fordux Mills in Southwold; Mr Girling took on the proprietorship of the *White Hart* at Blythburgh; but some of the older men, who had spent nearly all their lives in the service of the Southwold Railway, found times hard indeed.

Following the closure, the LNER announced arrangements – in the *Railway Gazette* (12 April 1929) and other sources – to take effect immediately to preserve through communications and bookings with Southwold. For passengers, the Eastern Counties Road Car Co omnibuses connected with all the principal trains calling at Halesworth Station. For goods and parcels traffic, a road delivery service between Halesworth, Southwold and intervening villages was proposed.

Looking back in the light of railway history, the closure of the Southwold Railway at first appears an inevitable example of the current trend of events. Road transport grew rapidly during the 1920s and was greatly encouraged by the availability of war-surplus vans and lorries and ex-soldiers trained to drive them. In 1929, the Southwold Railway, as it then operated, could never pay and the Board chose to cease operations forthwith rather than risk further loss in attempts to regain the traffic. From a materialistic point of view, their decision is justifiable but it was not very creditable to their enterprise nor pleasant for their employees.

The suddenness of the closure suggests, too, that the directors had hopes of precipitating a transport crisis in Southwold which would force upon the community the necessity of helping the railway to restart. There was indeed a strong local opinion that the line should be re-opened, at any rate for goods traffic, and in May 1929, Southwold Borough Council approached the Ministry of Transport to see what could be done. The MoT, however, regretted it was not in their power to render financial aid nor could they compel the railway company to maintain a service. However, the MoT informed the Borough Council by letter that, in the event of re-opening, everything possible would be done to smooth out legal questions. Sir Humphrey could not have written a better response for his Minister to deliver.

The Company's share and debenture holders made no move to encourage a re-opening, so the Borough Council decided to ask the Directors of the Railway if they were willing to sell and a letter to this effect was sent to Mr Ward, Secretary and General Manager of the Southwold Railway Company. Meanwhile, following an application by SR debenture holders to the Halesworth magistrates, the Bench appointed Mr Ward Receiver for the Company from 9 May 1929.

Mr Ward replied to the Borough Council letter he had received as Secretary and General Manager thus:

'Dear Sir,
'With reference to your letter of the 8th inst.
'As I have been appointed Receiver of this Company. will you please address your application to me. Yours faithfully, H.WARD'.

It seemed from this 'typical and paltry' letter (as one Southwold councillor put it) that the Company were not anxious to negotiate as it should not have been too difficult for Receiver Ward to consult with the late Secretary Ward and create a similarly evasive reply!

Fig 93: Former Station Master Girling on the platform of Southwold Station in the early 1980s. Mr Girling's memories have been very helpful in telling this story of the Southwold Railway's history and operation. It was a sad but pertinent chance that there is an Eastern Counties bus in the background.

PART 3

BUILDING AND WORKING THE RAILWAY

Another Preambulation

I have inserted another preambulation to introduce this part of our book because David Lee provides here a previously unpublished account of how the Southwold Railway was built and worked. His researches, some of the illustrations, and the human stories interwoven with the technical data are written by an author who was, for 19 years, a railwayman himself. Albeit David worked on the standard gauge GWR then BR railway, the principles, working practices and rules were what the SR emulated. What follows explains in a non-patronising way what is already familiar to railway-knowledgeable readers but is a mystery to others and, in the twenty-first century, is unknown to younger readers. Read on and enjoy!

Rob Shorland-Ball

Fig 94: Well ballasted SR track and wayside fencing east of Blythburgh.

CHAPTER 10

PERMANENT WAY AND CIVIL ENGINEERING INCLUDING THE BLYTH SWING BRIDGE

CONSTRUCTION AND INSPECTION

The Act of Parliament authorising formation and construction of the Southwold Railway had been passed in July 1876 but, because of difficulties in raising the necessary finance, the main contractor, Charles Chambers of Westminster, London, refused to enter into a definite contract until assured that the necessary finance and land would be acquired. Chambers was finally persuaded that all would be well and work started on 3 May 1878. Appeals were made to existing shareholders to encourage them to subscribe for additional shares, and some did.

The Great Eastern Railway had agreed to subscribe towards the cost of the Halesworth Station works, including the connecting footbridge from the standard gauge platform to the SR Halesworth Station. For this work, the GER Locomotive, Way and Works Committee had agreed a tender submitted by Messrs Stanley Hall & Company at a cost of £157 and to complete in four weeks.

In March 1879, the Chairman (R.C. Rapier) assured a public meeting that work was proceeding satisfactorily and that 'in a very few months you will actually see the iron horse marching triumphantly into the town'.

Fig 95: Track through Southwold Common cutting illustrating superelevation on a curve and quality of track-laying and ballast. The footbridge was a later addition in 1903.

SOUTHWOLD LINE.

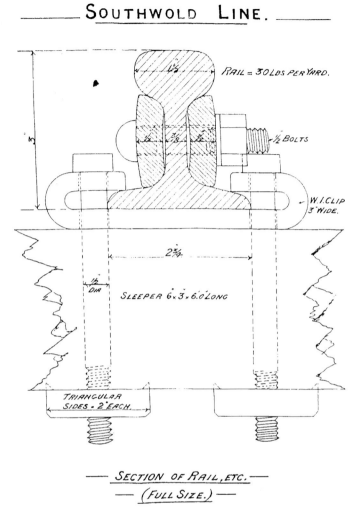

RAIL = 30 LBS PER YARD.

½ BOLTS

W. I. CLIP 3" WIDE.

SLEEPER 6 × 3 × 6.0 LONG

2¾

½ DIA

TRIANGULAR SIDES - 2" EACH.

— SECTION OF RAIL, ETC. —
— (FULL SIZE.) —

Fig 96: detailed drawing of SR track from GER Survey of the Southwold Line carried out in 1892 / 1894 in preparation for a possible take-over purchase by the GER.

(*The Southwold Railway*, Eric S. Tonks, published by the author, 1950.) Further details of the construction period have not survived in either the Chambers family papers or the local press; neither is there any certain knowledge of the locomotives Chambers used during construction.

Charles Chambers encountered, so far as it is known, no difficulties or need for major work in crossing the gently undulating terrain the line's formation followed, the only earth works of any note being List's Bank and List's Cutting (**Figs 59** and **60)** and the cutting through Southwold Common (**Fig 95**).

Other cuttings and further embankments were relatively minor works; the cuttings only a few feet deep, the embankments at a similar height. However, laying of the track was delayed because the component parts

of the siding points at stations and the rails allocated by the sub-contractor were not available until late June 1879.

The Company, on 3 September 1879, advised the Board of Trade that the line would be sufficiently completed for conveying passengers safely by 12 September and ready for inspection during the following ten days.

The inspecting officer appointed was Major General C.S. Hutchinson RE who carried out the official BoT inspection on Friday 19 September. The details of his Inspection are in Chapter 3. Hutchinson was also notified about three complaints received from local landowners which were investigated. The Railway Company was slow to respond to these concerns, but we know from subsequent evidence (**Fig 97**) that the Blythburgh bridge deck had to be propped and subsequently the props were replaced by concrete abutments (see **Figs 51** and **52** in Chapter 6).

Hutchinson's inspection report, dated 19 September 1879, states that he is generally satisfied with permanent way being laid to specifications agreed. Halesworth, Wenhaston and Southwold stations were completed and satisfactory and Hutchinson considered a platform height of only 9 inches was adequate for this Railway as the carriages had steps to the end platforms. He reported that the arrangements for signals and points interlocking were similar to those on another light railway and, because of the low speed, distant signals had been dispensed with. Working of the line by one engine-in-steam was considered satisfactory.

The size and relative complexity of the River Blyth Swing Bridge caused Hutchinson to describe it in great detail and to note its method of opening and the train safety arrangements necessary to ensure it could not be opened when a train was approaching. He also recommended that supports to bearings at the ends of the swing section girders required attention.

Fencing in some locations was not considered satisfactory and substitutions were necessary by post and rail fencing within six weeks; a further four locations needed attention also within the same time. The engines and rolling stock to work the line were considered to be satisfactory. Subject to Hutchinson's requirements being met he had no hesitation in recommending that the BoT should have no objection to the line being brought into use.

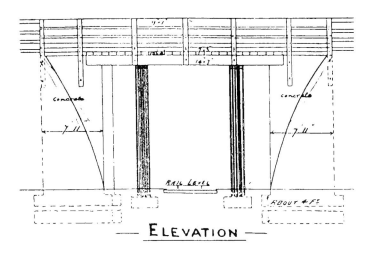

— SOUTHWOLD LINE. —
— BRIDGE AT 4 Mˢ. 72 CHˢ. —

— ELEVATION —

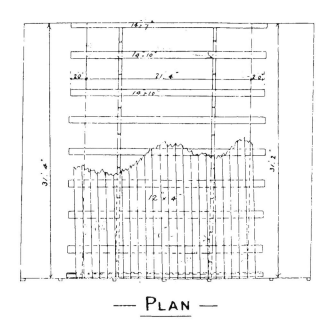

— PLAN —

— SCALE. 8 FEET TO AN INCH. —

Fig 97: From the GER Survey of the Southwold Railway, 1892 / 1894 by which time it had been necessary to place substantial props under the bridge and to improve the decking.

PERMANENT WAY

Specifications were drawn up by Engineer Pain for the track, so the permanent way was laid on stone ballast 18ins deep by 8ft 6ins wide (**Fig 106**). Gravel ballast was used between and almost covering the sleepers which were

Fig.98: Section of SR 30lb per yard rail.

6ft long by 6ins wide by 3ins deep at 2ft 4ins apart and originally for flat bottomed 21ft wrought iron, 30lbs per yard rails. Later the wrought iron rails were re-laid in steel 30ft long. **Fig 98** is a section of SR rail from the Southwold Railway collection at the National Railway Museum.

The rails were fastened mainly with dog spikes each side of the rail while at intervals of 7ft, steel single sole plates were placed under the rail and secured by a dog spike and a fang bolt, or two bolts in some cases. The triangular fanged nuts gripped the underside of the sleepers when tightened (**Fig 98 and 99**). Rail joints were 'fished' with a fang bolt, a double sole plate and 2 dog spikes. Curves were superelevated.

Fabrication of the points and crossings had been sub-contracted to Ransome and Rapier, who supplied rails which had been previously sent out to China where R & R had built and briefly operated the first railway in that country from Woosung to Shanghai. The Woosung gauge was 2ft 6ins and light rails weighing 26lbs per yard were considered sufficient for the 2 small locomotives supplied by R&R, *Celestial Empire* and *Flowery Land*, each weighing only 9 tons. When a heavier R&R locomotive, *Viceroy* of 11 tons, followed it was necessary to ship out what is

Fig 99: SR permanent way fastenings – dog spike, fang bolt and triangular fanged nut.

assumed to have been 30lbs per yard rails, probably early in 1878. The Woosung Road railway was officially opened on 1 July 1876 but was closed on 20 October 1877 and dismantled.

For some time, the rolling stock and dismantled permanent way from the railway was stored, unguarded and uncovered, at the port of Kaohsiung in southern Taiwan. The heavier 30lbs per yard rails were subsequently returned to the UK for allocation to the Southwold Railway contract but did not arrive in the UK until June 1879. The following note appeared in the R & R Order Book for job number 291, 'The following iron rails have come home [to the British Isles] and must be cut.'

Major General Hutchinson made a second inspection of the Southwold Railway in February 1880, when it was noted 3 items required further attention. He also commented, while inspecting Blythburgh station, that it was similar to Wenhaston but 'its use need not, I submit, be objected to by the BoT'.

RELAYING TRACK AFTER THE FIRST WORLD WAR

There is no record in the Company's accounts of any extensive track relaying until 1918, by which time much equipment needed replacing or repairing, the track being no exception, particularly on the curves. Except in 1906 when 1,600 sleepers were purchased, there is no record of any other track materials being bought until between 1918 and 1921 when a total of 50 tons of 30ft steel rails with fastenings were obtained. This material was mainly used to relay the curves at nine locations between 1918 and 1921, while the quantity of scrap rails displaced were sold as a result. Further scrap may have been sold in small lots without record. Scrap rail was periodically sold for various purposes including the Golf Course Bridge over the cutting at Southwold, (page 72 and **Fig 65**) and for supporting tree branches in Henham Park.

MAINTENANCE AND OTHER MATTERS

For maintenance of the permanent way, bridges, fencing, level crossings, hedge and grass cutting, the line was divided into two sections: No. 1 – Halesworth with a hut for tools, etc at Wenhaston and No. 2 – Southwold with a tool hut at Walberswick. Personnel for each Section was a Ganger and 3 Platelayers who could be called upon to assist with loading or unloading at stations and in other ways. The blacksmith at Southwold no doubt assisted when it was necessary to cut rails or other ironwork, the former being done by heating on site and cutting with a cold chisel.

In the absence of a telephone communication, the secretary, H. Ward, had to give all instructions by letter to the Gangers. A bundle of instruction letters for December 1908 to 1909 for Ganger J. Nichols of No. 1 Section is in Southwold Museum collections and a dated summary of concerns and instructions from relevant letters is quoted here. They give an insight into the day-to-day working, and problems, on the railway:

December 1908	Reminder about points being kept in good order in bad weather with special attention to snow in cuttings and level crossings.
2 February 1909	Work on widening necessary for the proposal to convert the line to standard gauge is only briefly referred to; ditches being filled

in – report on progress. Concerned about another ditch near Wenhaston and filling it in [see also 22 March and 11 June 1909].

5 February 1909 — 2.20pm up train was delayed for 5 minutes between the Water Mill and Ball's bridge (No. 4) by sheep on the line; the owners to be traced; how did the sheep get on the line?

25 February 1909 — Attention necessary at Halesworth to the barrow crossing under the foot bridge.

3 March 1909 — Gang to assist the carpenter in erecting the stage for the pump at the Quarry.

22 March 1909 — Report on progress on filling in ditches.

24 March 1909 — Gang to assist the carpenter in painting at Wenhaston and to give a coating of tar to the fencing and station roof and to the transhipment stage at Halesworth Station.

3 June 1909 — Water Mill Bridge (No.7) needed repair for which a baulk 9ft 6ins long by 9ins square was to be supplied.

11 June 1909 — Concern about another ditch at Wenhaston and filling it in.

26 July 1909 — Delay – and again on 26 July – to 5.35pm and 7.10pm up trains between Wenhaston and Halesworth caused by hay on the line; why had it not been removed?

12 August 1909 — Reference to The Railway Fires Act 1905 and prevention of line-side fires; a reminder that growth must be removed and burnt, nor left in heaps.

22 September 1909 — Iron work of all bridges must be prepared then painted.

13 November 1909 — Flooring to the new platform shelter at Halesworth Station must be of good old sleepers.

4 & 12 December 1909 — Trolley wheels need attention; send to Stratford for 'needful.'

New connections to the sidings at Halesworth and Wenhaston were installed during 1921 but not inspected by the BoT until 1928. In each case, the turnouts were locked with the Annetts Key attached to the Train Staff.

When built, the line was equipped with mileposts, placed on the right from Halesworth, and gradient posts placed on the left (**Figs 58** and **106**).

SWING BRIDGE OVER RIVER BLYTH (No.13)

The Southwold Railway crossed the River Blyth and its tributaries four times on the eight miles to Southwold. The largest bridge was a swing bridge over the Blyth just above Blackshore Quay and upstream from Southwold Harbour. **Fig 100** is of the original bridge, before rebuilding for widening and potential gauge change.

This bridge was a major engineering project in the construction of the line and Contractor Chambers sub-contracted the work to Mr Double who, it is understood, obtained the necessary iron work from Belgium. The original drawings have not been traced but in 1892, the GER Civil Engineer included a diagram of the un-rebuilt swing bridge in a set of drawings now in the Southwold Museum and at the NRM (**Fig 101**). The moveable section of the bridge was constructed from

Original swing bridge – 1879 - 1907

Fig 100: Original swing bridge.

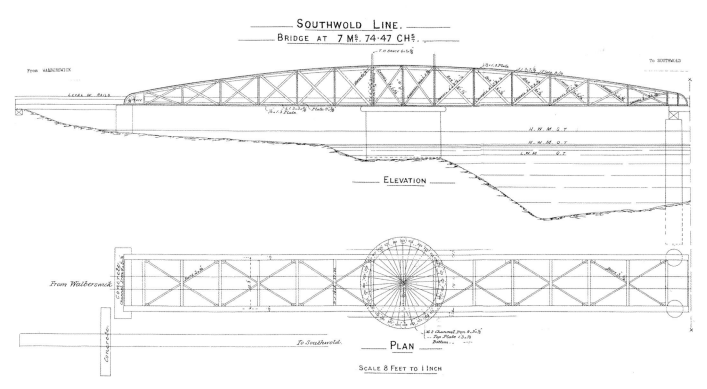

Fig 101: GER Civil Engineer drawing of the original swing bridge – 1892.

wrought-iron plate and channel section ironwork in a bow-string form with a span of 146ft. It turned on a central iron caisson supported on 12 piles screwed into the river bed to a depth of 44ft below rail level. On top of the caisson was circular wheelrace of 24 carrying wheels and approximately 19ft in diameter. There were two fixed land spans on either side off the swing span. The channel for river traffic was on the Southwold side and offered about 60ft between the central caisson and the two iron cylinders (which still exist today) supporting the river end of the Southwold land span. It was an Admiralty requirement that the bridge should be able to be opened for river traffic but apart from the occasions of opening the bridge to navigation in 1915 during the First World War, there are no other references to shipping movements.

Opening the bridge was entirely by manual labour provided by four members of Section 2 Southwold permanent way gang and probably the blacksmith accompanied by the Southwold Station Master with the Train Staff of the Southwold-Walberswick or the Blythburgh section to release the screw-bolt securing the bridge closed. One man of the pw gang in a rowing boat towed the bridge round; to open or close the bridge took about 20 minutes. The pw ganger was in charge of the operation and ensured that the bridge

Fig 102: Rebuilt swing bridge open in September 1907 while testing. Although there has always been general public interest in the swing bridge, it was opened so infrequently that pictures like this are rare and unusual. The men on the bank in the left foreground are holding a hawser attached to the bridge which is the only means of swinging it open, and closed. Note the bowler-hatted figure on the bridge; typically, if he is the Foreman, he is only supervising, not pulling on the rope!

was fully re-secured and the ends of the rails were correctly fish-plated.

When the bridge was open to navigation, the ends were protected by timber piers or dolphins to prevent any collision damage. Although the swing bridge was rarely opened for navigation (see **Fig 102**), its existence reflected the earlier history of the River Blyth Navigation and the one-time river ports of Blythburgh and Halesworth.

Merchants in Halesworth, seeking better transport for their goods, obtained the River Blyth Navigation Act in 1757 to improve the river between Halesworth and Blythburgh including locks at Bulcamp, Blyford, Mells and Halesworth. Quays were provided at Halesworth, Blyford and Blythburgh. The Navigation was opened in 1761 and continued in regular use until, in common with most river navigations and canals, competition from the Southwold Railway superseded it. From 1884 the Canal Commissioners 'declined all responsibility in respect of … maintenance of the banks, etc'. In 1888, receipt from tolls for use of the Navigation yielded nothing. Formal abandonment was finally confirmed under the powers of the Land Drainage Act (1930) on 19 February 1934.

CHANGE OF GAUGE
The Southwold Light Railway Order 1902 provided authority, among other matters, to alter the gauge to standard gauge making it necessary to rebuild all the bridge sections including the swing section which was only 11ft wide between the side spans. The initial proposals to change the gauge of the Southwold Railway to four foot eight-and-a-half inches came first with a new line to Lowestoft from Southwold, subsequently withdrawn, and then to Kessingland (see Chapter 5). Widening to standard gauge and then linking with the GER would have avoided the time and inconvenience experienced at Halesworth for transhipment of all goods and a change of train for all passengers.

Unfortunately, the Company's Minute Books may no longer exist and are anyway not available, so we have no date for the first consideration by the Railway's Board of a change of gauge. It must, however, have been no later than the 1890s because the Southwold Light Railway Order of 1902 provided the necessary authority.

We do know that the subject must have been discussed at the Board meeting of March 1906 because, with reference to a Minute of 29 September 1905, the following firms were asked to tender for rebuilding the swing bridge:

- Messrs Ransome & Rapier, Waterside Works, Ipswich, & 32 Victoria St, London
- Messrs A. Handyside and Co, Britannia Ironworks, Derby
- Messrs Francis Morton & Co, Hamilton Iron Works, Garston, Liverpool

Only Mortons replied; their tender for £1,352 10s was accepted and the work was completed in 1907. A report of an IMechE visit to the Garston Works in 1909 (copy from *Grace's Guide to British Industrial History*) illustrates the experience of this Contractor:

'MESSRS FRANCIS MORTON & CO, HAMILTON IRON WORKS, GARSTON.
These works are situated on the River Mersey at Garston, and cover 10 acres. They comprise a number of lofty and well-lighted buildings, specially laid out for the manufacture of all kinds of constructional steelwork, with large private dock free from dues, and railway-siding accommodation.

For upwards of seventy years the firm has been engaged in the manufacture of steel roofing, bridgework, fencing, steel telegraph- poles, dust-bins, castings, galvanized work, etc., and the company has shipped many thousands of tons of bridgework and constructional steelwork for H.M. Government and Colonial Offices, and also for the various large foreign railways. They have carried out several large swing-bridges, warehouses, wharf-sheds, etc., for the Mersey Docks and Harbour Board at Liverpool and Birkenhead, and are amongst the largest producers of this class of work in this country. The number of men employed is about 650.'

On the swing bridge new steel side girders were constructed and installed outside the original bridge structures which were then dismantled. No plans of the widened swing bridge have been located but the new one differed from the old in the angular configuration of the sides. In the centre of the swing section two radiused cross-bracings were installed overhead between the side spans (**Figs 100, 103** and **105**).

The original wooden fixed land spans on either side of the swing bridge were not replaced until 1914 when a contract was let to Joseph Westwood & Co of Westminster. The spans each side were not equal in length. The Walberswick span was about 30ft long and was replaced in steel to a similar form to the original. The Southwold span was longer, about 75ft, and was replaced by a single span steel structure similar to the swing span but lower in overall height and without any overhead cross-bracing. Subsequently there is no record of any maintenance work on the whole swing bridge until 1921/1922 when the wheelrace under the swing span needed some repairs which were contracted to Messrs Cocksedge of Ipswich. Between 1906 and 1908 three other bridges were widened: No 1 over Holton Road, Halesworth; No 4 – Mells Road Bridge – under Mells Road; no 11 under the Turnpike Road to Great Yarmouth at Blythburgh and, in 1908 Bridge 2, built in concrete, was widened in brick and completed that year.

Fig 103: The rebuilt and widened swing bridge showing the radiused cross-bracings between the two side spans which identify and date the rebuilt bridge in pictures.

Fig 104: Morton's workmen rebuilding the swing bridge –
4 September 1906.

Fig 105: Track-side view of Morton's workforce on
the rebuilt swing bridge.

Fig 106: Track over Woodsend Marshes towards Southwold Common cutting in the distance. Any standard gauge Lengthsman would be proud of this length: well ballasted, superelevation on the curve, no weeds, fences at the foot of the low embankment, clear drainage ditches, gradient post to the LHS and milepost to the RHS.

Fig 107: No 1 *SOUTHWOLD* working the 3.30pm down train near Halesworth, 3 July 1910.

CHAPTER 11

OPERATION OF THE RAILWAY AND TRAIN FORMATIONS

TRAIN SERVICE TO LONDON.

STATIONS.	UP TRAINS—WEEK DAYS.										SUNDAYS.
	a.m.		a.m.	a m.	a.m.	p.m.	p.m.	p.m.		p.m.	p.m.
Southwold .. dep.	7 25	..	7 25	..	10 0	..	2 23	5 25		7B 5	5 5
Walberswick ,,	7 30	..	7 30	..	10 5	..	2 28	5 30		7B10	5 10
Blythburgh (for Wangford) .. ,,	7 40	..	7 40	..	10 15	..	2 38	5 40		7B20	5 20
Wenhaston .. ,,	7 51	..	7 51	..	10 26	..	2 49	5 51		7B31	5 31
Halesworth .. arr.	8 2	..	8 2	..	10 37	..	3 0	6 2		7B42	5 42
Norwich (Th.) dep.	..	..	6 55	..	9 0	..	12 37	2 22	..	.. 5 56	..
Yarmouth (S. Tn.),,	..	..	7 37	..	10 0	..	2 35	3 30	..	.. 6 50	4 52
Lowestoft (Cen.) ,,	..	..	7 44	..	10 13	..	2 37	3 43	..	.. 7 4	5 2
Bungay .. ,,	..	..	..	..	10 5	..	1 47	3 24	..	.. 6 32	..
Beccles .. ,,	..	..	8 14	..	10 37	..	3 4	4 8	..	.. 7 28	5 32
Brampton .. ,,	..	..	8 24	..	10 47	..	..	4 18	..	.. 7 38	5 45
Halesworth .. arr.	..	..	8 33	..	10 55	..	3 18	4 26	..	.. 7 46	5 54
Halesworth .. dep.	8 24		8 34	..	10 57	..	3 20	..	6 30	.. ..	5 56
Darsham .. arr.	..		8 44	..	11 7	..	3 30	..	6 40	.. ..	6 9
Saxmundham.. ,,	..		8 52	..	11 15	..	3 38	..	6 50	.. ..	6 18
Leiston .. ,,	..		9 55	..	11 30	..	3A55	..	7 20	.. ..	7 22
Aldeburgh .. ,,	..		10 7	..	11 42	..	4A7	..	7 32	.. ..	7 34
Wickham Market ,,	..		9 6	..	11 29	..	3 52	..	7 3	.. ..	6 38
Framlingham ,,	..		11 18	..	12 53	..	6 8	..	7 28	.. ..	..
Woodbridge .. ,,	8 44	Mondays only.	9 20	..	11 44	..	4 3	..	7 18	.. ..	6 54
Bealings .. ,,	..		9 28	..	11 52	..	..	..	7 26	.. ..	7 1
Westerfield .. ,,	..		..	..	12 0	..	..	..	7 36	.. ..	7 10
Ipswich .. ,,	9 3	..	9 43	..	12 7	..	4 20	..	7 45	.. ..	7 21
Ipswich .. dep.	9 25		10 20	..	12D49	.	4 51	..	8 15	.. ..	7 30
Bury .. .. arr.	10 24		11 5	..	1 35	..	5 28	..	9 0	.. ..	8 29
Newmarket .. ,,	11 32		11 32	..	1 58	..	5 58	..	..	.. ..	..
Cambridge .. ,,	11 55		11 55	..	2 20	..	6 20	..	..	.. ..	..
Ipswich .. dep.	9 10	..	9 51	10 25	12 31	12 37	4 26	4 53	8 0	8 10 ..	7 35 8 18
Manningtree .. arr.	..			10 53		12 55		6 9		8 29 ..	..
Colchester .. { arr.	9 35			11 8		1 10		5 17		8 44 ..	8 42
Colchester .. { dep.	9 38			11 12		1 12		5 19		8 58 ..	..
Marks Tey .. arr.	..	EXPRESS.		11 23	EXPRESS.	1 28	EXPRESS.	5 37	EXPRESS.	9 9 ..	EXPRESS. ..
Witham .. ,,	..			11 37		1 30		7 38		9 27 ..	..
Chelmsford .. ,,	..			11 55		1 47		5 47		9 18 ..	..
Liverpool Street ,,	10 40		11 16	..	1 55	..	5 56	..	9 24	.. ..	9 10 ..

OCTOBER ONLY.

Through Tickets are issued between all the above Stations. Through Rates for Parcels, Goods, and Minerals to and from all Great Eastern Stations. The Through Rates for Fish to London are the same as from Yarmouth and Lowestoft.

A—Saturdays only.
B—After 31st October will run on Mondays and Saturdays only.
D—On Wednesdays passengers can leave Ipswich 12.20 and arrive Bury 1.12 p.m.

Fig 108: Southwold Railway Timetable [facsimile] 4 October 1914 to 31 March 1915 – page 20. **UP TRAINS – TRAIN SERVICE TO LONDON.** (© Rob Shorland-Ball)

The first two timetables, September and December 1879, have survived, together with a number for later years, but for the next 50 years much of the information on a regular basis comes from entries in the local weekly newspaper which included train times for both the Southwold Railway and GER at Halesworth.

The 4 October 1914 to 31 March 1915 timetable has survived and an accurate facsimile can be bought from the Southwold Railway Trust (Chapter 18). Its 50 A5-sized pages are more useful, today, for the social history of Southwold to be gleaned from advertisements and the rates, regulations, information for passengers and bye-laws of the Railway. The times of trains are on two separate pages on which the 'UP TRAINS – TRAIN SERVICE TO LONDON' is the first on page 20 (**Fig 108**) and there is no reference there to page 29 which shows the 'DOWN TRAINS.' (**Fig 109**)

David Lee has worked through his collection and his researches to provide a more specific analysis of the operation of the Southwold Railway.

Week day train services.

The first timetable for September 1879, with the only intermediate station open at Wenhaston, showed six trains each way:

	AM		PM			
UP trains – SOUTHWOLD dep:	08.30	11.08	12.42	02.28	04.10	06.24
DOWN trains – HALESWORTH dep:	09.15	11.58	01.12	03.22	05.31	08.14
Trains only stop at intermediate stations on notice being given to the Guard at start or by signal at the station to join. Conveyances meet all trains at Southwold and available at other stations.						

For December 1879 a pocket sized timetable was produced, including Blythburgh (now open), which showed only five trains each way and PM variations from the September timetable for UP and DOWN trains.

	AM		PM		
UP trains – SOUTHWOLD dep:	08.30	11.08	02.37	05.00	06.36
DOWN trains – HALESWORTH dep:	09.15	11.58	03.26	05.46	08.05
Trains only stop at intermediate stations on notice being given to the Guard at start or by signal at the station to join. Conveyances meet all trains at Southwold and available at other stations.					

Subsequently the station-to-station train timings remained basically at the same hours but there were variations in the minutes past the hour. The only complete changes were for adjustments caused by Great Eastern Railway alterations in timings at Halesworth to ensure connections with the Southwold Railway's trains. During the first nine years of the Railway's operation there was a difference in time between 'town time' and 'railway time' of five minutes which persisted up to 1888 (*Halesworth Times* 21 February 1888), though time had been set over the whole country to Greenwich Time by the Definition of Time Act 1880.

Readers who remember 'traditional' railway timetables will recall the text and graphic devices used to indicate whether particular trains were short workings or ran, or did not run, on particular days. The Southwold Railway pages illustrated in Figs **108** and **109** are masterpieces of typography and 'Printed by the Southwold Press, 6 and 8 Church Street, Southwold'. It is taken for granted that 'Weekdays' meant Monday to Saturday inclusive but beware the 12.37 ex-Norwich Thorpe which offers an up Southwold connection at 3.20pm then a Leiston and Aldeburgh connection via Saxmundham but 'A–Saturdays only.' Likewise the 7.05pm ex-Southwold was a 'Weekday' train but 'B–After 31st October will run on Mondays and Saturdays only.' These timetables are worth exploring with a *Pre-Grouping Atlas and RCH Junction Diagrams* (Ian Allan Publishing Ltd, 2014) to hand for geographical and railway reference.

Sunday services

Sunday trains: **PM** only	**UP** trains – September		**UP** trains – December	
SOUTHWOLD dep:	01.16	05.56	01.46	06.00
	DOWN trains – September		**DOWN** trains – December	
HALESWORTH dep:	02.00	07.25	02.26	07.25

TRAIN SERVICE FROM LONDON.

STATIONS.	a.m.	a.m.	a.m.	p.m.	p.m.	p.m.	p.m.		Sundays p.m.
Liverpool Street dep.	5 10	..	10 20	12 30	1 0	3 22	5 23	..	4 20
Chelmsford ,,	5 58	..	10 48	12 32	12 32	4 6	4 31	..	4 27
Witham ,,	..	..	10 33	12 22	12 22	3 20	4 51	..	4 47
Marks Tey ,,	..	..	10 35	12 56	12 56	3 38	5 11	..	5 6
Colchester arr.	6 22	..	11 25	1 35	2 5	4 32	5 20	..	5 31
Colchester dep.	6 25	..	11 28	1 37	2 8	4 35	5 26	..	5 35
Manningtree ,,	..	..	11 22	1 28	1 28	4 7	5 45	..	5 50
Ipswich arr.	6 46	..	11 50	1 59	2 30	4 57	6 49	..	6 7
Cambridge dep.	..	..	10 12	11 2	11 2	2 0	4 27	..	11 38
Newmarket ,,	..	..	10 37	11 43	11 43	2 41	5 11	..	12 14
Bury ,,	..	..	11 3	12 20	12 20	3E19	5 48	..	2 0
Ipswich arr.	..	..	11 40	1 16	1 16	4 17	6 40	..	3 0
Ipswich dep.	6 54	..	11 57	2 15	2 43	5 5	6 59	..	6 12
Westerfield ,,	7 3	..	10 24	2 24	2 52	5 14	7 8	..	6 22
Bealings ,,	7 11	..	10 32	2 32	3 0	5 22	7 15	..	6 30
Woodbridge ,,	7 18	..	12 15	2 39	3 6	5 29	7 22	..	6 38
Framlingham ,,	7 10	..	10 30	1 40	1 40	4 30	6 27	..	..
Wickham Market ,,	7 33	..	12 26	2 53	3 21	5 43	7 36	..	6 53
Aldeburgh ,,	7 10	..	12 7	2 37	2 57	4 15	6 36	..	5 46
Leiston ,,	7 29	..	12 20	2 50	3 10	4 28	6 49	..	5 59
Saxmundham ,,	7 46	..	12 38	3 6	3 33	5 56	7 48	..	7 6
Darsham ,,	7 55	..	12 47	3 15	3 43	6 5	7 58	..	7 18
Halesworth arr.	8 7	..	12 59	3 27	3 52	6 15	8 8	..	7 29
Halesworth dep.	8 9	11 28	..	3 29	3 54	6 19	8 10	..	7 31
Brampton arr.	8 18	11 37	..	3 38	4 3	6 28	8 20	..	7 41
Beccles ,,	8 26	11 45	..	3 46	4 12	6 36	8 29	..	7 50
Bungay ,,	8 55	12 14	..	..	..	7 59	..	..	..
Lowestoft (Cen.) ,,	8 52	12 8	..	4 9	4 33	7 12	8 51	..	8 15
Yarmouth (S.Tn.) ,,	9 5	12 23	..	4 25	4 50	7 17	9 8	..	8 30
Norwich (Thorpe) ,,	9 49	1 25	..	..	..	8 20	9 55	..	..
Halesworth dep.	8 40	..	1 5	3 35	4 0	6 20	8B15	..	7 33
Wenhaston ,,	8 49	..	1 14	3 42	4 9	6 29	8B24	..	7 42
Blythburgh (for Wangford) ,,	9 0	..	1 25	3 53	4 20	6 40	8B35	..	7 53
Walberswick ,,	9 12	..	1 37	4 7	4 32	6 52	8B47	..	8 5
Southwold arr.	9 17	..	1 42	4 12	4 37	6 57	8B52	..	8 10

Column notes: "Not on Saturdays"; "Saturdays only"; "London to Halesworth"; "Restaurant Cars, with Corridor Carriages, London to Halesworth"; "OCTOBER ONLY".

An Omnibus meets all Trains at Southwold. Conveyances can be obtained at Blythburgh and Walberswick.

B—After 31st October will run on Mondays and Saturdays only.

E.—On Wednesdays leave Bury at 4.10 p.m. and arrive Ipswich 5.2 p.m.

The Trains between Halesworth and Southwold will not run on Christmas Day.

Fig 109: Southwold Railway Timetable [facsimile] 4 October 1914 to 31 March 1915 – page 29. DOWN TRAINS – TRAIN SERVICE FROM LONDON.

The first timetables for the opening and December of 1879 scheduled two Sunday trains each way as illustrated. There were variations in times even during that short period, but basically the same hours were mentioned and any variations were in the number of minutes past the hour. During the winter months, November to April, the Sunday service of two trains was maintained to November 1883, then only one Sunday train and finally no Sunday service until 1928. In the summer months, May (or July some years) to October, a Sunday service of two trains was run, then only one and in some later years no service but, for 1927/28 from July to September four Sunday trains were timetabled.

Attracting passengers – Special Passenger Trains for Events.

During Bank Holidays in Summer after the First World War, the Company made great efforts to attract tourists and local people by issuing tickets at reduced fares, but no mention has been traced at that time of any additional trains, except as mentioned below. The last two years before closure saw great importance attached to this aspect for attracting traffic in competition with the motor buses.

The Company was very responsive to the need to supplement the timetable by running special trains for the extra traffic resulting from both day- and night-time events at Southwold, Blythburgh and Halesworth. The first reported occasion was in June 1880 following a concert by the Southwold Brass Band when a special left Southwold at 9.15pm. Similar functions were to follow over the coming years and included those that regularly took place including:

At Southwold
- Religious meetings and church outings
- Regattas
- Sports on Southwold Common
- Concerts at Southwold Pier, 'a Confetti Fete,' and concerts at other venues

At Halesworth
- Horse and Flower Show

At Henham Park
- Sports, cycling and military events.

In addition there were Special Events:-
- **1885**: An Auction Sale by the Southwold Corporation of land on the North Cliff. A large crowd of 400 intending buyers from London and Ipswich came to the Sale. The GER ran a special train from London to Halesworth, reported to be of 12 coaches. The Southwold Railway provided a double-headed 6-coach train which left Halesworth at noon.
- **1895:** Lifeboat Demonstration. It is said that the Southwold Railway had never carried so many passengers before.
- **1896**: A Special Practical Demonstration of the New Photography by Mr. Godfrey Martyn MRP on Whit Monday.
- **1908:** Parade at Henham Park disbanding 1st Norfolk Royal Garrison Artillery Volunteers from Southwold and 6 other towns before the Earl of Stradbroke, Colonel Commanding the Regiment. The parade took place on Sunday *(date and times not known)*: the movement of around 700 troops required some special trains from Halesworth and Southwold to Blythburgh which was the nearest station to Henham Hall.
- **1909:** Visit from H.M.Ships which anchored in the Southwold Bay while the officers were entertained by the Mayor (E. A. Holmes 1909-1911). A searchlight display was performed by the ships.
- **1913**: Display at Henham Park by the British Red Cross Society and the 3rd Howitzer Brigade, Royal Field Artillery, (TA), under the command of the Earl of Stradbroke. Following a firing exercise by the 3rd Howitzer Brigade the Red Cross Contingent, of 250 personnel, gave demonstration first aid to 200 'casualties.' Then followed an inspection of the 3rd Howitzer Brigade.
- *from* **1882**: During Whit Sunday and August Bank Holidays, bookings for Southwold started increasing annually from 1882; some 700 tickets were issued but there was seldom any mention of special trains running at those periods. There is also no reference to special arrangements by the Company for either of Queen Victoria's Jubilees.

Train time keeping.

There is no evidence to explain any bad time keeping of the Southwold Railway's scheduled daily train service, but there were periodical complaints about some services and even practical jokes by the Southwold cartoonist Reg Carter. The Company's misgiving about punctuality on their railway was often related to the time-keeping of GER trains which, unjustly, then caused public disquiet about the Southwold Railway's performance. When the Great Eastern Railway was founded in 1862, it combined all the railways of East Anglia including the former Eastern Counties Railway (ECR) which had a reputation for poor service. ECR unpunctuality was a household byword, making its reputation deservedly low. Some of the ECR's reputation was inherited by the GER, as continuing to be unpunctual and inefficient.

Before 1884, details of GER trains being late at Halesworth are not recorded but from that year to 1898, the Southwold Railway Halesworth Station Master, Walter Calver, reported to the Victoria Street, London, SR headquarters about the special arrangements he made for Easter, August Bank Holiday and Christmas necessitated by very late running of GER trains at Halesworth. Calver reported that either scheduled Southwold Railway trains had to depart late or a special train to maintain connections had to run. Late running of GER trains probably built up during the course of the day at the above periods, resulting in greater loss of time by the evening arrivals at Halesworth.

Late running by GER trains was not confined to holiday periods. In March 1894, an advertised excursion train run by the GER from Ipswich was shunted at Saxmundham for three other trains to pass, but that station failed to advise Halesworth what had been done. There is no indication that Calver ran a special on this occasion, though he wrote to SR Secretary Carne suggesting that the GER could have made other arrangements to avoid the delay. The worst incident of delay was following a tragic accident at Colchester on Saturday 7 July 1913 when the 5.23pm ex-Liverpool Street was delayed and finally arrived at Halesworth at 3.00am on Sunday 8 July. There is no record for the passengers' onward journey, but it seems there was a Southwold Railway special for them because it was reported that they arrived in Southwold at 4.0am 'tired after the wearisome journey.'

Train Operating and Train Formation.

An account of a typical day's operating on the Railway was outlined some years after closure in an interview with B.E. Girling, Station Master at Southwold at the closure of the line in 1929, and is reproduced with amplification or explanations as necessary. The two timetables below illustrate the services in the early 1920s which were introduced to win back business from competing buses and then the final few months before the Railway closed:

SOUTHWOLD RAILWAY: 9th July 1923, and until further notice							
UP trains – WEEKDAYS	AM		PM				SUNDAYS
SOUTHWOLD dep:	07.30	09.45	12.00	02.20	05.23	07.26	05.19pm
Walberswick dep:	07.35	09.50	12.05	02.25	05.28	07.31	05.24pm
Blythburgh dep:	07.49	10.04	12.19	02.39	05.42	07.45	05.38pm
Wenhaston dep:	08.00	10.15	12.30	02.50	05.53	07.56	05.49pm
HALESWORTH arr:	08.11	10.26	12.41	03.01	06.04	08.07	06.00pm
DOWN trains – WEEKDAYS	AM		PM				SUNDAYS
HALESWORTH dep:	08.40	10.45	01.00	03.45	06.37	08.12	08.00pm
Wenhaston dep:	08.51	10.56	01.11	03.56	06.48	08.23	08.11pm
Blythburgh dep:	09.02	11.07	01.22	04.07	06.59	08.34	08.22pm
Walberswick dep:	09.15	11.20	01.35	04.20	07.12	08.47	08.35pm
SOUTHWOLD arr:	09.21	11.26	01.41	04.26	07.18	08.53	08.41pm

Southwold Railway: 1st January 1929 until further notice					
UP trains – WEEKDAYS	AM		PM		SUNDAYS
SOUTHWOLD dep:	07.30	09.50	02.24	05.23	
Walberswick dep:	07.35	09.55	02.29	05.28	
Blythburgh dep:	07.49	10.09	02.43	05.42	————
Wenhaston dep:	08.00	10.20	02.54	05.53	
HALESWORTH arr:	08.11	10.31	03.05	06.04	

Southwold Railway: 1ˢᵗ January 1929 until further notice					
DOWN trains – WEEKDAYS	AM	PM			
HALESWORTH dep:	08.40	01.00	03.35	06.37	
Wenhaston dep:	08.51	01.11	03.46	06.48	
Blythburgh dep:	09.02	01.22	03.57	06.59	————
Walberswick dep:	09.15	01.36	04.10	07.12	
SOUTHWOLD arr:	09.21	01.41	04.16	07.18	

SOUTHWOLD RAILWAY OPERATION.

Based on notes from [retired] Southwold Stationmaster B.E. Girling and commentary below by David Lee. Up and down train times are related to the timetable pages in Figs **108** and **109**. To help to understand Mr Girling's references to Southwold Station, **Fig 110** is a landscape version of **Fig 68** Southwold Station final layout in 1929 in Chapter 6:

06.00am 'Loco Crew arrive and light up fire with dirty oily waste and old sleepers.'

Time shown for raising steam seems short. There was a general man on the Locomotive Foreman's staff who must have come on earlier to start the process of raising steam, hence the engine would be ready for work by 6.30am.

Instructions dated 20/4/1916 stated engine to be ready daily at 7.00am.

06.30am 'Steam raised sufficient to move; carry out any necessary shunting such as removing mineral wagons from the rear of the last down passenger train of the previous evening (Trains were always marshalled – Loco, Freight, Coaches, Minerals).'

No freight was carried on the last down train from Halesworth at night or the first up from Southwold in the morning.

After shunting: Porter pulled off signal; Stationmaster rang handbell; Guard blew whistle; Driver sounded loco whistle and the up train departed.

07.25am 'First UP train away. Milk was carried for Blythburgh and Wenhaston.'

The practice of ringing a handbell prior to departure was an old practice dating from the early days of railways but was continued on the Southwold Railway; there was no bell at Walberswick and it is questionable how often a bell was used at the intermediate stations.

'08.02am: UP train arrives at Halesworth. Loco off and runs round train passing behind the Southwold platform. Any empties in the rear of the coaches were next drawn off and pushed down to the coal tranship roads. There were two permanent transhippers at Halesworth whose wages were 30/- a week and who emptied 3 standard gauge 12 ton wagons.

'Note: The Freight tranship dock at the end of the line would hold 3 or 4 four wheeled trucks and the loco. The mineral tranship platform was at the rear of the passenger platform alongside the main line and about 100 yards south of Halesworth G.E.R. Signal Box. The Southwold Railway normally kept 1 or 2 coaches spare at Halesworth, 2 or 3 at Southwold and ran 2 or 3 on the train (see **Fig 30**).

'There was no provision for coal and water at Halesworth, but at the loco shed there was a tap [sic] that could be used for the loco tanks and six hods of coal were kept in the rear of the shed by the work bench in case of emergency. Despite the comparatively complicated track arrangement there was only one signal at Halesworth situated about 200 yards from the Southwold end of the platform and protecting the king point of the station.

08.40am 'First DOWN train departed. The handbell procedure was the same as at Southwold. This train carried mails (originally in the luggage van but later chained in the guard's

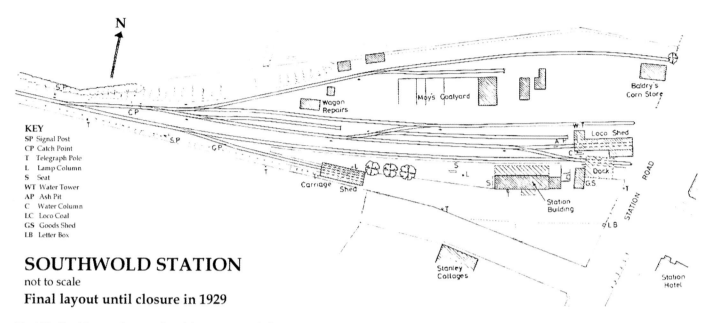

N

KEY
SP Signal Post
CP Catch Point
T   Telegraph Pole
L   Lamp Column
S   Seat
WT Water Tower
AP Ash Pit
C   Water Column
LC Loco Coal
GS Goods Shed
LB Letter Box

Wagon Repairs

Moy's Coalyard

Baldry's Corn Store

Loco Shed

Dock

Carriage Shed

Station Building

Station Road

Stanley Cottages

Station Hotel

SOUTHWOLD STATION
not to scale
Final layout until closure in 1929

Fig 110: Final layout for Southwold Station until closure in 1929.

compartment), newspapers, and freight from London and the North-East.'

The engine shed near Halesworth station had a chain pump for drawing water from a well and some coal could be taken onto the loco there. Southwold was the principal coaling point, but for Specials and permanent way / ballast trains, coal at Halesworth Station or at the Bird's Folly locoshed were sometimes useful.

9.17am: 8.40am DOWN train arrived at Southwold. Loco off, coal and water taken on if required; loco is run round and any minerals detached. The freight wagons on the front of the train were uncoupled and pushed down the length of the platform to the goods office by hand.

'The empties for Halesworth were next collected from the coal road and placed on the front of the train, between the passenger luggage van and the locomotive. The passenger luggage van always travelled at the front of the train on UP journeys and at the rear on a DOWN journey.

'The Goods Office at Southwold was on a platform beyond the passenger platform which could accommodate about 4 or 5 short wagons.'

10.00am   'UP passenger. This train usually carried the morning mails from Southwold.

'Train would consist of loco, any smaller freight in wagons covered with tarpaulin wagon-sheets and any other bulk loads such as sand or sugar-beet, the passenger luggage van, 2 or 3 passenger coaches.

10.37am   'UP train arrived at Halesworth. Loco off and run round to back of the train drawing off any mineral trucks, whilst the small freight was pushed down to the tranships stage by hand.

'The next booked train was the 1.00pm ex-Halesworth DOWN passenger but in the two hours before this there could be a permissively worked freight train. This ran if there were more than 7 or 8 wagons at Halesworth for Southwold and intermediate stations. The guard, in the absence of any guard's van, rode on the Engine. This train had no booked time but usually left Halesworth about 11.15am and arrived at Southwold about 11.15am. Though there was no official timing, all shunting and preparing and placing of trucks for the day at intermediate stations was done by the train engine; 2 minutes were allowed at each station for this work.'

Small freight was consignments of less than 1 ton and known as 'smalls'. Consignments in excess of 1 ton and full wagons were usually unloaded at Southwold in the long siding to the north of the goods yard also used by coal merchants.

11.50am 'DOWN permissive freight train arrived at Southwold onto the Station goods roads'. Coal trucks were placed in position for coal merchants and any Southwold freight placed for unloading. Empties and any freight for Halesworth, or intermediate stations shunted into order for UP Freight to minimise any additional shunting at intermediate stations. Coal and water for loco and depart on UP Freight for Halesworth and intermediate stations at 12.15pm. The train was never more than 14 wagons long.

Permissive freight trains: The need for running both DOWN and UP permissive freight trains was left entirely at the decision of the Halesworth and Southwold Station Masters. Timing of the two freight trains varied if the passenger train timings were changed.

12.45pm 'UP permissive freight train arrived at Halesworth and run straight into goods reception road. The Halesworth goods reception road was a continuation of the coal / mineral tranship siding.

'Loco off and run round to head of carriages standing in platform road or, if any freight at tranship platform, pick up this first and then back onto train.'

1.05pm 'DOWN passenger train and freight from Norwich, Ipswich and the North; no coal or minerals were carried on this train.'

1.42pm: 'DOWN passenger and freight train arrived at Southwold. Loco to coal and water; pick up empties, if any, and any loaded freight wagons.'

Not mentioned in the interview with Mr Girling is that, on the arrival of the

1.05pm down train at Southwold, the early turn engine men were being relieved by the late turn men.

2.23pm 'UP passenger and freight train.'

3.00pm: 'UP passenger and freight arrived at Halesworth. Loco runs round; empties off to freight road.'

3.35pm 'DOWN passenger departed Halesworth.'

4.12pm 'DOWN passenger arrived at Southwold.'

5.25pm 'UP passenger departed Southwold. In the winter this was the last UP train of the day and all the local carriers used to bring in their goods for despatch. This train also carried the day's production from Homeknit, Fordux Mills, and other local industry.'

Note: Goods Department clerks were hard pressed in making out the railway invoices when goods were handed in late.

6.02pm 'UP passenger arrived Halesworth. Loco runs round: light freight pushed by hand to tranship platform.'

6.20pm 'Last DOWN passenger train of the normal service. This train brought the London evening newspapers to intermediate stations and to Southwold.'

6.57pm 'DOWN passenger train arrived Southwold. Train left in platform exactly as it arrived. Loco to coal, water; lubricate then straight to Loco Shed. The whole operation was usually completed by 7.30pm and the crew and station staff went home.'

Winter Timetable 1914 - 1915 in **Figs 108** and **109:**

7.05pm UP passenger train on Mondays and Saturdays only.

7.42pm UP passenger train arrived Halesworth.

8.15pm   'DOWN passenger train on Mondays and Saturdays only.'

8.52pm   'UP passenger train arrived Halesworth. Train left in platform exactly as it arrived. Loco to coal, water; lubricate then straight to Loco Shed. The whole operation was usually completed by 9.30pm and the crew and station staff went home.'

The only security in those days was to lock the Station building and Goods Office and possibly the Loco Shed; otherwise the Station fore-court and Goods Yard were open to any access.

All trains had to carry a Red Tail Disc by day and a Red Tail Lamp by night. The Guard or Under Guard was responsible for ensuring that the Tail Lamp was burning (SR Rule 17). The Tail Lamp was an adapted policeman's belt lamp with a red shade.

The Southwold Railway Rule Book was re-issued on the authority of the Board of Directors on 4 October 1918 to come into effect from 1 January 1919.

The 50-page Southwold Railway Winter Timetable for 1914-15 is not only entertaining as a sort of railway sudoku but it also, over many pages of small print, gives rules and regulations for the operation of the Railway and the behaviour of passengers:

'**Compartments for Smoking**– Smoking is not permitted in the Waiting Rooms at the Stations and only in those compartments so designated.' The detailed regulations make entertaining reading and, of course, reflect the times over 100 years ago:
'NOTE: Motor Cycles charged with Electricity, Gas, Oil or other inflammable liquid or vapour are *not* conveyed by Passenger Train.

'**Dogs**: Dogs must be secured by a chain and collar and, if unaccompanied by a passenger, must be muzzled.

Charges: Dog conveyed with chain and collar, except when the weight of the Animal exceeds 1cwt – Above 10 miles and not exceeding 20 = £0.6d.

'**Light packages**, frail or very bulky in proportion to their weight . . . Banjos . . . Cases of Stuffed Birds . . . Mandolins . . . Stag's heads . . . Phonographs not on wheels . . . Symphoniums . . . Welsbach Lamps . . . **are only conveyed at Owner's risk** and the rates will be 25 per cent more than the ordinary Parcels rates.'

Train Formations
Mixed Trains

By the Regulation of Railway Act 1889 the Board of Trade regulations allowed:

'A limited number of mixed trains for the conveyance of goods and passengers, in which the goods wagons are not required to have continuous brakes, may be run, subject to the following –

a)   the engine and passenger vehicles of such mixed trains shall be provided with continuous brakes worked from the engine

b)   the goods waggons (sic) shall be behind the passenger vehicles with brake van in proportion of 1 brake van (per) 10 waggons (sic)

c)   total number of vehicles shall not exceed 25

d)   maximum average speed . . . between stations not to exceed 25 MPH

e)   such trains shall stop at all stations.'

Such were the main conditions for working mixed trains, but the Southwold Railway was not able to comply with conditions (a) and (b) while the Railway was limited to 16mph.

The siding connections with the running line at the Kett's Mill siding near Wenhaston and at Walberswick Station all faced towards Southwold so could only be served by DOWN trains so goods wagons to be put off or taken on must be set up in front of the carriages.

Up to 1908 at Blythburgh Station the siding connection faced towards Halesworth so could only be serviced by UP trains, goods wagons also being set up in front of the carriages.

The formation of mixed trains was therefore:

- DOWN trains leaving Halesworth –
- Loco + goods wagons for Wenhaston Mill and Walberswick Station + carriages + van 13 or 14 + wagon 9 or 10 + goods wagons for Blythburgh, Southwold Stations.
- UP trains leaving Southwold –

- Loco + goods wagons for Blythburgh (until 1908) + other goods wagons, loaded or empty, for Halesworth + wagons 9 or 10 + van 13 or 14 + carriages + empty wagons.

Vans 13 and 14 were for passengers' luggage and mails; 2 plank opens 9 and 10 were for ice, fish and milk. In addition to the above there were specific instructions as to what goods vehicles were to be included in each train by the Trains Working Notice dated June 1913.

Another reason for the train formation adopted was to ensure the van(s) were positioned by the barrow crossing at Halesworth Station to facilitate handling of any traffic for or from the GER.

When goods wagons were required for passengers' luggage they were to be thoroughly swept out and covered with a tarpaulin.

Goods trains

The working of a special goods train started in 1902 and, following the loop line being constructed at Blythburgh, instructions were issued dated 1 October 1908:

Working Special Goods Trains through Blythburgh Loop.
Length of loop between catch points = 214 feet
- Full Load: 1 Engine (19ft 7ins); 8 long trucks (173ft 8 ins); 1 small truck (12ft 10ins) = 211ft 1in

Lengths of Wagons, Trucks and Locomotives		
Small Wagons – SR Number	Large Wagons – SR Number	Lengths of wagons and trucks from buffer to buffer
3	2	
5	3	
7	4	
8	5	Nos 1 – 9, 11, 12: 12ft 10ins each
10	6	10: 12ft 8ins
12	7	13, 23: 12ft 2ins each
14	8	24 – 32 and MOY: 22ft 4ins
15	9	
Length of Locomotives buffer to buffer		
No 1	19ft 7ins	
Nos 2 & 3	18ft 3ins	

Distances between Stations

	From Halesworth		Between Stations	
	Miles	Chains	Miles	Chains
Halesworth	0	00		
Wenhaston	2	52	2	52
Blythburgh	4	70	2	18
Walberswick	7	45	2	75
Southwold	8	64	1	19

Point to Point timings (*in minutes*)

DOWN trains	Sept – Nov 1879	Dec 1879	1882	Aug & Sept 1911 - 1913	1917 - 1919	1920	1921
Halesworth	—	—	—	—	—	—	—
Wenhaston	10	10	9	—	9	9	11
Blythburgh	—	8	11	—	11	11	11

DOWN trains	Sept – Nov 1879	Dec 1879	1882	Aug & Sept 1911 - 1913	1917 - 1919	1920	1921
Walberswick	—	—	15	28	—	12	13
Southwold – arr and leave	24	19	2	5	15	5	6
TOTALS	34	37	37	33	35	37	41

UP trains	Sept – Nov 1879	Dec 1879	1882	Aug & Sept 1911 - 1913	1917 - 1919	1920	1921
Southwold	—	—	—	—	—	—	—
Walberswick	—	—	3	5	—	5	5
Blythburgh	—	13	12	—	15	10	14
Wenhaston	20	10	11	—	11	11	11
Halesworth arr and leave	14	14	11	28	11	11	11
TOTALS	34	37	37	33	37	37	41

These timings after 1882 remained fairly constant with periodical minor changes. The large change which took place in 1921 was the result of the BoT inspectors observing that the Railway's statuary speed limit of 16mph was being exceeded.

When goods trains were operated timings were similar so shunting at the intermediate stations had to be completed during the 2 minutes allowed for a stop and likewise at the Wenhaston Mill siding.

CHAPTER 12

SAFE WORKING OF THE LINE: SIGNALS, TELEGRAPH, TRAIN STAFFS, BRAKES, THE WORKING TIMETABLE

Signals

A railway the size of the Southwold Railway did not require a dedicated Signal & Telegraph Department, particularly in the early years. A telephone circuit to all stations – telegraph poles with a single insulator for the wire in **Figs 107 and 113** – was finally set up in 1899 and in 1908 at Blythburgh Station a central interlocking ground frame for all signals there was installed. Nevertheless, the SR had no designated staff as signalmen and maintenance was arranged as necessary with GER / LNER Railway Telegraph Linemen and Signal Fitters.

Signals were located at all the original turn-outs to sidings off the main running line. The SR adopted the old-fashioned slotted signal posts with 4ft long arms for each direction mounted side-by-side in a spindle through the post and concealed in the slot until operated. Both Home and Starting signals were operated by a rod up the post to the signal and connected to a hand lever at the base; the signal was detected at the toes of the hand-operated turn-out thus preventing the turn-out being moved once the signal was set. The signal posts were painted white with a flat iron cap which was painted black like all the metal work. The approach side of the signal arm was painted red with a white band and the reverse side plain white with no band. The driver observed the signal which was visible – or not visible,

Fig 111: No 1 *SOUTHWOLD* on the 6.30pm mixed down train at Halesworth, 3 July 1920.

Fig 112: The Wenhaston Station Master demonstrates a signal – lamp has been lowered.

Fig 113: A down train approaching Southwold Station Advance Home signal. 1920s.

meaning all clear – to the left of the signal post. In **Fig 112** the Wenhaston Station Master demonstrates the signal at his Station as a down train driver would see it. The signal lamp, which illuminates the spectacles two-thirds of the way up the signal post, has been lowered by the small iron windlass at the base of the post near the Station Master's left leg for cleaning and re-fuelling. The lamp was guided and held in position by parallel rails each side of the post.

For night working or during fog or falling snow, the green and red combined spectacles worked in conjunction with each signal arm and were illuminated by the twin bullseye oil lamp.

When later turn-outs were installed, for instance at the Harbour Junction, Halesworth, Wenhaston and Blythburgh, it is not certain whether additional signals were provided. It is a measure of the careful but rather slow and very old-fashioned working of the railway that they may not have been.

Fig 113 shows a down train approaching Southwold Station Advance Home signal. The driver, observing the signal arm to the left of the signal post at 'caution', knows that it is clear to proceed to the Home Signal

and the turnout ahead of his train is set for the platform road. The signal also carried a calling-on arm which, when off, indicated to drivers that the turn-out was set to the goods sidings. This arm had a cut in the end, but it is not known how it was coloured; it was probably fitted by 1918 to satisfy BoT up-to-date rules.

The porter/signal man is in position and behind him is a wooden shelter which might give a little protection from the weather if he needed to be present for shunting operations. Otherwise he could walk back to the platform once the train passed him.

The Railway had no signal boxes. The 5-lever ground frame at Blythburgh was adjacent to the station building and also controlled a Down Distant signal 325 yards from the frame towards Halesworth to improve the sighting of the Down Home signal.

Telegraph/Telephone circuit

When the railway opened in 1879 there was no communication between the stations, nor even with the first administrative headquarters of the railway in Richard Rapier's London office, except by written 'Train

Messages'. The later SRT London office, in Victoria Street, ultimately had a GPO telephone contact and in December 1899 a telephone circuit was installed between the SR stations. This was an omnibus open circuit with a code of bell rings to call up a particular station – thus:

- Halesworth   5 rings
- Wenhaston   4 rings
- Blythburgh   3 rings
- Walberswick   2 rings
- Southwold   1 ring

The main purpose of the telephone was to advise the following station when a train was departing.

Safe working – block working with the train staff and ticket system

The SR, like any single line railway, was potentially hazardous because Up and Down trains could meet head-on. That may seem unlikely and the SR had a 16mph speed limit enforced but bad weather, and the curves on the route meant that visibility could be poor. Railway companies operating on single lines were of particular concern to the BoT because of the potential for collisions. From 1858, no single line railway was permitted to work without a legal document under the Company's seal directing that:

- Only one engine may be in steam; if two are in steam they must be coupled together
- The Railway Operating System must be by Train Staff
- There must be telephone communication throughout the line.

In 1860 the BoT permitted single lines to be worked with a Train Staff and Ticket system and this change was incorporated in the Southwold Railway document, dated 20 September 1879, signed by R.R. Rapier and J.P. Cooper and embossed with the Company's Common Seal. Major Hutchinson's BoT Report which authorised the Railway to open and to carry passengers stated that:

'The points and signals have been arranged and interlocked similarly to the plan adopted on the Culm Valley Light Railway . . . and the line is to be worked with only one engine at a time.'

It was 20 years before there was telephone communication throughout the line, but block working was instituted immediately. In railway terms, a 'block section' was that part of the railway line onto which a train had been admitted from, for instance, Halesworth to Southwold. On the SR, this Down train was admitted to the block by the SR Station Master at Halesworth lowering the signal after the Guard had given the 'Right away' for his train. An additional security was the Train Staff – on early railways made of wood so a 'staff' – which was given to the driver by the Station Master and carried on the engine to Southwold. Without the staff no other train could be admitted to this block. On arriving, the driver would give the staff to the Southwold Station Master, who would give it back when the Up train was ready to depart for Halesworth. The SR Train Staffs were cast in heavy brass. The handle end was inscribed with the names of the Block Section stations between which the Staff could work.

The original single Train Staff was marked Southwold/Halesworth and incorporated another security measure. **Fig 114** shows two surviving Train Staffs, now in the care of Southwold Museum, and the reason why there are more than one will follow later. The first Staff terminates in an Annetts key which could unlock Annetts boxes securing the links to the turnouts from the running line to the sidings and for enabling the Blythburgh swing bridge to be opened. The key was invented by J.E. Annett of the London, Brighton and South Coast Railway. He patented the design in 1875 so it was still relatively new when the SR adopted it. In 1881, that patent was bought by Saxby and Farmer, the leading UK manufacturer of railway signalling equipment; coincidentally they both, like Annet, had worked for the LB&SCR.

One staff for the whole railway and one train operating was sufficient for the very early days of the SR but as business increased, a system was required which would allow two, or occasionally more, trains to operate at the same time. The Southwold Railway was not alone in this need and the BoT sanctioned the Staff and Ticket system and, if necessary, the introduction of more blocks along the course of a railway. On the SR the Station Masters, who were Staff holders, could issue a signed Ticket permitting the driver to proceed – with a copy of the Ticket – provided he had been shown the relevant Staff. This system also allowed more than one engine to be in steam on the railway but never in the

Fig 114: The left hand staff is for the Southwold to Blythburgh block section and that on the right hand for Blythburgh to Halesworth so two blocks with Blythburgh as a mid-point and change of staffs for a through train, which nearly all were.

same block section unless they were coupled together and double-heading a train.

The Train Tickets stock at the stations concerned was kept in a locked box, the key to which was attached to the relevant Train Staff for each Block Section by a length of chain (see **Fig 114**). The box could therefore only be opened when the Train Staff was present; the Train Ticket could then be completed and given to the driver as his authority to proceed together with a sight of the Train Staff to assure the driver that the Train Ticket was in order and it was safe for him to proceed.

The use of Train tickets was not frequent, but an example was the double-heading of the last Up train from Southwold at around 8.00pm with the engine from a Special goods train from Halesworth earlier in the day. The front engine driver was shown the Train Staff and given a Train Ticket while the Train Staff was carried on the second locomotive. At each station (except Walberswick which was no longer a Train Staff Station) the Train Ticket was cancelled and a fresh one issued for the onward journey. At Blythburgh, the Train Staff was changed for that to cover the Blythburgh to Halesworth block and a new Train Ticket was issued, as at Wenhaston.

By the early years of the twentieth century, the volume of traffic had increased considerably, especially for passengers during the summer months when up to

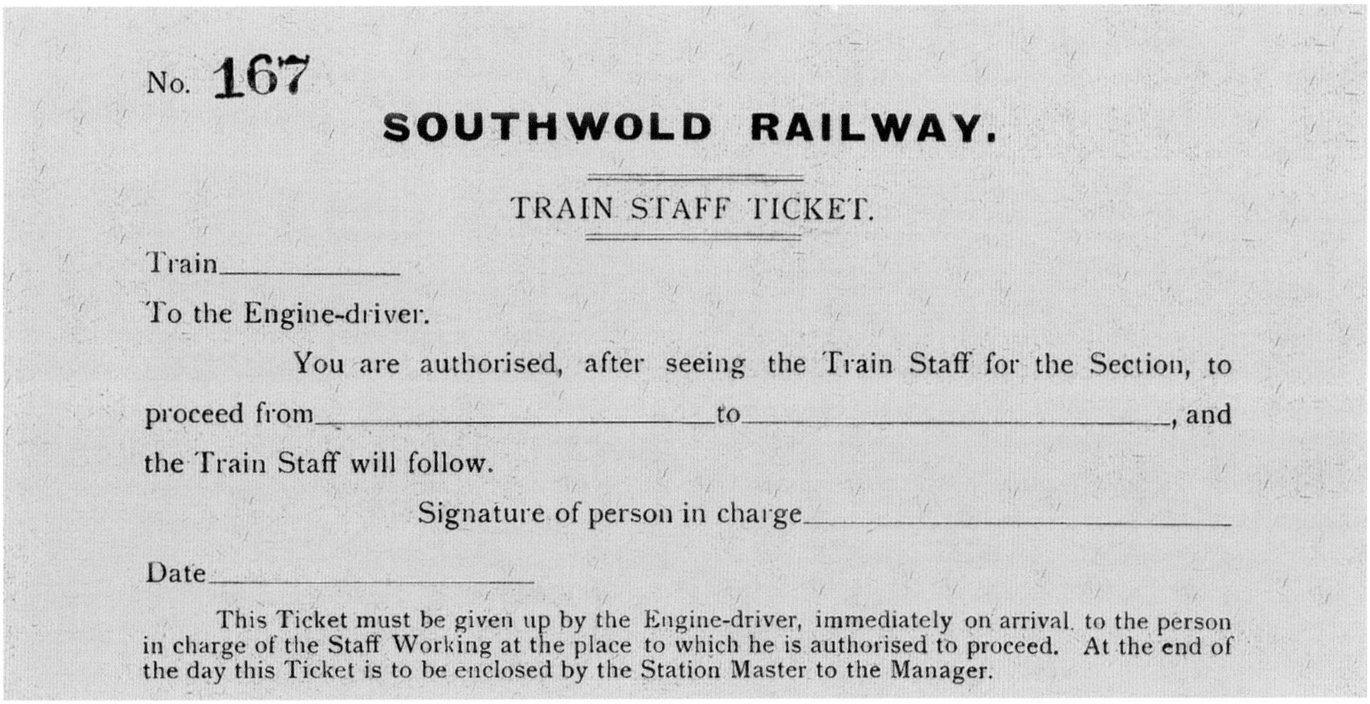

No. **167**

SOUTHWOLD RAILWAY.

TRAIN STAFF TICKET.

Train_____

To the Engine-driver.

You are authorised, after seeing the Train Staff for the Section, to proceed from_____ to_____, and the Train Staff will follow.

Signature of person in charge_____

Date_____

This Ticket must be given up by the Engine-driver, immediately on arrival, to the person in charge of the Staff Working at the place to which he is authorised to proceed. At the end of the day this Ticket is to be enclosed by the Station Master to the Manager.

Fig: 115: A Walberswick/Blythburgh Train Staff Ticket.

six trains, most of them mixed, worked each way. Goods traffic, too, was increasing so the Company requested BoT permission to run Special goods trains, covered by the Halesworth Station Master issuing a Train Staff Ticket for this train to proceed between the arrival of the Up passenger train at 12.10pm and departure of the 3.47pm Down passenger train. The times are approximate, so progress of the special train had to be confirmed by telephone to all stations. This arrangement was confirmed by the BoT early in 1902 and became the basis for train working for the next six years.

In 1907/8 a loop line was built at Blythburgh Station to allow trains to pass there. Engineer Pain wrote to the BoT proposing to increase the capacity of the line, as necessary, by a series of three Train Staff Tickets to be used as follows:

- TICKET A: UP special goods / passenger train from Southwold to Blythburgh and there to wait for a down train to pass before proceeding to Halesworth

- TICKET B: DOWN special goods train from Halesworth to Wenhaston, there to await orders to proceed to Southwold

- TICKET C: DOWN special goods train from Halesworth to Southwold authorising a clear run to Southwold.

The original Southwold / Halesworth Train Staff was to be retained and carried by the train following a special Train Staff ticket.

This unusual method of single line working envisaged the possibility of running six goods train every day – three in each direction – and may have surprised the BoT. Goods traffic continued to be very modest and on many days, it was not even necessary to run one special goods train. Nevertheless, in October 1908 the BoT suggested that the line be worked in two Block Sections, each being worked by a Train Staff and ticket system combined with the telephone. The Train Staffs for each section were:

Block Section	Ticket colour	Shape of head of Staff
Southwold / Blythburgh and Blyth Swing Bridge	Red	Round
Blythburgh / Halesworth	Blue	Rectangular

The BoT suggestion was adopted and Blythburgh became a 'Crossing and Train Staff Station.' The opening of the Harbour Branch required Walberswick, without a loop line, to become a 'Train Staff Station' so creating a third Block Section:

Block Section	Ticket colour	Shape of head of Staff
Southwold / Walberswick and Blyth Swing Bridge	Red	Round
Walberswick / Blythburgh	Green	Hexagonal
Blythburgh / Halesworth	Blue	Rectangular

This alteration facilitated the working of the Harbour Branch during the First World War when military and naval traffic was carried, but after the War the anticipated fishery business at the Harbour did not progress. In 1917 Walberswick Station was closed and the Southwold / Walberswick Block Section was withdrawn so working reverted to the 1908 arrangement. When Walberswick Station re-opened in 1919 it was not re-instated as a Train Staff Station.

This system, or a similar one, was universal for all single line railways so the Southwold Railway was not unique in its method of operation. The Company issued a Book of Regulations in 1879, re-issued in 1918, approved by the BoT and containing a number of references to safe working of trains. A Train Staff Regulation book was issued in 1908 which explained in more detail the mode of working.

Occasional instances of unusual or 'irregular' working was covered by a written Order from the Company Secretary and, for instance, permitted Special Fish trains on Sundays (when there was no passenger

Fig 116: The short-lived Walberswick / Blythburgh staff with a hexagonal head and no Annetts key.

Fig 117: Royal insignia at head of Act to Amend the Regulation of Railways Acts – 30 August 1889.

service) to run through without exchanging Train Staffs at Blythburgh. Drivers of such trains, including the trains required by the military at short notice during the First World War, were instructed to keep a sharp look out throughout the journey and to reduce speed while running through stations.

Brakes

In 1889, ten years after the Southwold Railway opened, parliament passed 'An Act to amend the Regulation of Railways Acts; and for other purposes'. This Act signalled a loss of patience by parliament, and the BoT, with railway companies. It was in the interests of public safety because of a series of serious accidents of which the Armagh collision on 8 June 1889 was the most recent. On a steep incline near Armagh, eighty people died, many of them children, after a portion of an excursion train, separated from the head end of the train because the locomotive could not haul all the carriages, ran away backwards down the incline and collided with a following train.

'**An Act to amend the Regulation of Railways Acts; and for other purposes. [30 August 1889]**
'Be it enacted by the Queen's most Excellent Majesty, by and with the advice and consent of the Lords Spiritual and Temporal, and Commons, in this present Parliament assembled, and by the authority of the same, as follows:

Power to order certain provisions to be made for public safety

(**1**) The Board of Trade may from time to time order a railway company to do, within a time limited by the order, and subject to any exceptions or modifications allowed by the order, any of the following things:

(a) To adopt the block system on all or any of their railways open for the public conveyance of passengers ;

(b) To provide for the interlocking of points and signals on or in connexion with all or any of such railways;

(c) To provide for and use on all their trains carrying passengers continuous brakes complying with the following requirements, namely:

(i) The brake must be instantaneous in action, and capable of being applied by the engine-driver and guards;

(ii) The brake must be self-applying in the event of any failure in the continuity of its action;

(iii) The brake must be capable of being applied to every vehicle of the train, whether carrying passengers or not;

(iv) The brake must be in regular use in daily working;

(v) The materials of the brake must be of a durable character, and easily maintained and kept in order. In making any order under this section the Board of Trade shall have regard to the nature and extent of the traffic on the railway, and shall, before making any such order, hear any company or person whom the Board of Trade may consider entitled to be heard.'

The Southwold Railway never had continuous brakes but could take comfort from the phrase in (v) above: 'the nature and extent of the traffic on the railway'. Apart from the locomotive brakes, the passenger trains only had limited brake power achieved by handbrakes screwed on, and off, by the guard. The goods stock only had handbrakes, which could only be safely operated when the vehicles were at rest, so mixed trains added weight but no more braking power.

The BoT acknowledged that many accidents would be prevented by the introduction of the '[inter] lock, block and brake' measures which the 1889 Act demanded. The Southwold Railway could comply with (1a) and (1b) in the provisions of the Act but (1c), which the Act stated must be complied with by 28 May 1892, was not, in the SR Board's view, achievable or necessary on their railway. A lengthy correspondence with the BoT ensued. The Company's reasons for not complying with provision (1c) may be summarised thus:

- Speed is restricted to 16mph
- The maximum number of trains per day is only six
- The distance between stations is, at the most, two-and-a-half miles
- All trains are mixed with carriages and wagons
- Three carriages are fitted with handbrake

- Regulations permit only one engine in steam at one time
- The line was opened in 1879 and has operated without an accident of any kind
- On several occasions when a driver observed an obstruction on the line he was able to stop the train using engine brake power only and without harm
- The gross receipts are a little over £3,000 per year. After deducting expenses and paying interest on capital, the Company has insufficient to finance another locomotive and any additional rolling stock and has no powers to raise additional capital.

The Directors desired to meet the new regulations but believed that the fitting of continuous brakes would not contribute any additional safety to the operation of the railway and considered them to be a potential cause of accidents while shunting. The Southwold Railway was almost certainly the only railway company in the UK and Ireland running passenger trains not fitted with a continuous braking system and continued so until closure in 1929.

The Working Timetable (Fig 118)

The timetable produced for the use of the railway staff; times of trains here are the exact time, correct to half-a-minute for arriving, passing, stopping and departing. The times in the Working Timetable may differ from those in the public timetables so it is a valuable resource for historical and operational research.

Fig 118 is such a resource, from David Lee's collection, for the Southwold Railway in the summer of 1913. Each train has a number, not disclosed in public timetables, and the Train Working Notes are always prefixed by the train number. After these numbers – 13 on the SR – there may be general notes or specific instructions. For instance: 'Halesworth to advise Blythburgh and Southwold each day before 7.00pm of all traffic going down by No 13.' Train 13 is a General Merchandise and Mineral Train so the three stations enumerated must ensure that there is siding space, if necessary, and any other special arrangements for particular consignments which are unloaded off Train 13, or needing to be loaded onto it.

Private: for use of the Company's Servants only

SOUTHWOLD RAILWAY.

TRAIN WORKING.

1st July to 30th September, 1913.

WEEK-DAYS.

UP.	1	3	3A	5	7	9	11	
	a.m.	a.m.	p.m.	p.m.	p.m.	p.m.	p.m.	
Southwold ... dep.	7 30	10 15	12 20	12 20	2 20	5 35	7 10	...
Walberswick ,,	7 35	10 20	12 25	12 25	2 25	5 40	7 15	...
Blythburgh ... ,,	7 45	10 30	12 35	pass	2 35	5 50	7 25	...
Wenhaston ... ,,	7 56	10 41	12 46	pass	2 46	6 1	7 36	...
Halesworth ... arr.	8 7	10 52	12 57	12 53	2 57	6 12	7 47	...

DOWN.	2	4	6	8	8A	10	12	13	
	a.m.	a.m.	p.m.	p.m.	p.m.	p.m.	p.m.	Mineral p.m.	
Halesworth ... dep.	8 40	11 33	1 33	3 35	3 35	6 26	7 53	8 15	Mondays to Fridays only.
Wenhaston ... ,,	8 49	11 42	1 42	pass	3 44	6 35	8 2	8 23	
Blythburgh ... ,,	9 0	11 53	1 53	pass	3 55	6 46	8 13	8 33	
Walberswick ,,	9 12	12 5	2 5	4 3	4 7	6 58	8 25	8 45	
Southwold ... arr.	9 17	12 10	2 10	4 8	4 12	7 3	8 30	8 50	

Nos. 1 and 3.—General Goods, Passengers' Luggage, and Empty Trucks may be attached.

No. 3A.—Empty Trucks may be attached. Will not run after the 31st July.

Nos. 2, 4, and 6.—General Goods. Passengers' Luggage only to be attached to rear, excepting Fish for Southwold.

No. 4.—Blythburgh to work down mails for No. 5.

No. 5.—Will commence running on the 1st August. Passengers' Luggage, and Empty Trucks from Southwold only, to be attached.

Nos. 5 and 8.—To reduce speed going through Blythburgh for the purpose of exchanging the Train Staff.

No. 8.—Will not run after the 30th August.

,, 8A.—Will commence running on the 1st September.

Nos. 7 and 9.—General Goods, Passengers' Luggage, and specially required Empty Trucks only to be attached.

,, 8, 8A, 10, and 12.—Passengers' Luggage only to be attached to rear, excepting Fish or Ice for Southwold.

No. 11.—Goods and Empty Trucks may be attached. Two Engines. To be worked by two Guards. On arrival at Halesworth additional Engine to shunt and make up No. 13.

Nos. 11, 12, and 13.—To work strictly in accordance with the Train Staff regulations.

No. 13.—General Merchandise and Mineral Train. To stop at each Station, and not to depart therefrom until called on by telephone by the next Station. In the event of the Telephone being out of order the Train must work to booked time, Driver and Guard keeping a sharp look out. If the departure of No. 12 is delayed, then No. 13 must **not** leave Halesworth until No. 12 has arrived at Blythburgh, and must **not** depart from Blythburgh until the Passenger Train has arrived at Southwold. Southwold to provide additional Guard, who must record the working and numbers and contents of trucks. Disc or side lamp of this train to be returned to Halesworth first train following morning.

Truck No. 10 to be attached to the rear of the Down and to the front of Up Passenger Trains for Fish, Ice, and General Passenger Train traffic.

Additional Engine to be kept ready to work Nos. 3A, 5 and 7 when required.

Trucks of Pigs and Sheep, also General Goods for Southwold, may be attached to the front part of any Passenger Train.

No Minerals, Timber, Grain, Flour, Empties, &c., to be attached to any Train except No. 13.

No Trucks to be detached or attached at the Water Mill Siding by any Passenger Train.

No Train of four or more Carriages to be despatched without an additional Guard; Halesworth to send additional Guard by No. 4 to assist to work up Nos. 3A and 5 when required.

Halesworth to advise Blythburgh and Southwold each day before 7.0 p.m. of all traffic going down by No. 13.

SUNDAYS.

UP			1	DOWN.			2
			p.m.				p.m.
Southwold ... ... dep.			4 55	Halesworth ... ... dep.			7 32
Walberswick ... ... ,,			5 0	Wenhaston ... ... ,,			7 41
Blythburgh ... ... ,,			5 10	Blythburgh ... ... ,,			7 52
Wenhaston ... ... ,,			5 21	Walberswick ... ... ,,			8 4
Halesworth ... ... arr.			5 32	Southwold ... ... arr.			8 9

Mineral traffic accumulated during Saturday to be worked down by Special, which must leave Halesworth at 6.0 p.m. Empty Trucks to be worked back on the return journey.

GENERAL INSTRUCTIONS.

The Staff are requested to use every endeavour to get the Trains away to time.

Passengers' Luggage and other articles must not be placed on the platforms of the carriages.

Passengers' Luggage must not be loaded into the open trucks unless such vehicles have been thoroughly swept out.

The Public are not to be allowed on the transfer stage at Halesworth.

H. WARD,

LONDON, *June 1913.* *Manager and Secretary.*

The Southwold Press, Printers, 6-8 Church Street, Southwold.

Fig 118: Southwold Railway Working Timetable and Staff Instructions 1 July to 30 September 1913 – **Private: for use of the Company's Servants only.**

CHAPTER 13

ACCIDENTS, MISHAPS, INCIDENTS AND FLOODS

Narrow gauge railways were not immune from accidents and sadly the Southwold Railway had two fatalities to its staff and one non-fatal accident but, so far as records show, it injured very few passengers. Of the fatalities to staff, one was tragic and the other unfortunate as a result of a rather foolhardy action on the part of the deceased.

No accounts of railway accidents make pleasant reading, but the details which are usually given in newspaper accounts and BoT/Ministry of Transport Reports can be an informative historical record. They may also tell us much about the operation of the railway concerned, especially many years ago, so this chapter is an informative part of the story of the Southwold Railway.

Fatal accidents

The first accident happened early in the existence of the Company on the morning of Wednesday 14 November 1883 at Walberswick station as the 9.07am down train from Halesworth entered the station. Usually it proceeded along the shallow cutting towards the station where the Driver – John Cutting and Fireman William Todd on this occasion – generally reduced speed. However, Driver Cutting could see that there were no passengers waiting but he saw Edward Court, aged 17, Walberswick Clerk-in-Charge, was holding something. Guard (Arthur Wright) gave the signal to proceed but when Driver Cutting felt a jerk, [and Fireman Todd warned him], he stopped the train about ten yards beyond. The incident was witnessed by Fireman Todd who may have crossed over the footplate to look back along the train; the driver was on the right hand side but looking forward. At the inquest, Fireman Todd said Court had a basket and some leggings under his right arm and with his left hand caught hold of the iron hand rail at the leading end of the carriage. Guard Wright called out to him to get on behind so if he fell he would take no harm but bruising. Court ignored this helpful advice and he seemed to miss his footing. He was unable to help himself, twisted round with his back to the carriage, fell between the carriage and the platform and the carriage ran over him. Both the Driver and Guard ran back when the train stopped to assist him, but Court was fatally injured. Court's body was placed in the First Class compartment and carried on to Southwold then to a temporary morgue in the Marquis of Lorne Inn on the High Street.

The inquest was held that evening before Coroner H.F. Vulliamy Esq. The medical evidence, given by Mr F.H. Vertue, was 'that death had ensued from shock to the system caused by the wounds received'. The Coroner concluded that no blame was attached to anyone and the jury returned a verdict of 'Accidental death from being run over by a train'. The funeral took place at St. Edmunds Parish Church, Southwold, on Sunday afternoon 18 November and was attended by all the Company's employees while a large number of townspeople and friends gathered as spectators. Burial was in the churchyard on the north side of the church and Edward's family erected a memorial (**Fig 119**) which mentions the Southwold Railway. The vicar who took the funeral service alluded to the sad event with much feeling in his sermon at the evening service.

Court had been employed by the SR Company since the line opened, first as a porter at Southwold and, shortly before his unfortunate death, as a booking clerk (and as Clerk-in-charge) at Walberswick Station. He was considered a singularly bright and promising 17 year old lad. It seemed, however, that Court made a habit of boarding a moving train in the way that Fireman Todd reported; Guard Wright had repeatedly told him to get on behind but, sadly, the young and active Court thought he knew better.

The Company reported the incident to the BoT (Railway Department) but no report of an enquiry has been traced; it is only a statistic in the annual report on accidents for 1883.

The other fatal accident was at Wenhaston Station on Friday 24 December 1926. The victim was Station

Fig 119: Memorial in St Edmund's Churchyard, Southwold, recording the death of Edward Court 'WHO LOST HIS LIFE ON THE SOUTHWOLD RAILWAY NOV 14 1885 AGED 17 YEARS'.

Master Harry Girling and the story can be told in words and pictures because it illustrates some of the Railway's working practices. The caption and picture of **Fig 120** is the starting point.

The up train had left Southwold at 10.05am and arrived at Wenhaston Station platform at 10.35am.

Station Master Girling, assisted by the Guard, decided to loose-shunt two wagons off the train into the Station siding, mid-way along the passing loop shown in **Fig 121** sketch map, via the points at the Halesworth end of the station. These points were adjacent to the level crossing and, immediately beyond them, was under line bridge 8 which had no timber decking (**Fig 122**).

Such loose-shunting was usual practice, if required, but there were only a few minutes in the working timetable to allow for this operation; perhaps Mr Girling was in a hurry?

Let us suppose that the wagons Mr Girling required at Wenhaston were the two coupled to the vans (see the train in **Fig 120**) so he would first uncouple them from the vans. The engine would then draw the five 4-wheeled open wagons over the level crossing and probably onto Bridge 8 to be clear of the points leading to the passing loop shown in **Fig 121**. After changing the points, Girling, on the platform, gave the signal to set back into the passing loop to the Fireman who was on the same side of the engine as Girling. The Fireman informed the Driver who was on the right-hand side of the footplate in his driving position. As the setting back movement of the five wagons began, at about walking pace, Girling stepped between the wagons, walking with them, to uncouple the first two.

Fig 123 shows the figure-of-eight coupling Girling needed to lift to separate the two wagons he intended to keep at Wenhaston. Originally all the SR goods vehicles were fitted with 'chopper' buffer-couplings similar to the sketch in **Fig 124**.

Fig 120: an up mixed train arriving at Halesworth SR Station with, in this example, five 4-wheel wagons, two 4-wheel vans and at least two of the Cleminson Patent 6-wheel carriages. No record now exists of the consist of the up train in the Wenhaston accident but let us suppose it was the same as the train at Halesworth.

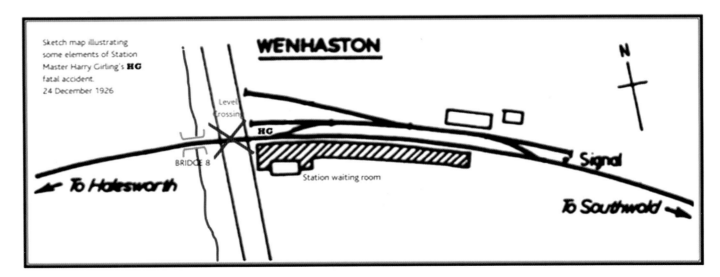

Fig 121: Wenhaston Station layout sketch map illustrating some elements of Station Master Harry Girling's fatal accident, 24 December 1926.

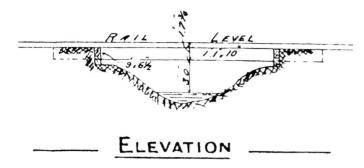

ELEVATION

SR UNDER BRIDGE No 8

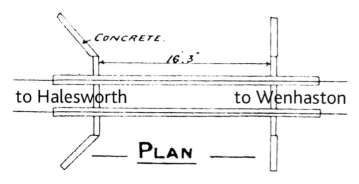

to Halesworth   to Wenhaston

PLAN

Fig 122: Elevation and Plan of SR underbridge No 8 at Wenhaston.

The principle seems, at first sight, to be similar to the figure-of-eight loop in **Fig 123**, but what was missing from the SR chopper-type buffer couplings was a bridle to secure the chopper when it was down and coupled to an adjoining vehicle. In August 1921, two wagons became uncoupled because the chopper bounced upward after a driver abruptly closed his regulator. The SR Company's solution was the figure-of-eight loop which replaced the chopper and was pinned into place once down and connected.

All Station Master Girling needed to do, while the buffer couplings were being pushed together, rather than taut in the pulling position, was to pull out the locking pin and lift the figure-of-eight into the position in **Fig 123**.

It was a dry morning and the rails were not greasy. A witness to the whole operation was standing at the level crossing gates. He saw Girling on the platform side of the wagons then heard a scream and groaning and saw Girling under a wagon. The fireman, looking back from the left-hand side of the loco footplate, saw Girling step between the wagons to uncouple the two for the siding as the train

Fig 123: Figure-of-eight coupling link.

Fig 124: Sketch of 'chopper'-type buffer coupling.

moved slowly back and next saw a uniform cap fly into the air. He immediately called out to the Driver, 'I believe we are over the Station Master.' The driver stopped the train at once, the Fireman pulled Girling out and he was carried to the waiting room. Dr. Melville Hooker was called, found Girling in great pain and suffering from shock; he administered morphine and supervised removal to the hospital at Halesworth where Girling died.

At the inquest, Dr Melville described the injuries sustained as the worst combination of injuries that he had ever seen. He stated that Girling died from shock caused by the injuries. When asked how the accident had happened, he replied that he understood Girling's foot was caught in a check rail, he was bowled over by the still slowly moving train and one of the wagons passed over him. The Coroner summed up that it was clearly an unfortunate accident for which no one was to blame. The jury returned a verdict of 'Accidental death' stating that no one was to blame.

An MoT report on the accident was critical about the practice of going between moving vehicles to uncouple them and surprise was expressed that the Company's Rule Book did not contain a clause warning men against this dangerous practice. The Company subsequently inserted a warning as Rule No 98.

The report also commented that bridge 8 (**Fig 122**), only ten or twelve yards from the siding points, was not boarded on each side of the rails or between them so it was impossible for a man to uncouple there before a propelling movement into the passing loop started. The report recommended boarding-in to provide a suitable walkway for men, when necessary, to pass along the side of a train.

Whether the presence of the unboarded bridge had any bearing on the accident will never be known, or whether Girling realised the considerable risk he was taking in going between moving vehicles but was anxious not to delay the passengers in the train any further.

As often happens after a railway accident and the subsequent MoT report, good can come from ill and improvements are made which contribute to operating safety. Both these fatal accidents can be attributed to staff misjudgements but in both cases, it is reasonable to assume that the staff in question were trying to keep trains on time and not cause unwelcome delays which would have to be reported to the General Manager in the London office. The Southwold Railway had no more fatal accidents but there were other matters which delayed trains and they are described chronologically in the next section. They, too, contribute to our understanding of the working of the railway so are a useful historical record.

A Non-Fatal Accident

Another accident occurred at Walberswick, thirty-eight years later, which caused damage to rolling stock. There were no reported injuries to passengers.

Runaway wagons: On Bank Holiday 3 August 1921, as the 4.00pm up goods train to Halesworth was passing Tinker's Farm, just beyond mile post 7, two wagons became uncoupled. They coasted back down the gentle gradient and dashed into the rear of a down train stationary in Walberswick station. The impact is described as being so violent that one of the wagons, loaded with coal, was thrown off the line, while two box vans and three carriages were badly damaged at the headstocks. There were no reported injuries to passengers on the down train, though they must surely have been aware of the collision if the shock damaged the carriage headstocks. The Company did not report the incident, but they learned that the National Union of Railwaymen, presumably on safety concerns for the staff, had made a report of the incident to the MoT. The Company therefore held an enquiry on 10 August 1921 when it was determined that:

- the Driver had shut off steam too quickly after breasting the summit of the incline;

- the sudden slowing of the loco caused buffering-up of the train and the chopper coupling between the train and the last two wagons disengaged;
- the Fireman, Guard and Assistant Guard failed to keep a lookout so did not observe the detached wagons running back down the incline.

Fines were imposed on the train crew and the Assistant Guard received a serious warning. (**Fig 125**)

The MoT did not hold an enquiry but as the incident had been brought to its attention, a meeting was held with Colonel Pringle of the MoT, the Chairman and the Manager. The question of speed, couplings and provision of Brake Vans in the rear of all trains was fully discussed. The whole matter was left to the Company to reconsider and submit proposals to the Ministry.

Colonel Pringle had observed that the running time of 37 minutes allowed between Halesworth and Southwold included stops at stations. To maintain booked timings, therefore, particularly if any shunting was required, the trains must be exceeding the speed limit of 16mph between stations. The Company in their submission proposed that the running times of trains should be increased by four minutes, thereby making the journey 41 minutes against the present time of 37 minutes and that all vehicles should be fitted with 'figure of eight' couplings. The Ministry agreed with the proposals as a temporary measure, stating that should the low speed be increased in future, the question of providing a braked vehicle in rear of mixed

trains would have to be considered. In reference to the question of fitting continuous brakes discussed during the 1890s, the Ministry were now of the opinion, in the interests of public safety, it was not necessary to insist on the Southwold Railway Company's carriages being equipped with continuous brakes.

Disruptions caused by inclement weather.

Good weather conditions gave the Southwold Railway increased passenger traffic in the summer months but inclement weather, especially winter storms, sometimes caused serious damage by flooding or complete washouts of embankments. Falling snow also disrupted train services. The SR was particularly vulnerable to flooding near Wenhaston, Walberswick and across Woods End Marshes before Southwold.

On the opening day in September 1879 the railway service was disrupted by flooding at Wenhaston, following heavy rain, and as a precaution no trains travelled any further so Southwold had to wait for the arrival of their first train until the next day.

The earliest recorded damage was during December 1881, when a severe NE gale blew off part of the engine shed roof at Southwold. This did not disturb any train services but in 1892, during the night of 17 February, there was a heavy snow storm with high winds. Despite some drifting, the first train up from Southwold at 7.30am and the return at 9.10am from Halesworth both ran right time. More drifting snow subsequently caused 23 minutes delay to the following 10.50am up train but the GER Halesworth Station Master held the main line

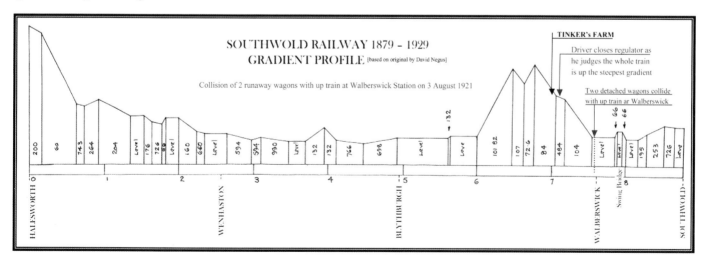

Fig 125: annotated gradient profile for the Southwold Railway showing where a too-rapid closing of the loco regulator caused a sudden buffering-up of the train which disengaged a chopper coupling.

down train so that SR passengers could connect. There was no record of any further disruption during the rest of that day.

The next recorded weather incident, in December 1894, was considerably more serious. On Saturday 22 December, when the 10.55am up train arrived at Halesworth, SR Station Master Walter Calver noticed, and reported, a broken window in carriage No 6 caused, he believed, by gale-force winds in a heavy north-easterly gale. Although the gale abated during Saturday evening, the sea broke through defences on either side of the town on Sunday evening and the embankment between Walberswick Station and the swing bridge was scoured away for at least 300 yards leaving the rails and sleepers suspended.

On Monday morning 24 December 1894, the Southwold Station Master Frederick Handford walked to Halesworth to advise Station Master Walter Calver of 'the unfortunate stoppage'. At that time there was no telephone communication between stations and because all engines and carriages were kept at Southwold it was not possible to run any trains between Halesworth and Blythburgh. Four buses were hired for a service in lieu and to maintain connections with GER trains. GER stations were advised from Halesworth of the situation and asked not to forward any traffic to Halesworth for the SR. Walter Calver made three reports to the Company Secretary; that quoted below illustrates how dedicated staff were to the Company – even on Christmas Day:

'Dec 26 1894 to 17 Victoria St. London
'On Tuesday Xmas Day I started out [from Halesworth] at 7.00am, walked to Wenhaston and gave Spoole* instructions from Mr. [Engineer] Pain. I walked back to Halesworth and loaded a Box Truck with sleepers. Porters Spoole, Sallows, Farmer and myself pushed the Truck to Blythboro.' [We had a] large horse to take it up Lists Bank where we went on to Breach in road [ie. the washed-out embankment] and assisted in the repair until 4.30pm Myself, Spoole and Sallows walked home leaving Farmer at work with the others. On reaching Halesworth at 7.45pm we were quite knocked up.
'Yours truly W. Calver'
* Spoole at Wenhaston was the ganger of No. 1 permanent way gang.

Restoration of the embankment and relaying the track took almost four days then, on the night of Thursday 27th December, an engine with one coach was able to pass over the new bank and proceed to Halesworth in time to connect with the last GER train (down) 7.59pm at Halesworth, after which normal working resumed on the following day.

An estimated total work force, including volunteer fishermen, of at least 30 men spent Christmas working hard so Mr Engineer Pain supplied the whole gang with roast beef, plum pudding and beer from the Swan Hotel, Southwold, for four days.

This incident must have been an early example of a railway company providing an alternative bus service for passengers in an emergency, while it was remarked by the *Halesworth Times* that 'an experience of this kind at mid-winter is calculated to make us devoutly thankful for the existence of the much abused Southwold line.'

Less than three years later on Monday 29 November 1897, Southwold was struck by another severe gale which again did serious damage to the foreshore of Southwold's sea front and breached the railway embankment across Woodsend Marshes (**Fig 126**), while water on the road into Southwold was reported as being level with the tops of the railings on house front walls thus cutting off the town from the Station. Train services were not affected until the afternoon of Monday when the 1.10pm down train could not proceed beyond the River Blyth swing bridge. Passengers, parcels, mail and goods traffic were taken across the river in three or four boats to Blackshore Quay and thence by road into Southwold. An engine and at least two coaches and six wagons were now marooned near the swing bridge. It was possible to operate the train service between Blythburgh and Halesworth, so passengers, parcels and mails were then conveyed by road between Southwold and Blythburgh – passengers were charged 9d. The extent of damage to the embankment must have been greater than in 1894 and took at least seven days to repair; normal working was not resumed until Wednesday 8 December.

Fortunately the gale abated so on Wednesday 1 December over 30 tons of fish was carted from Southwold Harbour to Blythburgh where some was transferred to rail but several carts had to continue to Halesworth. Three loaded wagons at Halesworth SR Station were unloaded in order to convey ballast material from the Bird's Folly quarry at Holton to the breached embankment site (**Fig 127**).

Fig: 126 A view from the swing bridge (behind the photographer) towards the Southwold Common cutting after the 1897 gale and floods scoured out the Woods End Marshes embankment.

Periodically, in 1904, 1906 and 1910, more disruption was caused by high winds, high tides and flooding but the permanent way gangs, and other staff too, continued to give noble service and made great efforts to sustain normal services. Occasionally, bus services were hired in to maintain the SR timetable.

During the last week of August 1912, a violent storm caused wide spread disruption to railway services in East Anglia. Southwold Railway services ran normally until Monday 26 August when, after the last down train, flooding occurred between Wenhaston and Blythburgh and during the night a tree was blown down severing the SR stations' telephone line. SR services were resumed on Wednesday 28 August but GER trains continued to be delayed. Saturday 31 August was probably the GER's worst day, but the Southwold Railway was able to minimise visitors' discomforts by running their delayed connecting trains after midnight into Southwold.

In 1916, services were disrupted twice within three months. On Thursday 13 January, the highest tide for twenty years on the East Coast caused extensive flooding over a wide area of Norfolk and Suffolk including Southwold as reported in a letter by Secretary H. Ward to Board member W.C. Chambers:

'Dear Sir,
'I much regret to inform you that in consequence of a severe gale from the north-west early on Thursday last, the 13th inst., the sea overstepped its normal boundary and great volumes of water came over on

Fig 127: Workmen, re-ballasting the Woods End Marshes embankment.

to the low lying parts of the Town on both sides, thus completely cutting off Southwold from the outside world, from about 5pm on the Thursday until the afternoon of Friday. The height of the tide broke all previous records by half an inch.

'The river wall broke in many places and large volumes of water rushed out and covered the adjoining marshes and lands. The main line between Southwold Cutting and the Swing Bridge was breached in 2 or 3 places about the Junction to the Harbour Branch, to a depth of between 2 and 3 feet. The water covered the line at the bend below Lists' Wood and along the Blythburgh curve, but fortunately did no damage at either of these places. The water in the vicinity of the Harbour Junction subsided sufficiently to enable the men to quickly repair the damaged places, so that running was resumed about 3pm on the Friday.

'The Harbour Branch, I regret to say has suffered rather severely, the bank at Blackshore being partially broken away to the extent of about 230 feet, and a large hole made in another part. The Ferry Road where the branch crosses has been washed away for about 12 yards to a depth of from 2 to 4 feet. It will take about 800 cubic yard of material to repair the whole of the damage, and I think the bulk of this will be available in the Southwold Cutting.

'Yours truly, H. Ward.'

The breach by the level crossing at Ferry Road was repaired by Southwold Corporation staff using ballast taken from the Cutting for which a temporary siding was constructed from spare rails and controlled by one of the Harbour Branch Junction Annetts Key Boxes.

Three months later, another fierce storm hit the town during the evening of Tuesday 28 March blowing down trees including several across the line between Walberswick and Wenhaston causing disruption to normal working which was not resumed until the 10.05am train on Wednesday.

After the 1916 storms there were no further reports of severe weather or disruptions to train services until Wednesday 9 August 1921, when a heath fire of great intensity broke out near Blythburgh Station; it was witnessed by train passengers who talked of seeing 'giant flames' over an area of about 100 x 50 yards.

A few months later in November, the severest of gales 'for many years' blew down a shelter on the pier and 'the top of the engine shed [roof] at … [Southwold] was removed'. Train services not affected.

On the last weekend of 1921 and the first of the New Year, Southwold suffered a high tide which made the town an island by flooding the surrounding marshes but there is no report of train services being affected. However, in the following week on Wednesday 4 January 1922, East Anglia had a heavy snow storm with high winds causing a drift up to seven feet blocking the line between Walberswick and Blythburgh so cancelling the train service until the 10.05am up train on Thursday 5 January.

Another 'heavy snowstorm – deep drifts filled up by Blythburgh' and the Cutting through the Common took place over Sunday and Monday morning 15-16 January. The drift was ineffectively charged by the engine of the 7.30am up train, but staff had the line open to resume normal working by midday.

By contrast, over the 1922 Whitsun Bank Holiday the weather was of 'a brilliant character' so that on the Monday 200 passengers were booked from Halesworth to Southwold.

The last record of inclement weather to cause disruption to services was in 1924 on the night of Tuesday 21 and Wednesday 22 October when heavy rain and flooding caused damage to the track at Wenhaston; train services were suspended until the next morning.

Miscellanea, some humorous, which delayed train working.

The first recorded non-fatal accident was in 1883 being reported by the Halesworth Station Master, Walter Calver, who advised management in London that:

'after the last down train on Thursday 30 August four bullocks strayed onto the line, one being hit, at the second crossing past Mr Kett's field. Calver was on the train so, with the Guard, went back to find the animals [and discovered] a gate open. The bullocks were herded into the field; the gates closed and fastened [and] found in good order.'

The location was probably an accommodation crossing; the night was dark; Jackson was driving.

The Railway's first reported incident of a train being divided when running was on 11 September 1897 as Walter Calver notified in his letter to the secretary:

'Sept 11 1897
'To – H.Carne Esq. 17 Victoria St. London From – Halesworth

Dear Sir.
'I beg to inform you after our 1.20pm had left GE Signalman informed me he could see some trucks detached from our train, as the train was going

down the bank. I followed on with porter Spoole and Aldred *xxxxxxxxx (not readable)*. [We saw] trucks No 25 and 14 standing on the line about 50 yards this side of Kett's Bridge. I left Spoole with the two trucks and sent Aldred on to Wenhaston with instructions for the Driver to stop at Kett's Siding. I stopped at Ketts Siding and stopped the 2.20pm, detached the engine, went [back] and attached the two trucks and placed them in Ketts Siding, came on with train to this Station, caught our connection of the 3.14pm The two trucks were loaded with passengers' luggage taken on by 3.45.

'Yours truly, Sgd W. Calver'

Some SR trains were divided for operating reasons, particularly up trains approaching Halesworth on a 1 in 66 gradient which often caused a heavily loaded train to stall. A stalled train was divided, and the first parts taken forward into the station, the engine returning for the remainder of the train. In such circumstances railway companies usually issued special train loading and working instructions, but none have been traced for the SR.

The first recorded failure to lift the train up this bank was in late July 1897. Following division of the train, engine No. 1 took vehicles forward to the station. Due to insufficient brake power the remaining carriages ran back, to the consternation of the passengers, coming to rest near Mile Post No.1.

Almost four months later, on 1 December 1897, during restoration of the embankment washout at Woodsend Marshes as recorded previously, the last up train worked from Blythburgh and driven by the locomotive Foreman, consisted of two carriages and six wagons loaded with fish. The loco failed to lift the train up the bank so it was divided but no runaways were recorded. However, on August Bank Holiday evening 1899, a heavily loaded six coach train had to be divided and the rear three carriages ran back to Wenhaston. Presumably there were no injuries and passenger views are not recorded.

Instances of trains failing on the Halesworth bank were becoming more frequent; in 1900, the Station Master reports on an incident:

'April 16 1900
'To: A.C. Pain Esq. 17 Victoria Street. From: Halesworth

'Dear Sirs,

'I beg to inform you the 2.20pm train from Southwold this day stopped on Halesworth Bank and set back again to get a run at the Bank but stopped again at Ballast Pits.

'I went down as quickly as possible with a sprag* but before reaching the train several of the passengers had started walking up the line. What passengers remained I had removed into the front coach, uncoupled [it from] the train and ran [it] up to the station and sent engine back for remainder of train.

'Our train was made up as follows:

3 coaches, 3 trucks, engine No. 1 Driver Laws; Guard Wright.

'We delayed GE down trains 8 mts.

'I beg to suggest that 2 good sprags* should always be carried in Guards Van.

'Yours truly (sgd) W. Calver'

*A 'sprag' was a specially shaped piece of round timber for wedging under a wheel or between the spokes and against the underframe to prevent a vehicle from moving.

There were no further reported mishaps until 1925, when at Halesworth on Saturday 3 July the 1.00pm down train, very shortly after starting, was diverted into the siding east of the line, used for permanent way purposes (see Halesworth final layout **Fig 29**, page 54). The stop block at the end of the siding was demolished and the leading wheels of the engine were derailed. After re-railing by SR staff, the loco, though slightly damaged, was able to work the train to Southwold three hours late. Passengers did not suffer any injuries though some were alarmed; some were half-day excursion ticket holders off a London train but there were no complaints. Throwing stones or placing obstructions on the line, by juveniles and adults, and sometimes causing damage to railway property were not unusual for the Southwold Railway from the early years of operation. The first report by the Halesworth SR Station Master in July 1881 was of a GER employee throwing a stone, resulting in an end window being broken in carriage No. 5.

In October 1888, a more serious offence was reported when a piece of stone, weighing about 4lbs, was placed against a rail on Holton Road Bridge in the path of the last down train. Both Driver and Guard felt the train shake on passing the location so reported the incident to the Station Master when they arrived at Wenhaston. The following morning the Halesworth SR Station Master also received word of the incident by letter from Wenhaston (remember the SR had no telephone connections between stations until 1899) and contacted the police.

Just two years later on 9 October 1890 as the 10.30am up train passed Ball's Bridge (No. 4), Driver Hammond saw a boy throw something at the train so reported to the Station Master on arriving at Halesworth. It so happened that the Police Superintendent was on Halesworth platform and he ordered a man to go and investigate; these local police had an idea who was responsible!

The next recorded incident, in 1892, came to the knowledge of the Halesworth Station Master from the local police sergeant who, in March, had observed four local boys trespassing on the line at Holton. No action was taken by the police, but the SR Secretary was informed so he could warn them not to repeat the offence.

Two years later on 27 June 1894, a boy was caught throwing a stone near Halesworth. Station Master Calver took out a summons against the lad; two other lads and Driver Hammond were cited as witnesses.

On 23 June 1896, near Holton Road Bridge, a 6-year old boy threw a stone as the 2.15pm up train was passing, breaking a window in carriage No. 4. Again, the police sergeant happened to be present on the platform and found the culprit who admitted the incident. He was from Norwich, staying in Loam Pit Lane, Holton. The Sergeant took the boy to the people he was staying with, explaining what he had done, and reprimanding him. Because he was under age, summonsing was not possible and probably not really desirable.

The three following incidents are different from, and more serious, than the stone throwing local lads.

A passenger, claiming to be a regular traveller on the Southwold Railway, wrote in July 1900 to the BoT expressing concern for the safely of operating staff. The passenger was worried about the Guard passing between carriages to examine tickets while the train was in motion. He pointed out that the Guard ought to have better facilities to pass between carriages because, the writer believed, it was not possible to do so over the couplings 'on account of the danger of falling between [the carriages], so he goes on the outside planks [sic] and the stretch at curves is too far and too dangerous … he has fallen off I believe once'. The BoT, who had not received reports of such instances in the previous three years, requested the observations of the Company's Directors. In reply on 1 August 1900, Claude Pain stated that the 'Guard was permitted to step from one platform to another on one side of trains while it was running'. On the question of a bridge between carriages, he stated:

'it was fully considered before the line opened. Each carriage was over 40 feet long [so had] considerable horizontal movement going round corners and slight vertical movement through inequalities in the road and uneven loading … if a bridge were provided it would open up a source of serious risks. [A] Guard did fall once but [was] uninjured [and there had been] no other accident since [the Railway] opened. In all, 93,000 trips [had been] run in perfect safety, apart from one incident. The Directors consider they are not prepared to take a greater risk by making any change.'

The BoT explained the Director's response to the passenger but he persisted in his concern for the guard's safety, requesting further details. The BoT were not prepared to pursue the subject any further and consulted Colonel Yorke of the Railway Inspectorate Department, who considered the passenger a busy-body but urged that something should be done for safety reasons.

Lieutenant Colonel Van Donop of the Railway Inspectorate was required to call next time he was in the area. In his report of 16 January 1901 he stated that the Guard had to stretch 2ft 9ins on straight track and 3ft 3ins on the sharpest curve but in view of the speed limit he did not think there was much danger to the Guard. However, Mr Pain agreed to reduce the stretch by one foot thus making the maximum distance to stretch between carriages 2ft 3ins. New lengthened foot boards were fitted and the Company so advised the BoT on 8 May 1901.

No record of Guard Wright's reported previous fall has been traced but must have been some time during the latter part of the nineteenth century. His successor, Guard Palmer, is also said to have fallen off when passing between carriages, rolling down the embankment across Woodsend Marshes. The Driver became aware of his fall and set back to meet him walking towards the train. No report or date of this incident has been traced.

Some years were to pass before another unusual incident was to befall the Railway. At Blythburgh on 3-4 September 1912, the station booking office was broken into. 9 shillings and 11 pence and the bicycle of the relief clerk in charge, G.T. Moore (Clerk at Southwold), was stolen. The thief, who had been in trouble previously, presumably cycled along the A12 to Great Yarmouth where he was arrested and was ultimately sentenced to four months hard labour.

A mischievous incident that did not cause any problems or delay to train operation occurred near Walberswick on 14 September 1912. A holiday maker with two relations from London had cause to cross the railway when one of them saw a notice board on a nine foot pole which he pulled up and threw across the line but then decided to place the pole between the rails. A young boy was witness to the incident and informed the Gamekeeper who saw the pole and board between the lines and, finding the perpetrator having a picnic nearby, asked what right he had to trespass on Sir Ralph Blois' property? The pole and notice board were removed but the culprit would not give his name although it was gleaned he was staying in Southwold.

The Gamekeeper subsequently traced him and a case was taken before the Halesworth Magistrates Court. The Defendant was represented by E.R. Cooper, a Southwold solicitor, who explained that the post was only stuck in the ground, would have fallen at a touch, and would be visible by the train driver for at least 200 yards. The Bench, however, considered there was a case to answer. The Defendant said he had no malicious intent, he did not wish to cause injury to any person or the train, he only did it as a joke and offered an apology to the Managing Director of the Southwold Railway.

The solicitor for the Company said there was no desire to press the case, did not acknowledge it was serious but wished to let it be known that such incidents would not be allowed on their line. The Bench came to the conclusion that no Jury would convict. It was recorded that the Defendant had been guilty of a very foolish joke, for which he was sorry, so the case was dismissed.

Case dismissed?

A dismissal may be granted by a court that has exercised its discretion in evaluating a particular case. The case of the notice board planted in the 3ft gauge SR track can reasonably be evaluated as a foolish joke. However we authors wish to put our case that this chapter should not be dismissed because it is very much part of the 'Tale of a Suffolk Byway'. The two fatal accidents reveal much of the operating methods

Fig 128: We are not complaining!

of the Railway. The non-fatal mishaps – like the guard rolling down an embankment, or the thief who cycles into the arms of the law on his stolen machine – give colour to this story of Suffolk life,

The loyal service which the SR employees gave to their railway, and their pride in helping passengers, running their trains right time (which is a very genuine railway expression), or restoring storm damage, contributed to the affection for the Railway which still exists today. Be thankful that you were not in the carriages which ran away from near Halesworth to Wenhaston but enjoy the fact that no-one was hurt and, apparently, no-one complained.

Fig 129: We are not complaining – but we wish we could get away to the beach . . .

CHAPTER 14

DIRECTORS, MANAGEMENT AND OPERATING STAFF

People stories are as important as technical and historic data in telling a connected and holistic tale of an undertaking like the Southwold Railway. Their stories are especially relevant in this book because only the Operating Staff were really local people. The Directors and the principal office managers were based in London and generally met and worked there. The physical and social distance between them and the Railway they directed and managed may be argued as one of the reasons why the Railway Company lacked substantial capital resources or local authority contacts and goodwill in Southwold and in Suffolk.

The summaries of the Directors' lives and achievements are from David Lee's meticulous researches, but it is typical of some aspects of the Southwold Railway Company's history that little is known about Charles Chambers and his two sons, Walter and Herbert, who were all Directors and railway contractors; what David has discovered or deduced about them is recorded below.

DIRECTORS:

Arthur Cadlick Pain CE (1844-1937): Arthur Pain had been involved with at least eight light railway or tramway projects, some standard and some narrow gauge, before he became concerned with the Southwold Railway in 1875. Not all of these projects materialised but he consistently advocated the benefits of such railways in rural and thinly populated areas which were generally unattractive to the major railway companies.

Pain was educated at Winchester School and served his pupillage under the County Surveyor for Devon from 1862 and 1864 and became an assistant to a variety of engineering projects including waterworks. In the 1860s, he became Resident Engineer to the Duke of Devonshire's Estate and in 1866 set up his own practice and became a Member of the Institution of Civil Engineers in 1877. In 1872 Pain was appointed engineer to the standard gauge Culme Valley Light Railway which

Fig 130: Portrait of Arthur Pain in retirement; permission to reproduce here by his great-grandson, Simon Pain.

was completed in 1876. His office was at 5 Victoria Street in London and that address ultimately became the Head Office of the Southwold Railway.

He became Managing Director of the Southwold Railway Company from 1885 to 1903 then Chairman until 1929, but also retained his initial responsibility as Engineer until his son Claude succeeded him in that post in 1912. He died in 1937 aged 93.

Claude Pain CE (1881-1956): son of Arthur Pain, he served his practical training with his father from 1889-1901 and set up his own engineering practice. Claude continued to assist with some of his father's projects including the reconstruction of the Blyth swing bridge and the construction of the Southwold Harbour Light Railway. As Engineer to the Southwold Railway from 1912, he was commissioned into the Royal Engineers in 1916, served in the First World War, then rejoined the Southwold in 1919. He became a Director of the railway in 1929.

Richard Christopher Rapier CE (1866-97): He was educated at Christ's Hospital, London, then apprenticed to Robert Stephenson & Co in Newcastle-upon-Tyne, where he was afterwards appointed an assistant. He subsequently entered the Orwell Works of Messrs. Ransomes at Ipswich and became Ransomes' London representative. He was so successful that new works – Waterside Iron Works under the name of Ransomes and Rapier-were constructed at Ipswich for the special manufacture of railway plant and materials. Mr. Rapier was managing director of these works at the time of his death.

In 1872, he interested himself in introducing railways into China, and in conjunction with Messrs. Matheson and Co. had a share in the construction of the Shanghai and Woosung Railway. He was one of the chief promoters of the 3ft gauge railway from Halesworth to Southwold and became chairman from 1877 to 1897. He was connected with various important enterprises and was a member of the Institution of Civil Engineers, the Institution of Mechanical Engineers, the Geological Society, and other scientific and technical societies. He was elected a member of the Iron and Steel Institute in 1874.

Charles Chambers (1830 – 1903): Walter Charles Chambers (1855 – 1938) and Herbert William Chambers (1862 – 1941) were sons and engineers. Little is known about Charles Chambers and David Lee has found no reference to his engineering training or when he started as a railway construction contractor. He had a contract for the Kingsbridge to Salcombe Railway in 1864 but withdrew in 1871 after very little had been achieved. It may have been significant that Arthur Pain was working in Devon at this time and, perhaps, met Chambers.

From 1870 he had contracts for three branch lines in Radnorshire which were completed in 1874/75 and in May 1878 he was engaged to build the Southwold Railway – probably his only narrow gauge railway – which was ready for BoT inspection in September 1879. In 1883, Charles Chambers became a Director of the

Railway and then Chairman from 1897. He continued with railway contracting work after the Southwold opened, sometimes working with his sons. His London office was at 5 Victoria Street until 1899 when he retired and his sons took over his business.

CHAIRMEN OF THE SOUTHWOLD RAILWAY COMPANY

Colonel Heneage Bagot-Chester	1875 – 1877
Richard Rapier	1877 – 1897
Charles Chambers	1897 – 1902
Arthur Pain	1903 – 1929 and continued as Engineer
Claude Pain	1929 – 1960

SECRETARIES TO THE SOUTHWOLD RAILWAY COMPANY

H.R. Allen	1875 – 1877	Solicitor in Halesworth
T.H. Jellicoe	1877 – 1880	Solicitor in Southwold
A.C. Pain	1880 – 1884	also Manager and Engineer
H. Carne	1884 – 1900	Died in office
H. Ward	1900 – 1910	(Came from Great Northern Railway) –
	1910 – 1929	Manager and Secretary –
	1929 – 1933	Receiver

OPERATING STAFF

Little is known about many of the operating staff because whatever records the Company kept are no longer available or, as far as we know, in existence. However, David Lee has worked meticulously through whatever sources he could find including local newspapers, trade directories, census records, and contacts he has made with former staff, or their friends/descendants, in Southwold, the Blyth valley and Halesworth. Where possible, he has shown dates of appointment and of leaving – in some case from obituaries showing date of death and giving a potted history. Trade directories sometimes alter their publication dates, so some dates of appointment have to be estimates. Nevertheless, this part of our story is a fascinating picture of Suffolk life on and around the Railway from the 1870s to the 1960s when the Southwold Railway Company was finally wound up.

These staff records are in roughly chronological order and the dates relate to a reference to a particular place which David Lee's researches have uncovered:

Edmond Stanley: probably second SM at Walberswick (or Clerk / Porter in Charge) 1883-94.

History: 1809 (Melton Constable); 1902 (Bulcamp); 1815 (Wells-next-the-Sea) Master of 70 ton fishing smack *ECLIPSE*. 1861 Census (Walberswick). Probably the oldest employee of the Company.

Walter George Bridal: Southwold SM 1881-83.

History: 1844 (Faversham, Kent); 1881 Census (Living with family at 14 Station Road, Southwold); Not known why he came to Southwold but may have known Arthur Pain who gave him position as SM. 1885 Headmaster, or Assistant Teacher at Tudor House School overlooking Southwold Common. Possibly re-named the School as 'Walden's Boarding and day school for young gentlemen' for which Pain was a referee. Was Secretary to the River Blyth Ferry Co. Ltd. 1889 (Emigrated to Australia); 1900 (Australia).

William George Jackson: SR Locomotive Foreman 1879-1916.

History: 1851 (Ipswich); Jackson started work with Ransome & Rapier in Ipswich in 1874 and went as part of the R&R team to China in 1876 as engine driver and in charge of the locomotive shed for the Woosung Road between Woosung and Shanghai. On opening day, 30 June 1876, he drove the R&R 0-6-0T *Celestial Empire* hauling the first train. In 1879 Richard Rapier, Chairman of the SR, appointed Jackson as the railway's Locomotive Foreman. In 1876 he built *Shanghai Cottage* on Station Road. 'Southwold' where he and his wife gave parties when they dressed in Chinese costumes and he told stories of 'adventures' in China. He is probably the origin of some of the myths about the Chinese origins of some SR locomotives and rolling stock.

Arthur Edgar Wright: SR Guard 1879-1914

History: 1863 (Walberswick) 1924 (Dovercourt). Father was a mariner, so he initially went to sea then succeeded

Fig 131: Guard Wright in his frock-coat uniform.

in his application to join the SR and was employed as a Guard from September 1879. He lived in Southwold. Wright was much admired by SR staff and passengers and noted for his genial disposition and courteous attentive manner.

Walter (Wally) G. Upcraft: Clerk on Southwold Station Parcels Office 1916-18(?); Southwold Station Goods Clerk 1924-26; SM Blythburgh 1926 – 1929.
History: 1903 (Reydon, Southwold); 1984 (Reydon). A long-shore fisherman who was a 'Jack of all Trades' with a strong calling to the sea. He went back to fishing after his short service at Southwold Station and in February 1924 joined a Lowestoft steam drifter. Offered an SR job so left the drifter in May and worked on the Railway until closure in 1929. Then more fishing; Eastern Counties Road Car Co conductor and driver; Southwold Harbour Master; Trinity House Pilot.

Bertie Edward Girling: Southwold Station Booking Clerk 1900-12; SM Blythburgh 1912-26 ; SM Southwold 1926-29.
History: 1888 (Bungay). Initially followed a maritime career then joined the SR in 1900 and worked through to closure; he was retained for a further month to close down and lock up all the stations. Then he worked for Fordux Mills in Southwold; as Clerk in the Southwold office of Eastern Counties Road Car Co Ltd to 1938 then to Harrogate for LNER. Back to E. Anglia in 1945 as landlord of the White Hart, Blythburgh, until 1959; retired to Wenhaston then Southwold.

Southwold Railway Company and its staff

The Company seemed to be a fair and even-handed employer. Wages were comparable with similar jobs on the GER. Uniforms were supplied and all operating staff in contact with passengers wore blue serge suits, fastened

Fig 132: No 3 *BLYTH* on up train with Station staff: left to right: Finch (Booking Clerk); Stannard (Driver on footplate); Moore (Fireman); Self (Doy's dray driver); Cox (Porter / Shunter); Case (Lad Porter); Calver (Southwold SM 1900 to 1908); Bailey (Goods Porter - under tree).

Fig 133: Southwold Station staff on the goods stage: - left to right – King (Porter); Stannard (Driver); Steadman (Goods Clerk); Fisk (Porter); Moore (Foreman Porter); Jackson (Loco Foreman).

with plain nickel buttons with a raised rim. Jacket lapels were adorned SR, possibly in green worsted, and similarly the caps 'giving an air of military efficiency'. Guard Wright wore a frock coat with 'Guard' on the left lapel and SR on the right. His cap had an SR badge and oak leaves round the peak, both in gilt. Station Masters wore a similar cap.

Uniform issues, and replacements, were every second year. Drivers were allowed two suits of dungarees and caps every year. All staff were issued with an overcoat every two years so the Company did recognise the winter chills and icy winds that low-lying Southwold experienced every winter. When an East Anglian spoke of a lazy wind one knew that 'this wind never goes round; it goes straight through you'.

The Company's finances were never strong so, in 1921, wage cuts became necessary. At a meeting in the Angel Hotel, Halesworth, on Sunday 21 October 1921, the financial position was explained to the staff and during what is reported as a friendly discussion

the necessity for wage reductions was agreed. Further reductions followed in 1922, 1923, 1924. In 1925 there was a further reduction from 20 October which, it was reported, 'the staff took in a good spirit'. Perhaps they recognised that they were lucky to still have jobs. Since the First World War ended, Britain's economy had struggled and the volume of British exports in the mid-1920s was only about 75 per cent of its pre-war figure so there were high levels of unemployment.

Station Masters

The social status of Station Masters was well established and recognised by the time the Southwold Railway opened in 1879. In the nineteenth century, they were almost invariably male and were responsible for the management of other staff working on their station and for safety and the efficient operation of the station. They tried to ensure that all trains leaving their station were 'right time,' that passengers were courteously welcomed and that parcels and goods arriving and being despatched did so correctly. At small country stations like those on the SR, there were few staff to assist so SR Station Masters often undertook several jobs, like booking clerk, porter and signalman as well as their overall care for their domain. They could attain a respected status in their community, controlling the principal means of transport, receiving daily newspapers, Royal Mail, and, once the internal station-to-station phones were installed, be a source of news.

STATION	STATION MASTER	IN SERVICE	ON LEAVING
HALESWORTH	D Price	1880 - 1881	to Wenhaston
	F W Hansford	1881 - June 1883	to Southwold
	W Claver	July 1883 - 1902	to Southwold
	H A Wright	1902 - 1929	——
WENHASTON	D Price	1879 - 1881	to Halesworth
	G Goldsmith	1881 - 6 July	to Blythburgh
	H A Wright	1881 - 1902	to Halesworth
	P F Dyer	1902 - 1907	Left service
	A A Singer	1907 - 1912	Left service
	J Button	1912 - 1913	Left service
	H B Girling	1913 - 1926	Fatal accident
	W J V Nichols	1926 - 1929	——
BLYTHBURGH	no record	1880 - 1881	possibly covered by a clerk from Southwold
	F W Hansford	March to June 1881	to Halesworth
	G Goldsmith	1881 - 1902	Left service
	W Pullen	1902 - 1912	Left service
	B E Girling	1912 - 1926	to Southwold
	W G Upcraft	1926 - 1929	——
WALBERSWICK	E Court	1882 - 1883	Fatal accident
	E Stanley	1883 - 1894	Retired, aged 85
	W Pullen	1894 - 1902	to Blythburgh
	W J V Nicholls	1902 - 1917	to Southwold
	Station closed	1917 to 1 July 1919	
	W Beard	1919 - 1923	Left service
	W Bird	1923 - 1926	Left service
	W J V Nicholls	1926 - 1929	——
SOUTHWOLD	J Leigh	1879 - 1881	Left service
	W G Bridal	1881 - 1883	Left service
	F W Hansford	1883 - 1902	Retired
	W Calver	1902 - 1905	probably Retired
	C H FitzHugh	1905 - 1916	Left service
	H J Clarke	1916 - 1926	service terminated
	B E Girling	1926 - 1929	——

Fig 134: Doy's dray and driver George Self in Southwold Station yard.

Communicating with Head Office

SOUTHWOLD RAILWAY.

DIRECTORS.

ARTHUR C. PAIN, Esq., J.P., Chairman,
17 Victoria Street, Westminster, S.W.
W. STEELE TOMKINS, Esq.,
32 Victoria Street, S.W.
WALTER C. CHAMBERS, Esq.,
The Beeches, Kington, Herefordshire.
HERBERT W. CHAMBERS, Esq.,
Parliament Mansions, S.W.

AUDITORS.

J. F. CLARKE, Esq., F.C.A.,
41 Coleman Street, E.C.
J. J. MAYHEW, Esq.,
Southwold, Suffolk.

Manager and Secretary .. .. .. H. WARD.

Offices :—17 Victoria Street, Westminster, S.W
Telephone : Victoria, 5125.

Fig 135: from page 5, Southwold Railway Timetable 4 October 1914 to 31 March 1915.

The summary in **Fig 135** of Company Directors and the Head Office staff – Mr Ward, the Manager and Secretary – is a reminder of the practical distance between the operating staff and the Company's principal day-to-day decision maker.

Eventually, internal station-to-station telephones were installed but the communication with the London head office was by letter. By a fortunate chance David Lee discovered and was able to preserve Station Master Calver's Wet Letter book from when he was Halesworth Station Master from 1883 to 1902 (**Fig 136**). Its numbered pages are copies of letters sent out by the Halesworth Station Master. It might be supposed that Southwold Station was the principal station and therefore the most senior Station Master. He, too, must have had such a copy book but it was Halesworth that was in contact with the GER, to which the Southwold was a feeder, and therefore more frequently in touch with Secretary Ward in London.

Such a copy book, or Wet Letter Book, became standard practice in offices from the 1870s. Such a book was a development of the earlier process of making copies on single sheets of paper and Google is an invaluable aid in explaining its use:

'A typical book might contain up to 1,000 sheets of very thin and unsized paper bound into a hard cover. The paper had to have a good mechanical strength when damp . . . With the book open, sheets of waterproof

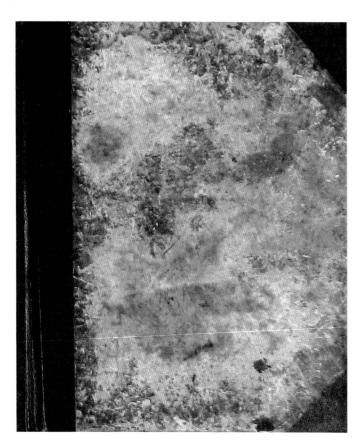

Fig 136: Front cover of Halesworth Station Master's Wet Copy Letter Book. The book belongs to David Lee and he has had it professionally rebound because it was falling apart; the hard front shown here illustrates the long-service wear and tear on a book over 100 years old.

(oiled) paper were placed behind both the right-hand and left-hand pages. The letter to be copied was placed, with the ink uppermost, on the right hand page, while the left-hand page was dampened so that it would take the copy. The book was then closed and the entire book was squeezed in a screw press (copy press, letter press), the hard covers ensuring an even distribution of pressure. When removed from the press, the book was opened, the original letter retrieved and the copy allowed to dry.

'While the advent of the typewriter and carbon paper around the turn of the century made the copy book redundant for some business correspondence, its use for copying handwritten letters is said to have continued until the 1950s'.

Dr Brian Davies – <www.archifdy-ceredigion.org.uk> Ceredigion Archives – is the record office for the county formerly known as Cardiganshire or (in Welsh) Sir Aberteifi.

The Halesworth book is a valuable reference source for the daily operation of the Southwold Railway so David Lee has transcribed a number of letters and added a gloss below each one. Here is a selection:

'To: Mr. Hansford BLYTHBURGH
From HALESWORTH   June 6 1881
re An unclaimed fish box

'Dear Sir, There is a box lying here for Lord Dunwich [probably Viscount Dunwich of Henham Hall] addressed to Halesworth Station. The GE people refuse to hand it over to us and state they will forward by carrier. Can you see the Henham people for them to instruct GER to hand goods over to carrier. Reply and oblige.
'Yours truly D. Price'

D. Price was the first Station Master at Halesworth to about the end of June 1881. This letter reflects the potential difficulties when two railway companies are working from the same station even though at Halesworth there were separate platforms for GER and SR and separate facilities for parcels and goods. The nearest station to Henham Hall was Blythburgh but if the fish box had been handled by and labelled from a GER station, the GER men at Halesworth would not release it. And if it was released to the SR, how to get it from Blythburgh Station to Henham Hall?

An appropriate carrier was, however, another difficulty. White's Guide for 1885 does not list any carrier taking in Blythburgh but there was a carter there who perhaps, on occasion, would call at Halesworth. The Southwold Carriers only took in Darsham, Lowestoft and Yarmouth so they went NW of Southwold and not E towards Blythburgh or Halesworth.

Summer weather may have posed another problem if the fish box could not be delivered quickly!

'To: Manager A.C. Pain Esq
From: HALESWORTH   August 6 1881
re Timber rails felled near LIST'S CUTTING

'Dear Sir, I saw Mr. Farrow today *re* your conversation as to traffic from LIST'S cutting. He does not mind which arrangement is acted on only wishes his own men to unload; they would only number 3 or 4 at the outside & not 10 or 12 like last time.

And I having to give a decided answer today I have arranged to drop 4 or 5 wagons off the 11.00am up train from Southwold on Tuesday morning next when Mr. Farrow will be there to see them loaded, and run the Engine down from Halesworth to fetch them & Mr Farrow will try your plan ie. to leave the trucks overnight and have the loaded wagons fetched to Southwold before the starting of the 7.45am train on Wednesday morning so as to see by which arrangement he can load the most rails.

'Mr. Farrow had to take an answer to the firm tonight so that I felt compelled to lean towards his plan in preference to yours for he threatened to send his own Traction Engine and cart them to DARSHAM. Should these arrangements not meet with your approval will you kindly advise me how to proceed after the 2 trips above arranged for & will you kindly forward an order to Jackson to be out earlier on Wednesday morning & run the trip required.
'Yours obediently, F.W. Hansford'

Mr Hansford succeeded Mr Price in 1881. Jackson was the SR Locomotive Superintendent and often drove locomotives. The 'rails' were fencing rails cut, it seems, in the woodland and loaded directly onto wagons on the Railway between Blythburgh and Walberswick. This was a usual practice when no station was near.

'To: Engineer & Manager A.C. Pain Esq
From: HALESWORTH   9 July 1883
re Takeover at Halesworth Station

'**Dear Sir**, I beg to inform you I took charge at this station this day and found everything correct.
Yours truly W. Calver'

W. Calver takes over at Halesworth and, below, writes to his predecessor who is now at Southwold.

'To: Mr. Hanford SOUTHWOLD
From HALESWORTH   July 9 1883
re Extended working for Special train

'Dear Sir, Of PM Special Train from your station tonight for Wenhaston. Will you run the above Train thro, to Halesworth; please reply
Yours truly W. Calver'

There was no telegraphic communication between stations until 1899 so all advices had to be by letter.

'To: Secretary H. Carne Esq. 5 VICTORIA STREET
From: HALESWORTH   July 8 1886
re EXCESS FARES

'Dear Sir, I beg to inform you the only way this can be checked [*prevented*] is to have all tickets examined at this Station before the departure of our Trains. As the booking is done by GER people we cannot tell who have booked & who have not [but] I believe if this was done for a time it would put a check on.

'There are times when we have passengers run over [the footbridge from GER platforms] after the bell have rung & not time to book. I believe there are some who never think of booking, please allow me to have the tickets examined for a time.
'Yours truly W. Calver'

There were even fare dodgers in those days! A hand bell was rung at all Southwold Railway stations before the train left.

Follow-up reports were made of a number of passengers without tickets being told to book.

'To: Secretary H. Carne Esq. 5 VICTORIA STREET
From: HALESWORTH   April 10 1885
re REDUCTION OF TRANSFER CHARGES

'Dear Sir, I beg to inform you Rowe agree to reduction of 1d pr ton of coals and would like Bricks to remain the same. I beg to suggest the following Rates:
    Coal Salt Cement Manure Lime: 3d. per ton
    Bricks & Coke: 4d. per ton.
    Pipes & Stone: 6d. per ton.
'The amount of work Rowe can get through will enable him to earn a good wage at the above Rates as the amount of Traffic we have keeps Rowe always employed. I feel sure Rowe will accept these rates. If you approve please so advise Rowe.
'Yours truly W. Calver'

It seems that Rowe, the Transfer Porter, was only paid by the tonnage he shifted from the main line wagons into SR wagons. The tonnage of Minerals for 1885 was 4,550 which would have included all the above except bricks which were not entered as 'Minerals.' In 1889 it was suggested Rowe be replaced by two men at 14/- or 15/- per week each, as being more economical. Rowe was paid £78.00 a year.

'To: Secretary H. Carne Esq 5 VICTORIA STREET
From: HALESWORTH   November 8 1889
re OCCASIONAL ADDITIONAL DUTIES FOR PLATELAYERS

'Dear Sir, Ganger Sporle wish me to ask you if the platelayers [can] go down to Wenhaston Station to meet the 7.17pm Train from Southwold to see if they are required to assist in loading Fish, and if they are not required, will they be paid for so doing?

'I informed Sporle I would ask the question and I knew you would not pay [except] when they worked.

I beg to say I think this a very unfair question for Sporle to ask. On wet days these men lay up in their Huts & they have several privileges allowed them what other Company's do not for their men. I know when they have pigs to kill they have an hour or two off-duty to do it [yet] cannot give 10 minutes of their time for the interest of the Company but wants to be paid for it. This is a very disgrateful Spirit for a man to have.

'Yours truly W. Calver'

This reveals some interesting aspects of labour relations and paints a familiar picture of platelayers being unable to work on the permanent way but 'laying up in their huts', on wet days. The outcome of the Wenhaston fish loading dispute is not known but it seems SM Calver believed the men were 'trying it on.'

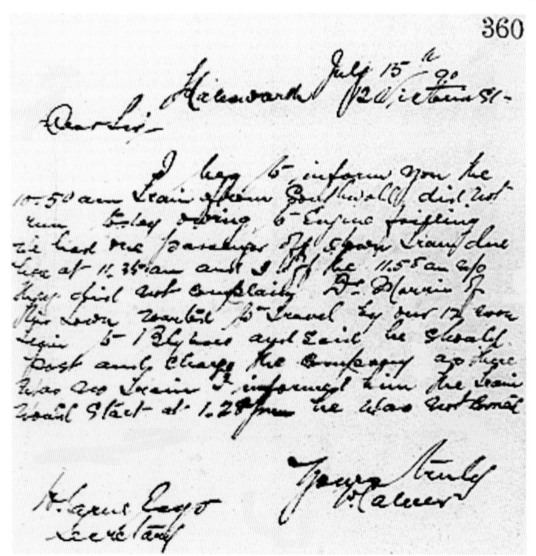

360

Fig 137: Letter from Halesworth Station Master W. Calver's Wet Copy Letter Book to SR Secretary Carne, 15 July 1890. Calver wrote a neat, round hand but deciphering this letter is not easy!

PART 4

ROLLING STOCK

Fig 138: Fireman Albert Stannard and Driver Nealey Fiske on their footplate.

CHAPTER 15

LOCOMOTIVES

The suggestion has been made that Messrs Ransome and Rapier [R&R] supplied locomotives for the opening of the railway and in *Eighty Years of Enterprise 1869-1949* published by Ransomes & Rapier Ltd it is stated that they built two such engines. There is, however, nothing in the SR records to substantiate this; the only five locomotives the railway ever possessed are described below. It is just possible that R&R supplied engines to the contractor during the construction period but again there is no evidence of this. The probability is that R&R did not consider the three engines contracted in 1875/76 for the Woosung and Shanghai Railway as suitable for use on the Southwold Railway, so Chairman R.C. Rapier possibly sub-contracted supply of motive power to Sharp, Stewart. On the other hand, the circumstances might equally have been as follows, but the position is uncertain.

The Director's Report to the Ordinary Meeting of 28 February 1877 mentions a conditional contract with the Bristol Carriage and Wagon Works Co. of Lawrence Hill, Bristol, for the supply of 'Engines, carriages and wagons', but this was not entirely put into effect and in the middle of 1878, when construction of the line was well in hand, Charles Chambers (the Contractor) submitted to the Board a proposition from Sharp, Stewart & Co Ltd (Atlas Works, Manchester) to supply locomotives and rolling stock, for which they were prepared to accept debentures to the extent of two-thirds of the order. The Board considered this at their Meeting on 23 August 1878 and, after further negotiations, on 1 December 1878 Sharp, Stewart were given the order to supply three locomotives on the terms mentioned, though the firm stated that they would not be able to supply one or more before May 1879.

DRAWING No 1   No 1 *SOUTHWOLD*   No 2 *HALESWORTH*   No 3 *BLYTH* — Sharp Stewart

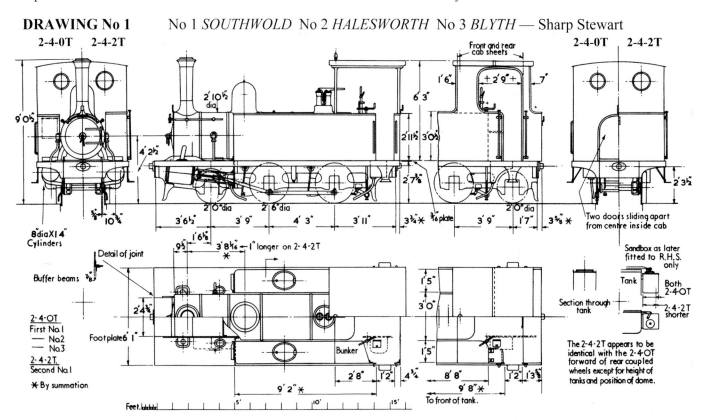

Fig 139: The first three Sharp, Stewart locomotives.

These engines were 2-4-0 side tanks of the makers' own design fitted with Stephenson's link inside frames valve gear and similar to others supplied for light passenger work. The numbers, names and maker's numbers were as follows, supplied in 1879:

No 1 *Southwold* Sharp, Stewart 2848
No 2 *Halesworth* Sharp, Stewart 2849
No 3 *Blyth* Sharp, Stewart 2850

The principal dimensions of those original locomotives were as set out in the table:

Driving Wheel diam	Leading Wheel diam	Cylinder Bore x Stroke	Boiler Wkg Pressure	Heating Surface	Water Capacity	Weight M.W.O.	Weight empty
2ft 6in	2ft 0in	8ft x 14in	140 psi	189sqft	300 gals	11ton 16cwt	9ton 0cwt

Traffic did not provide enough money to pay all the debenture interest so, in 1883, these financial arrangements were terminated and No 1 was returned to Sharp, Stewart. Subsequently they resold the locomotive in 1888 to become No 1 on the Santa Marta Railway, Colombia, where it was employed on banana plantations until withdrawn in 1932. The remaining two locomotives were hired from the makers for £150 per year until purchased outright in 1890.

The 1890s showed a steady rise in the volume of all kinds of income-generating traffic and a replacement for the original No 1 was therefore purchased in 1893 from Sharp, Stewart's Atlas Works, Glasgow; to the makers this was No 3913 and to the SR it was again

No 1 *Southwold*. In principal dimensions the loco was identical to the others but was longer (17ft 0in against 15ft 0in), possessed a pair of trailing wheels that made for smoother running in reverse (there were no turntables on the railway), a cab affording greater protection for the footplate men and a coal bunker at the rear. The only other difference was the weight in working order of about 13tons 15cwt and a water capacity of 400 gals. When new none of the locomotives were fitted with sand boxes (**Fig 140**).

Of the three engines, one was kept at Halesworth from 1914 with coaches as a spare in case floods should preclude a through service, one at Southwold in regular use and the third either spare or under repair; the engines

Fig 140: No 1 *SOUTHWOLD* 1879 to 1883.

Fig 141: No 2 *HALESWORTH* in maker's lined grey 1879.

Fig 142: Ex-Southwold. Railway No 1 working on the Santa Marta Railway, Colombia, c1900.

were worked in rotation to keep all of them serviceable. Running repairs were carried out at Southwold, in or in the vicinity of the engine shed. For major overhauls, the locos were usually sent to the GER works at Stratford, but not always – Nos 2 and 3 were rebuilt at Southwold with a new boiler in 1901 and 1900 respectively and carried brass plates 'Rebuilt 1901' and 'Rebuilt 1900'. New boilers were again fitted in Southwold to these

Fig 143: No 2 *HALESWORTH* in steam on a GER flat wagon after overhaul and awaiting return from Stratford Works to Halesworth. 1909.

engines in 1920 and 1925 respectively but this time no plates were affixed.

Detail alterations in later years included the provision of stays to secure the cabs for Nos 2 and 3, fitted from the front of the cab to the top of the tanks, presumably because in their declining years the cabs had become loose. The original livery of these engines was green lined black edged white, but by 1914 at least and probably earlier, this had given way to blue with red lining as used by the GER; the final livery was plain

black, though the locomotives were always kept smart, with brass work gleaming.

The Company's last engine was ordered in January 1914 in the anticipation of heavier traffic from the harbour branch which would require additional motive power. No 4 *Wenhaston* – delivered in July 1914 – was an 0-6-2 side tank built by Manning Wardle & Co Ltd. Leeds (their works number 1845) and was much more powerful than the earlier engines (**Figs 144** and **145**). The principal dimensions of No 4 were:

Driving Wheel Diameter	Trailing Wheel Diameter	Cylinder Dimension Bore x Stroke	Boiler Working Pressure	Heating Surface	Water Capacity	Coal Capacity	Weight M.W.O.
2ft 6in	1ft 9in	82ft x 14in	160 psi	223sqft	500 gals	14.75cwt	19tons 4cwt

It had Walschaert's valve gear, steam sanding and was provided with swinging windows in the cab and seats for the engine men. It was painted in the maker's

standard dark green lined with light and dark green, which livery was retained to the end; frames, cylinders and wheels were black, lined red. *Wenhaston* was well

Fig 144: No 4 *WENHASTON*. Manning Wardle works photo. 1914.

liked by the footplate men, although much heavier on coal, and less prone to slip on wet rails which they very often were in the damp Blyth estuary. In the twilight of the SR's active career, *Wenhaston* was worked very hard. In 1928, the locomotive was thoroughly overhauled at Southwold, when a brick arch (supplied by the makers in February) was put into the firebox to reduce fuel consumption. Saving money on coal for the locomotives was evidently in the minds of the Board when, in 1928, they considered tenders and specifications for vertical-boilered locomotives by Sentinel, Clayton and Atkinson-Walker but none were ordered.

No 1 *Southwold* 2-4-2T was also due for heavy repairs in 1928 but the likely cost was prohibitive to the slender financial resources of the Company. The locomotive was therefore withdrawn from stock and, after standing on blocks outside the Southwold engine shed for some months, was finally scrapped on the spot in May 1929, a month after the railway closed. The other three engines were immured in the sheds at Southwold and Halesworth at the closure and remained there until the railway was dismantled 12 years later.

By 1900, after twenty-one years of almost continuous use, the original two locomotives needed only minimal repairs. Ten years later saw the start of a need for heavy repairs and replacement of boilers as Nos 1 to 3 became older. Nearly £3,000 was expended on heavy repairs and

replacing major parts but that, and the cost of routine maintenance, meant that their continued existence was economically doubtful.

In 1913, director H.W. Chambers, in writing to his brother director W.C. Chambers, on the question of paying a dividend on the Ordinary Shares, states, 'It is a question if the time has not come when the locos are costing more to keep up than they are worth, and that we must buy a new one very shortly.' He was right and No 4 *Wenhaston* was ordered in January 1914.

During April and May 1912, train working experiments were carried out by firing the locos with coal alone, coke and coal, or coke alone. There were six trials over distances of 494 and 530 miles and costs per mile came out between 2.19d for all coal firing and 3.06d per mile with coke alone. Coal was demonstrably the favourite but no decision is recorded so presumably no change was made. However, it was noted that firing with coal meant smoke was considerable when standing at stations, but there was little smoke nuisance in the carriage when coke was used.

Fig 146, showing No 3 *Blyth* at Southwold on a still and apparently windless day, demonstrates the smoke nuisance which a steam locomotive can cause if it is burning a rather soft coal. It seems probable that *Blyth*'s driver has the blower on to enliven the fire which will account for the column of smoke bursting out of

DRAWING No 2   No 4 *WENHASTON*   —— Manning Wardle

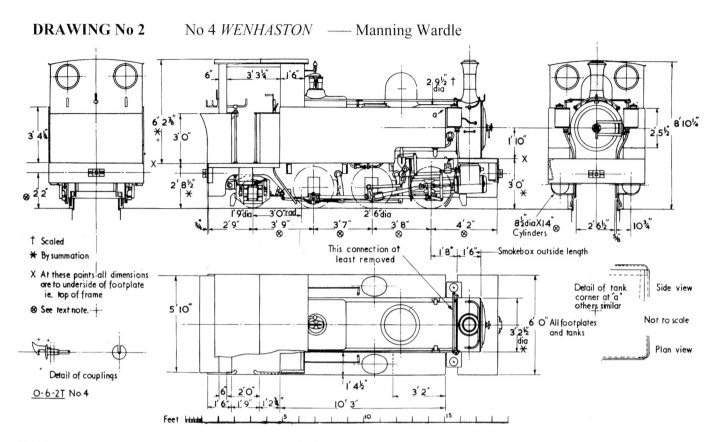

† Scaled
✳ By summation
X At these points all dimensions are to underside of footplate ie. top of frame
⊗ See text note. ┼

Detail of couplings
O·6·2T No 4

Detail of tank corner at "a" others similar   Side view

Not to scale

Plan view

This connection at least removed

Smokebox outside length

Fig 145: No 4 *WENHASTON* 0-6-2T was a more powerful locomotive than the Sharp, Stewarts and liked by footplate crews. It became the last working locomotive on the railway.

Fig 146: No 3 *Blyth* shunting at Southwold on an apparently windless day.

the chimney. Although *Blyth* is not at the platform in **Fig 146,** it would be quite usual for a driver at the head of an up train to use the blower to ensure he had a good head of steam before setting off to Halesworth.

Few instructions or requirements for locomotives to be prepared and steamed up for the day's work have been traced, but surviving timetables show that a locomotive must be ready by 7.30am for the first up train which was booked off Southwold at that time for many years. An interview with Mr Girling, the last Station Master at Southwold, explained that loco men arrived at 6.00am to be ready for shunting by 6.30am for the 7.30am departure. It seems unlikely, however, that steam could be raised in only 30 minutes. There was a 'general man' on the Locomotive Department staff who probably came on duty earlier to start the lighting-up process but no schedule has been traced to confirm this supposition.

Likewise, few other instructions for enginemen, apart from a Rule Book (1912 edition), have been found, though the following circular has been located:

Notice to Drivers and Firemen
(undated but probably 1920s)
Speed Restrictions: To reduce speed when running down List's Cutting, when approaching the bridges

at the Water Mill, and when passing the curve at end of Holton Road Bridge from Halesworth.

Engine Whistle: One whistle to be given when approaching an intermediate station and two whistles when a truck is to be detached.

One whistle when approaching the Southwold Cutting.

In 1926 Drivers were required to complete a detailed form headed 'Daily Statement of Engine Hours and Duties', under four categories: time taken; coaching; freight; mixed and ballast.

The staff of the locomotive Department was six men: Loco Foreman, two sets of Enginemen – Driver and Fireman – and a general man who did cleaning work in the shed and served as relief fireman. The Enginemen worked alternate weeks early or late turns usually changing footplates on arrival of the down trains at around 2.20pm daily. After the reduction of Engineers' hours in 1919 the Southwold Railway men, by 1926, worked alternate weeks:

First week: 6.00am to 3.00pm. (early turn)

Second week: 9.30am to 12.30pm. then 1.30pm to 7.30pm. (late turn)

Fig 147: Fireman Adamson on No 4 *Wenhaston* footplate and A N Others.

The men worked in pairs or 'Sets':

Driver H.J. Stannard + Fireman A.G. Stannard (for 20-years)

Driver N.C. Fisk + Fireman R.J. Adamson

The original Locomotive Foreman was W.G. Jackson, who was one of the railway's most colourful and best-loved characters (**Fig 148**). The story that the carriages came from China and were originally painted yellow with green dragons on the side, probably started as an embellishment of one of the tales he loved to tell, for in 1876 he had driven the first train in China, on the Woosung Tramroad. Soon after he came to Southwold he built Shanghai Cottage, which was the scene of many lively parties. Mr & Mrs Jackson used to don Chinese costume and the former regaled his guests with highly-coloured accounts of his adventures in the Far East, and even on the Southwold Railway; for there were plenty of mildly humorous incidents which imagination improved as recollection faded. Jackson retired in 1916, when he was replaced by J.H. Belcher, whose enthusiasm for small railways had been fortified by several years' experience as Engineer on the Selsey Tramway. The post changed hands twice more, first to F. George (from Stratford) and finally to S. Poynter, who came from Messrs Richard Garrett's Works at Leiston.

Once closure loomed, and came about, the Railway was featured comprehensively in photographs and, during the closing weeks, on film. Personal memories were not much recorded whilst the Railway was working, or even when it laid derelict, but after it was gone, in 1941, and after the Second World War, informed research began. In the 1950s, Eric Tonks wrote and self-published his book on the Railway and he was followed by others including Arnold Barrett Jenkins, David Lee and Alan Taylor. A number of former servants and officers of the Southwold Railway were still living in the town or nearby and several were contacted for their memories. Information from B.E. Girling (last Southwold Station Master) – whose particulars of daily working are in Chapter 11 – and N.C. Fiske (Driver) has been woven into the following notes on locomotives, carriages and the goods rolling stock. They were collated by David Negus (Engineer and member of the

Fig **148**: Southwold Railway Locomotive Foreman William Jackson on the SR from 1879 to 1916.

Southwold Railway Trust) who at one time lived in Wenhaston where former Driver Fiske also lived.

Locomotives

It is reasonable to suppose that the contractors who built the Southwold Railway over the period 1878-9 must have used locomotives for material haulage, for at least part of the work, but there seem to be no records available. What is clear is that the three locomotives ordered from Sharp, Stewart & Co could hardly have played any part in the construction phase as they did not arrive until shortly before the opening of the Railway.

Sharp, Stewart & Co were very well known throughout the Victorian period, with a hard-won reputation for the high quality of both design and construction. By far the greater part of their construction output was of standard-gauge locomotives destined for many of the numerous main-line railways of the period. From the 1850s onwards, they produced several series of standard designs, particularly of 2-4-0 tender and tank locos for passenger work and 0-6-0s for goods traffic, many of which were long-lasting in service.

Included in their output was a small class of outside cylindered 2-4-0 tank locos for the North Staffordshire Railways, constructed in 1874 (Works numbers 2445-2447). With a weight, in working order, of some 42 tons, there was, of course, no comparison with the tiny locos destined for the Southwold Railway – except that the latter exhibited many of the recognizably Sharp, Stewart features of the North Stafford locos, but on a much smaller scale – and with proportionately longer chimneys. The neat, clean lines were typical of the mid-Victorian period. The production of narrow-gauge locos was but a small part of Sharp, Stewart's output and the designs for the Southwold locos incorporated as much as might be appropriate of main-line practice. Southwold drivers were proud of their locos and were encouraged that they were not 'industrial' types such as contractors would use.

It is interesting to note that, contemporaneously with the Southwold locos, Sharp, Stewart built two three-foot gauge 2-4-0Ts for the Manx Northern Railway. Works No 2885/6 of 1879. The latter were some 25 per cent larger in size than the Southwold locos but were very similar in appearance, the main difference being the provision of upper sides to the cabs, with conventional openings.

The lack of upper cab sides for the Southwold locos has sometimes provoked rather unfair comment. In the late 1870s many newly constructed tank locos were provided with vestigial cabs, little more than a front spectacle plate – for instance both GER and Midland 0-4-4Ts, among others; at least the Southwold locos were better than that!

Examination of the makers' drawings shows that the leading wheels were provided with radial axle-boxes, with a total of 2in of side play. The side play was not controlled, leading to the locos 'boxing' at speed (relative speed, that is, on the 16mph Southwold maximum). The Manx Northern locos, apparently, suffered from the same problem, which was exacerbated by the greater permissible speed of 45mph allowed because all Manx stock had automatic brakes.

Careful examination of photographs reveal that the Southwold locos, when new, had chimneys in which the base and cap had rebates such that the barrel matched the smallest part of the base or cap in diameter. These were soon replaced with chimneys where the barrel fitted within the base or cap. Later still, the design of the cap seems to have been changed to a more elongated form.

The locos, when new, had marine-type coupling rod bearings but these were soon changed to the more normal small loco type with adjustable keeps.

Sharp, Stewart designs provided generous wheel-bearing surfaces which meant that the axle-boxes, to contain the larger bearings, allowed slightly less room within the frames for access and maintenance. This restricted space meant the eccentric-sheaves for the Stephenson's valve gear had to be set relatively close to the loco centre-line. For the outside cylinders the valve chests were, necessarily, set immediately inside the frames. The small valve chests of the locos protruded a little further into the frame spaces than did the axle-boxes. This led to the valve spindles having to be operated by separate shafts, parallel to the valve rods proper and linked to them by two short cross links, supported by the motion plate and a further plate just to the rear of the valve chests. This seems to have been a variant on the 'swing link' version of the Stephenson motion much used by Sharp, Stewart but may be unique to the Southwold locos. The Manx Northern 3ft gauge Sharp, Stewart locos had much larger valve chests than the Southwold examples, so their valve spindles may have lined up directly with the valve rods.

The rear cab plates of No 1 (original), 2 and 3 were unusual in having sliding doors, with an arched top – presumably to allow tube cleaning to be done from either the smoke-box or the fire-box ends.

The rear of the side tanks, proper, more or less coincided with the front spectacle plate, the twin coal bunkers being situated immediately to the rear of the tanks. Heavy handling of coal seems to have dented the sides of the bunkers showing up, particularly, on photographs of newly repainted locos.

The 'new' and replacement 2-4-2T No 1 *Southwold* arrived in 1893 from Sharp, Stewart's Glasgow works which was then home to most of their activities. For the most part, it matched the earlier designs, with only subtle changes in dimensions. It is presumed that the requirement was that the new loco should be only marginally longer than the earlier locos. What looked in photographs like a more substantial cab was deceptive;

both front and rear spectacle plates were developed from the upper cab sides. This allowed the rear bunker to have space for some 15cwt of coal and the side tanks were now extended almost to the front of the cab-side openings.

On this loco the rear truck also had 2in of side-play and this development improved the loco ride and overcame the tendency for 'boxing' found with the original No 1. According to Driver Neil Fiske this was the fastest and most comfortable loco; despite the supposed 16mph allowable maximum speed, Fiske was adamant that 25mph was achieved frequently, under suitable conditions! Perhaps the loco was better balanced. Good track conditions were all-important with all three of the Sharp, Stewart locos because wet and greasy rails did give rise to adhesion problems especially up the lengthy rise to Halesworth.

It is not known why the SR Board decided to go to Manning Wardle for their fifth loco in 1914; perhaps their relationship with Sharp, Stewart had deteriorated over the years.

0-6-2 tank No 4 *Wenhaston* was fairly typical of a number of small locos produced by Manning Wardle. Some slightly larger ones for the 2ft 6in gauge Sittingbourne & Kemsley Light Railway exhibited the same, rather angular appearance.

The rear Bissel truck allowed considerable side-play but this time, there was a very strong central control spring which gave rise to a lot of trouble. The frail 30lb per yard rails were hardly man enough for *Wenhaston's* axle loading of about 6 tons but the main problem was at turn-outs. All too frequently, No 4 went straight on, particularly if it was in reverse, so derailments were not uncommon. According to Driver Fiske, the Railway prevailed upon Manning Wardle to produce a new control spring, of lesser strength. The fitting of this, out in the open air in Southwold Station Yard, was fraught with difficulty, as can well be believed! It seems to have been successful, however, and *Wenhaston* proved quite popular - even if it did gulp down coal.

It was still a fairly simple and crude loco – but it did have one feature which proved very popular – it had a coiled steam pipe within each of its four sand-boxes which ensured that the sand was always dry. Adhesion was pretty good. The frugal SR Engineer dismantled one of *Wenhaston's* front sand boxes and tried it on one of the Sharp, Stewarts; it certainly proved to be successful, for the other two were similarly equipped with one new sand-box apiece. *Wenhaston* continued with one instead of two front boxes but the two internal rear sand-boxes were retained. They were more-or-less under the cab

Fig 149: 0-4-2T No 1 *SOUTHWOLD* outside Southwold Engine Shed. Driver Collett on footplate, Fireman Moore on step and Driver Stannard with oil can c1908.

seats so good in the winter for the crew, but a bit warm in the summer!

Close examination of the many photographs will show that the Sharp, Stewarts were little altered over the years (apart from chimneys), although the 2-4-0Ts did need stays to support the front spectacle plates, and new No 1 needed a patch on the bunker, where the coupling hook had obviously caused a hole to develop. All of the locos were provided with home-made timber side cheeks to their cabs to reduce the chill of winter winds.

All four locos were provided with tool-boxes, which presumably held the prickers, etc. for fire-box cleaning and probably held a set of traversing jacks in case of a minor derailment.

Before going on to the rest of the rolling stock, a word about the buffer-couplings. These, so-called, 'Norwegian' or 'chopper' couplings were of the simplest possible design, without any side-play, slack-gathering device, or safety bridle. The slack movement was sufficient to cause considerable wear to the coupling hooks and, in some photographs, this wear is very noticeable. It was, perhaps, inevitable that this wear-and-tear would eventually lead to a de-coupling, which happened to a goods train, fortunately without any injuries. The 'figure-of-eight' couplings which were then fitted prevented a repetition but did lead to much slower shunting and, informants recall, a number of somewhat squashed fingers.

Fig 150: 2-4-0T *HALESWORTH* heads a mixed down train at Southwold.

CHAPTER 16

CARRIAGES AND WAGONS

PASSENGER CARRYING VEHICLES

In the absence of the Director's Board Meeting Minutes, no trace has been found how decisions were made as to design specifications or with whom the building contract should be placed, but it is probable that either Arthur Pain or Richard Rapier were the best-informed Directors. The latter is the most likely decision maker because his business, Ransomes and Rapier of Ipswich, had obtained carriages for the Shanghai and Woosung Railway (S&WR). Rapier also wrote: *Remunerative Railways for New Countries* (E. & F. N. Spon 1878) which contained woodcut illustrations of carriages from the catalogue of the Bristol Wagon & Carriage Co. Ltd. (BW&C Co Ltd) of Lawrence Hill, Bristol.

The carriages for the Southwold and the S&WR were very similar in design, as confirmed by **Fig 151**. The S&WR carriages, however, were 4-wheeled 15ft long, 1st Class and 2nd Class, and 18ft long 3rd Class for a 2ft 6in gauge railway. The Southwold Railway carriages, though longer and for the 3ft gauge, were panelled and moulded to the same design with similar seating arrangement. Six 6-wheeled carriages were ordered from the BW&C Co Ltd on 6 May 1879 and were delivered to Halesworth where a photograph of one was taken

Fig 152: SR carriages after unloading from standard gauge flat wagons at Halesworth in 1879.

INTERIOR OF FIRST-CLASS CARRIAGE.

FIG. 39.

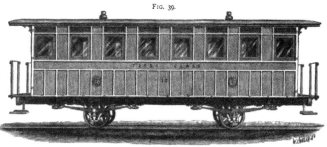

EXTERIOR OF FIRST-CLASS CARRIAGE.

Fig 151: Interior & exterior views of 1st class carriages for railways of 2ft 6ins – (Shanghai & Woosung Railway [S&WR]) – to 3ft 6ins gauge from: Richard Rapier. *Remunerative Railways for New Countries* (E. & F. N. Spon 1878).

after unloading (**Fig 152**). Two were 1st and 3rd Class composite brakes (Nos. 4 and 5) and four provided 3rd Class accommodation only (Nos. 1, 2, 3 and 6).

The original plans have not been traced. However, when researching the BW&C Co Ltd's correspondence with the BoT at the former Public Record Office, Kew, (now the National Archive), David Lee found a covering letter dated 3 September 1879 which referred to a number of plans including that of a '1st and Parliamentary Composite Carriage' which had also been entered in a Register of Plans. Disappointingly, it transpired after a further search that none of the plans any longer existed.

A contemporary account in *The Railway Record*, 1 October 1879, entitled 'The Model Three Feet Gauge' states of the Southwold Railway:

'[Six] passenger carriages have been built by the Bristol Wagon Works Company, (sic) … are 30ft long, composite 1st and 3rd Class only; they weigh 6-tons each [have Cleminson Patent six-wheel under-frames] and hold 40 passengers. The passengers are seated *vis-a-vis* with ample space for the ticket-collector to walk

from end to end of the train, each carriage having a platform and balcony, with doors at the ends.'

The *Railway Record* account explains that the coupling between the carriages was invented by James Cleminson of Westminster Chambers. Photographs show the pin securing the 'Norwegian' (or 'chopper' hook) style couplings between the carriages. The pin had a weight attached to it presumably to ensure that the chopper hook should not disengage unless the pin was removed or not put in place (**Fig 154**).

These couplings were of the simplest possible design, without any side-play or a slack gathering device. The slack was sufficient to cause considerable wear to the coupling hooks and, in some photographs, this is very noticeable.

Cleminson also invented and patented the system of a flexible 6-wheel-base fitted to the Southwold Railway carriages and some of the freight vehicles. This arrangement allowed the centre pair of wheels to have lateral movement when negotiating curves and was connected to the two outer pivoted pairs of wheels. A longitudinal beam connected the centre pair of wheels

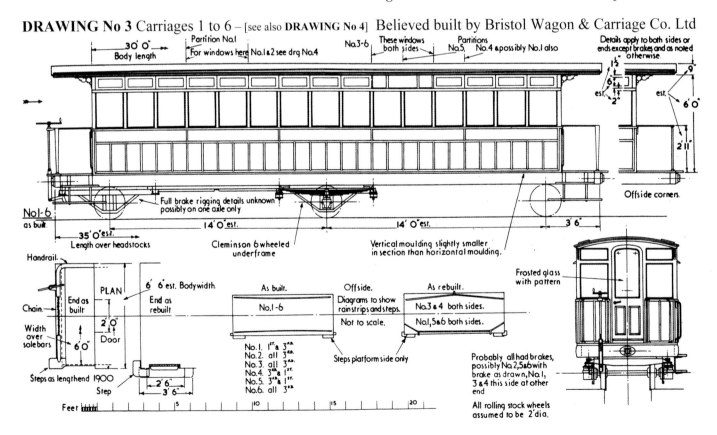

DRAWING No 3 Carriages 1 to 6 – [see also **DRAWING No 4**] Believed built by Bristol Wagon & Carriage Co. Ltd

Fig 153: Measured drawing of Carriages 1 to 6 as originally delivered with open verandahs.

Fig 154: Detail of an SR carriage coupling showing the weight securing the pin which locked the chopper coupling in a closed position.

to the end wheels by a double joint. The centre wheels moved outwards on a curve, so the double joint also moved outwards. As it was connected to the wheels at either end of the carriage, they moved radially. In theory, as the coach was on a uniform curve, the centre axle was as far to the outside as need be to ensure that two outer axles were following a radial path, and if imaginary lines were drawn from the three axles they should meet at the centre of the curve.

Unfortunately the Cleminson theory and the reality of railway practice did not quite agree as SRT Volunteer and SRT member David Negus DMS CEng MICE has helped us to explain. The flanges on the wheels tried to keep the wheels at right-angles to the rails at the point of contact but the Cleminson system was trying to hold the wheels to the radius of the curve so there were stresses which caused flange wear, rail wear and wear on the wheel bearings. When the carriages entered or left curved sections of track, either the leading or the trailing wheels were not quite at right-angles to the track. The centre pair of wheel frames relied on a rubbing pad under the carriage for a bearing surface

to assist the sideways movements associated with the Cleminson system. Wind-blown sand, particularly in the Walberswick cutting, got in between these bearing faces and was probably the cause of the groaning noises some passengers reported hearing from under the carriage floors. Driver Fiske recalls that there was 'an awful lot of wear on the wheel-frames and links'.

Nevertheless, the Southwold Railway was not alone in buying 6-wheeled vehicles using the Cleminson system and was not the first; the North Wales Narrow Gauge Railway, opened 1877, and the Manx Northern Railway which opened in September 1879 also adopted it.

Fig 153 is a measured drawing of the Southwold carriages and illustrates some of the details of the bodies. For instance, hand brakes were fitted to the Composite carriages only, with the hand operated control located on the veranda at the 3rd Class end.

The carriage sides were completely straight with the waist divided into two rows of panels; five long upper panels over thirty vertical lower panels were all bordered by bolection mouldings. Above the waist were fifteen fixed window-lights over which there were quarter lights, at least six of which opened for ventilation, some bearing advertisements for Adnams beer and for other traders. The body ends had large lights, with an upper fixed light, each side of the central door, fitted with an etched glass panel, over which was an opening quarter light. The verandas were fitted with iron railings round the north side and end to the centre coupling with an opening protected by chain completing the end, but there was no chain across the south side entrance. Fall plates were not provided over the centre couplings, but to enable the Guard to move between carriages a short foot-board was fitted, projecting beyond the headstock. Following a minor accident to a Guard this was later extended (see Chapter 13).

Inside the 3rd Class compartments of all carriages was an open saloon with wooden bench seats ranged along the side walls and, after 1904, covered with a strip of carpet. The only form of heating in cold weather was for straw to be strewn ankle-deep on the floor. Lighting was by oil lamp at each end of the saloons, while blue cloth curtains were fitted to the south side windows. There are no recorded details of floor covering. The 1st Class compartments occupied three side lights in length, presumably with bench seating along the sides and upholstered in blue cloth but not as luxurious as the illustration in **Fig 151.** Entrance was by a door in the end off the veranda and a door in the partition between each section. Heating for 1st Class passengers was provided by metal foot warmers filled with hot water, presumably from the engine, whilst relatively dim lighting was supplied by an oil lamp. The 1st Class compartment floors may have been carpeted. The 1st Class compartments of the two Composites, carriages 4 and 5, were at the Southwold end; the railway had no turntable so the carriages remained heading as they were delivered.

In 1912, it appears that the Directors were considering the condition of the carriages and their appeal to the

Fig 155: Third class carriage No 2 as built with an open end; it was never rebuilt. The next carriage has an enclosed verandah-end which improved conditions inside, especially in winter.

public because by then the stock had been in service for 33 years. A tender was sought from the BW&C Co Ltd for two 8-wheeled twin-bogie carriages, but clearly the tender price was too much for the Company's slender finances so the subject was not considered further. However, at about the same time consideration was given to converting a carriage from 3rd Class to a 1st and 3rd composite brake. No 1 was selected. There is no reference to the subject in Agendas to Board meetings, but the accounts for 1911 and 1912 show far higher costs for carriage maintenance at £55 and £62 in respective years from which it can be assumed that conversion took place over that time. The 1st Class compartment was at the Halesworth end of the carriage. (**Fig 156**)

The initial cost of the carriages is not obtainable from the accounts, but a common practice of most railway companies during the nineteenth century was to settle the cost partly in shares: BW&C Co Ltd received £400 of 4 per cent Preference shares and 15 £10 Ordinary shares, issued in the name of Albert Fry – one of the founders of BW&C Co Ltd – in 1851, and transferred to the Leeds Forge Co. Ltd in 1925 after a take-over by that Company in 1924.

The Southwold Company's financial position meant that instalments on the balance were in arrears during the first half of 1883, so a payment of rent was arranged with the suppliers; this cost was charged to revenue and paid off by the end of 1886.

Maintenance of locomotive, carriage and wagon costs can be found in the Company's accounts including a significant increase for repainting in 1890 when two carriages were overhauled and repainted and again in 1898. The derailment of three carriages of the 3:40pm down train at Walberswick on Monday 4 September 1905 caused damage to the running gear of two carriages which required repairs.

In 1912, when the Board discussed the condition of the carriages, the Chambers brothers, in correspondence, were of the opinion that it was better to spend £100 to £150 on new springs, as some were now flat but new springs were not purchased until 1916, after 37 years use.

Fig 156: Carriage No 1 First Third composite in the 1920s. It was converted from Third in 1912.

DRAWING No 4 Carriages 1,3 & 6 as rebuilt   and (below) 6-wheeled Wagons

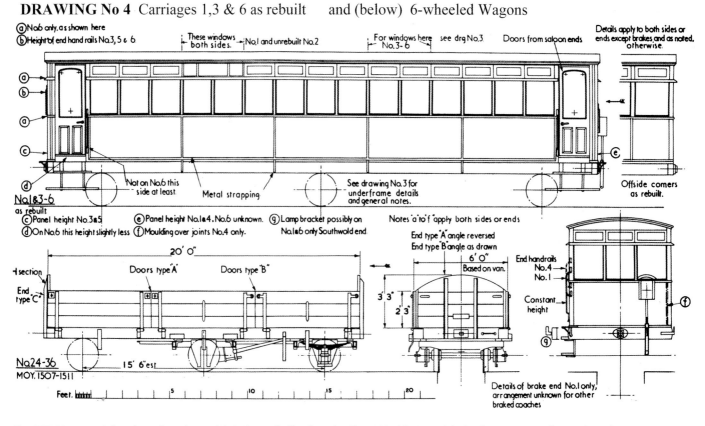

Fig 157: Measured drawing of carriages 1,3 & 6 as rebuilt after the First World War with the former verandas enclosed.

During the First World War, maintenance had been at a minimum while the use of the whole fleet had been extensive, resulting in heavy wear and tear. By 1919, the carriages were 40 years old at which age their economic life was usually considered to be expired and, as there is no record of any heavy repairs being carried out, the fleet was generally in a bad condition. Arrangements were therefore made with English Bros. of Wisbech to recondition the bodies during the winter months, so carriages were sent away one at a time over the following years. In the process of reconditioning the carriages, the original waist panels and mouldings were replaced by five large panels covering the whole of the waist with mouldings along the waist under the window. The end verandas were enclosed using the original end door to the platform. The ends above the waist had three fixed lights with upper lights of which the centre one was hinged to open for ventilation.

Fig 158: Passenger comfort. Interior of a third class carriage; note the strip of carpet along the wooden benches.

So far as can be ascertained the interiors were not altered expect for re-upholstering the 1st Class. Enclosing the verandas created a compartment in the Brake Composites for the guard, in which a vertical brake wheel attached to the end wall replaced the original 'T'-form handle.

FREIGHT ROLLING STOCK
Vans

The bi-annual accounts and returns required by the Board of Trade up to 1912 only included statistics of the number of passenger-carrying vehicles and of freight wagons conveying all goods, but from 1913 details were also required of 'Luggage, Parcel and Brake Vans'. The Southwold Railway Company entered two such vehicles.

When the Railway opened there were no covered freight vehicles and, in the absence of Board Minutes, it is not known what decided the purchase of the vans. but the half-year accounts from June 1880 to December 1884 show parcel traffic was steadily increasing from 9,834 to 17,852 items which needed better protection from the elements than being in an open wagon and sheeted, as did passengers' luggage and GPO Mails.

The makers were the Midland Railway Carriage & Wagon Co. Ltd of Birmingham (MRC&WCo Ltd) with whom an order was placed for two vans during the first six months of 1885; vans 13 and 14 were delivered later that year.

Certain features of the original goods wagons built by MRC&WCo Ltd were identical to these vans. Measuring ten feet long by six feet wide with a wheel base of five feet, the vans had outside timber body framing, to which was fastened inside horizontal side sheeting. Sliding doors were fitted each side opening towards the Southwold end. A hand brake was fitted on the platform side, with a long lever and pin rack and operating a wooden brake shoe. In keeping with all vehicles, central combined buffer couplings were fitted. Examination of the underside of the surviving van body 14 revealed a rod attached to the end of each buffer coupling leading through the under frame middle bearer with a spring on the reverse side, presumably a form of auxiliary draw gear. There is no reference in the Directors' meetings to either vehicle until 1918 when it was noted 'these Vans have arrived at a condition when it is impossible to repair any farther locally and it is considered absolutely

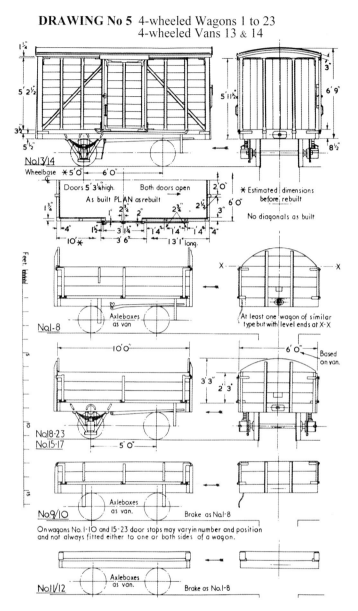

DRAWING No 5 4-wheeled Wagons 1 to 23
4-wheeled Vans 13 & 14

Fig 159: Measured drawings of original and rebuilt vans and the 4-wheel wagons. 6-wheel wagon dimensions are on Drawing 4 – **Fig 157.**

necessary to have one rebuilt'. No. 14 was sent to English Bros of Wisbech during January 1918 and returned in March; No. 13 followed immediately and was back by late October 1918.

In the process of rebuilding, both vans were lengthened by three feet and the wheel base increased to six feet which amounted to them being almost new vehicles. It is most likely that the only original components reused would have been the running gear, couplings, door with top and bottom runners, and possibly the two ends. All other material must have been new. To lengthen them,

Fig 160: 4-wheel van 13, delivered new in 1885 and shown before rebuilding in 1918.

Fig 161: 4-wheel van no 14 as rebuilt and lengthened in 1918. The van body was discovered and returned to the Southwold Station site in 1962 then subsequently moved to the East Anglian Transport Museum, near Lowestoft.

an additional outside frame upright was inserted in each side quarter with diagonal bracing from the top of the door frame to the base of the corner post. See **Fig 161** of the surviving Van 14 and compare with **Fig 160**.

The tare weight of 2.6.0. was painted on the sole bar beneath the door and an 'English Brothers' nameplate was affixed thereon.

When Van 14 was seen in the 1970s at the East Anglian Transport Museum, the surviving body was painted inside pale green with horizontal steel rails three feet long attached to the sides about three feet from the floor, projecting about three and half inches, presumably for securing bicycles and perambulators. The floor boards were laid from side to side. A bracket was fitted for a tail lamp at the ends at the right hand corner frame.

FREIGHT ROLLING STOCK
4-Wheeled Wagons

The decision to procure freight vehicles was probably made by Richard Rapier as suggested in the case of the carriages. An order was placed with MRC&WCo Ltd for twelve open wagons of three different designs in 1879, and they are assumed to have been delivered by September that year. All wagons were 4-wheeled, 10 feet long (overall 13 feet) by 6 feet wide with a 5 foot wheel base. Eight (Nos.1 to 8) had 3-plank drop sides with radiused ends 5-planks high; Nos. 9 and 10 were 2-plank dropsides, the ends level with the sides, and were used mainly for carrying milk in churns and boxed fish; either wagon was included in the formation of most trains. Finally, two (Nos. 11 & 12) had 1-plank fixed sides; they were classed as Timber Wagons in the BoT returns and were fitted with bolsters. The load of all these wagons was 4 tons and the tare weight around 2 tons but latterly there was no such information painted on the sides in the traditional way. It has not been possible to ascertain the initial cost of these wagons.

There was an interval of seven years, despite rising freight tonnages, before further wagons were added. Three (Nos. 15 to 17) were ordered from MRC&WCo Ltd in 1892 and in 1894 six further 4-wheeled wagons (Nos. 18 to 23) were ordered from the same firm. Both batches were of the same dimensions as the original wagons with drop sides, but the curvature

Fig 162: 4-wheeled dropside open wagon No 4 of 1879 with high ends. Behind is a standard gauge Southern Railway wagon. Photographed at Halesworth in the 1920s.

Fig 163: Maker's photo of 4-wheel, four plank drop-side wagon No 16.

of the ends were flatter being of one board which made them slightly lower. The load was increased to 5 tons. Of the 1892 batch, the makers' photograph shows No. 16 with 4-plank sides with ends level with the sides (**Fig 163**).

Whether this was a trial by either the makers or the Company is not known, but it clearly was a disadvantage because the 4-plank dropside would have rested at an angle to the ground when lowered compared to the 3-plank sides which came down clear of the ground. No.16 ran in traffic for some years – it is in the background of a tinted postcard dated around 1904 – before being cut down to 3-plank sides with ends level.

FREIGHT ROLLING STOCK
6-Wheeled Wagons

Larger wagons were ordered in 1896 when 6-wheeled wagons with a loading capacity of 7 tons came from Thomas Moy Ltd. coal factors and wagon builders, Peterborough. Three wagons (Nos. 24 to 26) arrived during the latter part of the year. Three years later circumstances necessitated further additions to the fleet when six more (Nos 27 to 32) were ordered from Moy

early in the year to the same design as those of 1896 and arriving late in 1899. The fleet then remained static until the opening of the Harbour Branch in the autumn of 1914 when four more identical wagons (Nos. 33 to 36) were obtained from Thomas Moy Ltd. and were delivered by the end of that year in anticipation of increased traffic. The total wagon fleet of 4-wheel and 6-wheel vehicles was by then thirty-four and no further additions were made until 1922 when two second-hand 6-wheeled wagons (Nos 37 to 38) were purchased from Thomas Moy and in 1926 one more (No. 39) came from the same firm.

All these additional wagons were to the builder's standard design with minor variations. They had sides of three drop doors of 3-planks with ends of four planks and radiused tops similar to the earlier 4-wheelers. Length was 20 feet by 6 feet wide mounted on a Cleminson 6-wheeled Flexible Wheelbase, similar to the carriages, giving a wheel base of 15 feet 6 inches. The design and construction of all the 6-wheeled wagons originated from those privately owned by Moy, the tare weight being around 4 tons 2 hundredweight.

Fig 164: 6-wheeled three plank wagons nos 31 & 37 of 1899 and 1922 respectively being shunted by No 3 *Blyth* at Southwold in 1928.

Volunteer and SRT member David Negus DMS CEng MICE adds a comment on the 6-wheeled wagons and their Cleminson flexible wheelbases:

'The much shorter wheelbase of these wagons, compared to that of the carriages, would have reduced the out-of-line effects on entering and leaving curved sections of track. That was just as well as they would have had to negotiate turn-outs, and perhaps indifferent quality track in some sidings, much more regularly than the carriages.'

WAGON RUNNING GEAR, BRAKES AND BUFFER COUPLINGS

All wagons had a wheel diameter of about two feet with six 'bow' type spokes; the axle-boxes were grease- or fat- lubricated. The twelve original wagons, the two vans and subsequently wagon numbers 15 to 39 appear to have been fitted with oil-lubricated axle boxes. For a period, some 4-wheeled wagons were fitted with canvas covers over the axle boxes when they were used for conveying gritty and dusty ballast following the washout of the embankment across the Woodsend Marshes in 1897.

The centre buffers originally incorporated a coupling hook of 'chopper' form which dropped over a pin in the adjoining coupling, but no bridle was provided to prevent the hook jumping out when the stock buffered-up abruptly. This was the cause of the accident at Walberswick in 1921 (see Chapter 12), following which the MoT Inspecting Officer recommended a 'figure of eight' form coupling be substituted. This

was effected from October 1921 following which strict instructions were issued that: 'when a truck is detached the new coupling *must* be laid [back against] the wagon end and on no account left {in place projecting] from the buffer'. This instruction was reiterated in April 1922 stating that if any irregularity is discovered it must be reported to the Manager with the name of the defaulter. Coupling hooks and their figure-of-eight successors were fitted at the Halesworth end on all vehicles (see **Figs 123** and **124**).

Continuous brakes were not fitted to any of the rolling stock, though hand operated brakes were provided on all open wagons and the two vans in the form of a large wooden brake shoe bearing on one wheel; on the centre wheel of the 6-wheeled wagons. The hand brake was applied by a long lever held down by a conventional pin rack attached to the sole bar on one side of a vehicle only. It is difficult to see from photographs on which side the brake lever was attached, sometimes because the wagons were tarpaulin covered or the details in the photographs are not clear.

WAGON MAINTENANCE

Repairs to wagons, lifting to change wheels or side springs, and painting – when finance allowed – was effected in the open at Southwold in a short spur off the north siding near a small workshop. Wheels requiring to be turned on a lathe were sent to the Garrett works at Leiston.

The Railway maintenance staff consisted of a carpenter and a blacksmith.

FREIGHT TRAFFIC and how it was loaded.

The Southwold Railway never had any wagons specifically built for livestock, though a cattle pen was built at Halesworth. Sheep, pigs and calves, the latter usually in sacks tied around their necks, were carried when the wagon was covered with a net; the number of pigs per wagon varied according to size of pig and the wagon used.

Traffic liable to damage by netting could only be conveyed in the open wagons when tarpaulin covers were used. A stock of 53 was recorded at closure in 1929, measuring 14ft x 10ft of best flax, dressed black and lettered SOUTHWOLD RAILWAY on both sides.

Sugar beet growing in East Anglia started experimentally at Snape from 1911; the beet had been introduced from Holland whence the crop was exported for processing but in 1916, a factory was opened at Ipswich following which the crop was grown in the Blyth Valley. By 1927, forwardings of beet traffic were recorded from Wenhaston. To accommodate this new traffic, a trial was made by the Company to increase the capacity of at least two 4-wheeled wagons by adding a fixed plank to the sides and levelled ends to No. 22 and one other. This traffic could have been of considerable benefit to the Company had the sugar beet business been able to survive.

The size of a consignment was clearly a limiting factor as it was on any railway, but the Southwold Railway's narrow gauge and consequently limited loading gauge meant that, for instance, forestry traffic was beyond the Railway's capacity. Despite the two bolster-fitted Timber Wagons (Nos 11 and 12), an offer to transport trees measuring between 20 and 48 feet in length with girths up to 7 feet, which were quite usual in the wooded areas nearby, had to be refused. Fortunately, because the Southwold was an independent railway it was never a common carrier, so traffic offered could be refused even if its dimensions and weight were within the Southwold's capacity.

PRIVATELY OWNED WAGONS OF THOMAS MOY LTD.

Thomas Moy Ltd., with head office at Colchester, were coal factors with depots all over East Anglia, West London and railway wagon builders with works at Peterborough. In common with many coal merchants, collieries, quarries, gas works and some manufacturers, Moy also had a privately-owned fleet of standard gauge wagons, in some cases colourfully painted and identified in large letters, probably for publicity purposes as well as for their owner's convenience.

Moy extended their fleet to the Southwold Railway where it had three wagons, probably being the only English narrow gauge railway on which privately-owned wagons ran. These three wagons

Fig 165: 4-wheeled open wagon loaded with coal on a mixed train. The photographer was on the open veranda of the carriage behind the wagon.

Fig 166: Private-owner 6-wheeled wagon No 1511. Maker's photograph mid-1880s.

were numbered 1507 to 1509 and on each end bore the letters A to C respectively by which Southwold Railway staff generally recognised them. These wagons were mounted on Cleminson 6-wheeled Flexible Wheelbases, similar to the carriages. The sides comprised three doors of 3-planks each with ends a plank higher than the sides and radiused. The tare weight was around 4 tons with loading of 7 tons. The wagon handbrakes were of the same pattern as those on the Southwold's 6-wheeled wagons. These wagons were quite likely to have been on the line at its opening in 1879, or very soon after, as in 1885 two (probably A & B) were sent to Peterborough on 1 July and 10 August respectively for repairs and C on 30 November 1886.

In 1922, Moy built two further wagons (1510 & 1511), D & E respectively, of nearly identical design and two of their former wagons were sold to the Southwold Railway (Nos. 37 & 38) and in September 1926 a third wagon (No. 39).

These 6-wheel Moy wagons were the envy of the Halesworth Station Master who repeatedly requested similar wagons during the struggle to clear trans-shipped traffic until the Company finally introduced its own wagons of identical design from 1896. Moy's wagons usually only conveyed the coal transhipped from *their* standard gauge wagons but, when available, arrangements were made for the Southwold Railway to hire them from at least 1885.

INADEQUATE ROLLING STOCK AND LIMITED FACILITIES TO HANDLE THE RISING VOLUME OF FREIGHT TRAFFIC

When a branch or extension to a standard gauge line was constructed to a different gauge to the parent line, usually considered cheaper to construct but probably not much more economic to operate, an immediate problem arises with the need to transfer all freight between the two systems. Beside the Southwold Railway the following other instances were:

- Lynton & Barnstaple Railway at Barnstaple
- Leek & Manifold Railway at Waterhouses (but this railway did have Transporter Wagons)
- Ffestiniog Railway at Minffordd
- Corris Railway at Machynlleth
- Vale of Rheidol Railway at Aberystwyth
- Welsh Highland Railway at Dinas
- Welshpool & Llanfair Railway at Welshpool

David Lee has been able to discover information about complaints from the parent railway (GER and LNER) and sometimes from the Southwold Railway's freight customers about delays. In the case of the Southwold Railway, it served a small but developing seaside town during the latter years of the nineteenth century and the early 1900s when much building material and other supplies were required As the population and some industry developed, so those commodities, particularly coal and building materials, increased in volume. In 1881 the population was 2,107; by 1901 it had increased to 2,800.

The freight traffic consisted of minerals, which included coal in bulk, general merchandise, usually in small lots of under one ton in cases, barrels or bags. For the latter, there were few difficulties in transhipment: it only required a narrow platform between the standard gauge wagon and the narrow gauge wagon, with the floor of each wagon and the platform at the same height. Then the traffic could be man-handled or barrowed between the two vehicles. Coal, minerals and other bulky traffic, however, required much physical effort on the part of the SR Transfer Porter. The need for his work depended on the weather, particularly during autumn and winter when such traffic was heavy, and the availability of Southwold Railway wagons; three narrow gauge wagons were required to clear one standard gauge wagon of coal.

Complaints were usually from the GER about standard gauge wagons, always referred to as 'GER trucks' regardless of the actual ownership of the wagons, and they were received by Halesworth Station Master Walter Calver. He was made well aware of the inadequate supply of Southwold wagons as early as 1885 when Moy's larger 6-wheel wagons had to be hired over a period of six months. By 1888 he wrote a letter to the Secretary, Mr H. Carne, asking, 'could you arrange with Mr. Moy to use his wagons – we badly want more wagons and larger than those we now have'. There is no evidence of this arrangement being effected, until a return dated June 1890 which included reference to the iron lantern for Southwold lighthouse, weighing 8 tons and carried in two Moy wagons C and B on 27 March 1890.

In the previous year the Railway had been greatly handicapped in carrying 300,000 bricks for building the new Southwold lighthouse, replacing the Low Light at Orford Ness which had been successively rebuilt after destruction by fire, storm damage, rough seas and coastal erosion (ref: *Southwold Lighthouse –History and Context*. Chris Cardwell. Southwold Museum. 2017). The Halesworth Wet Copy Letter Book shows Mr Calver writing to Wenhaston and Blythburgh Station Masters requesting quick discharge and return of wagons in their sidings.

Unless there is any explanation in the Minutes of the Directors' Board meetings, it would be interesting to know why the wagon fleet was only increased by nine 4-wheeled wagons of only five tons capacity between 1892 and 1894 when the freight traffic was steadily increasing and Southwold was growing. It seems that the London-based Directors and management were not responding to the local situation. It was not until late in 1896 that three larger wagons were ordered being followed by six more of the same in 1899 bringing the fleet to a total of 26 wagons. The most likely reason for the Board not making adequate provision to cater for increasing traffic was inadequate finance in the 1880s following the return of engine No. 1 *Southwold* to the makers and clearing the debt for the original supply of rolling stock in 1883.

In the years following opening of the railway the tonnage of minerals, mostly coal, and general freight increased year by year as extracts from bi-annual accounts show:

Year	Coal & Minerals	General Goods	Total Traffic
all traffic figures are in tons			
1880	3,052	1,960	5,012
1885	4,555	3,199	7,754
1890	5,712	2,907	8,619
1895	6,817	4,938	11,755
1900	9,313	7,103	16,416

The original fleet of small low capacity wagons may initially have been adequate for conveying the traffic on offer, but by 1885 difficulties and delays in trans-shipping all traffic, particularly coal, were beginning to be felt and the problem continued into the early years of the twentieth century.

Complaints were frequent from consignees and the Goods Manager of the GER. There were staff shortages at Halesworth because the one Transhipment Porter was doing nearly all the coal and mineral trans-ship work. At Southwold, consignees were slow in discharging vehicles but, because they were important local customers, the Company did not raise demurrage charges for detention of wagons. On occasions there were no Southwold Railway wagons available at Halesworth, while on some days in summer there were too many wagons to be attached to the first down passenger train at around 8.40am. In 1900, Mr Calver suggested a goods train to run during the summer months but it was to be a few years before this happened. The GER considered the Southwold traffic to be an inconvenience and they were responsible for shunting the main line wagons to serve the Southwold's transhipment siding. At times the GER transfer siding was blocked by GER traffic and, in 1887, it was reported not to be long enough by Walter Calver. He believed a siding to hold 30 wagons was necessary, but it was not lengthened to accommodate 18 wagons until 1896. Moreover, it is recorded between 1892 and 1896 that coal intended for Southwold was held back in main line wagons at Lowestoft, Beccles and Saxmundham.

Despite complaints and delays to their own traffic to and from Halesworth, the GER did not increase their staff or shunting power; there was only one Shunting Horse

available at Halesworth. Wagons of coal could often be held for days waiting to be transhipped with between 10 to 50 wagons waiting for clearance on most days during the heavy coal demand period. Clearance was at an average of nine per day when Southwold Railway wagons were available.

Eventual introduction of three long 6-wheel wagons came late in 1896. Following that the situation did not improve much as loaded wagons continued to accumulate at a slightly lower level following a drop in traffic during 1897. The GER continued to complain about delays in clearing wagons, traders at Southwold were not assisting by discharging promptly, and Station Master Calver continued complaining that there were still insufficient wagons to move the traffic. In 1898, the number of wagons awaiting to be transhipped were at a similar level to former years so, finally, nine more long 6-wheel wagons were obtained between 1896 (3 wagons) and 1899 (6 wagons).

David Lee's analysis of Mr Calver's letters between 1892 and 1901 reveals the scale of the problem:

from Halesworth Station Master's letter book – 1895 to 1901							
Year & dates	Page No	Wagons waiting	Annual Totals	Year & dates	Page No	Wagons waiting	Annual Totals
1892				**1898 / 99**			
28/10	422	24		5/8	551	22	
15/11	425	10		7/9	553	31	
9/12	429	26		28/9	554	41	
15/12	430	14	74	8/10	555	39	
1895				6/12	558	50	
20/09	499	42		7/1	559	21	204
11/11	501	40		**1901**			
15/11	502	39		25/6	575	22	
20/11	504	51		20/7	577	20	
23/11	505	40		27/7	579	30	
27/11	506	35	247	18/9	582	24	
1896				3/10	583	36	132
2/2	514	30					
2/8	519	38					
12/8	521	21					
1/9	525	50					
3/9	526	49					
21/9	528	36					
26/9	530	74	298				

Complaints about delay continued, but there is no more of the detailed information which analysis of Mr Calver's Wet Copy Letter Book has provided. Nevertheless, this is a well-documented indication of the problems which the Southwold Railway faced and which the Board failed to remedy. The two possible solutions which they might have followed were:

i) Convert the Railway to standard gauge so that transshipment became unnecessary at Halesworth.

ii) Adopt the use of narrow gauge Transporter Wagons which could carry the standard gauge wagons to Southwold or, if their loads were destined for an intermediate station, they all had – or in due course developed – sidings to which the Transporter Wagons could be shunted for unloading.

The Southwold Railway Board did consider a standard-gauge conversion, secured parliamentary authority for it and undertook some preparatory work which has been explored in earlier chapters. However, both 'solutions' were capital intensive and neither would necessarily be cost-effective once their operation had been thoroughly investigated and increased revenue estimated. Chapter 17 examines these 'solutions' in a little more detail.

Fig 167: No 3 *BLYTH* with an up goods train in the siding at Southwold Station c1908.

PART 5

A DERELICT RAILWAY – THE END OF THE TALE?

Fig 168: 'Eyore' would not welcome a fence across 'his' railway!

A DERELICT RAILWAY FROM 1929 TO 1941 TO 1963

After the closure of the railway and the running of the last goods trains, the line remained relatively undisturbed throughout the 1930s.

The track between Southwold and Blythburgh ran between wooden fences and, being on the sandy soil of Southwold and Walberswick Commons or embanked round the Blyth Estuary, suffered relatively little from encroaching vegetation (**Fig 169**).

However, the unkempt hedges of the Blythburgh to Halesworth section soon straggled across the line and the track was hidden in many places by willow-herb, ragged robin and other marsh-loving weeds. Alders, sprouting between the rails, rapidly reached several feet in height and parts of the line near Wenhaston became waterlogged (**Fig 170**).

The stations, which were never very substantial structures, soon assumed a neglected and desolate air as timber walls rotted and weeds crept over the platforms. Station interiors, seen through the broken windows, were littered with rubbish. At Wenhaston, the double signal was still, forlornly, at danger and a coal weighing machine and pan were rusting in the station yard. Chicken houses invaded the permanent way at Blythburgh and at Walberswick a solitary signal and ruinous shed were in a gorsey wilderness.

Southwold Station presented probably the dreariest picture of all, with empty sidings, the dismal black sheds, some used as coal offices, and the goods yard and sidings used by coal merchants (**Figs 172** and **174**). No 4 *Wenhaston,* remaining at Southwold, was soon too

Fig 169: Walberswick Station, looking towards Southwold, in 1935.

Fig 170: Wenhaston Station level crossing c1935.

Fig 171: Wenhaston Station building, boarded-up and desolate; the Station nameboard survives – c1932.

Fig 172: Southwold Station 1931. In the background is the Southwold HomeKnit factory and the Station Hotel.

Fig 173: No 1 SOUTHWOLD partially dismantled and subsequently scrapped on site at Southwold Station in May 1929.

rusted for even committed enthusiasts to lever it out of the Engine Shed for photographs and No 1 Southwold, which had been partially dismantled before the Railway closed, was scrapped in May 1929 (Fig 171).

The only cheerful note was provided by the row of three chestnut trees on the platform, especially in their spring and autumn glory. Halesworth looked less woebegone because dilapidated rolling stock still

Fig 174: Southwold Station detail – L to R: Water tank; Engine Shed; Goods Office. 1937.

Fig 175: Winter at Halesworth Station 1937. Carriages at the platform and SR goods wagons in the engine run-round loop. The second carriage in this view was accidentally (?) burnt out by a tramp who had a home in it.

standing at the platform at first gave an impression that all was not yet lost; that traffic might return.

Unfortunately, time, weather and occasional vandalism made a re-opening seem less likely as the 1930s progressed. For instance, coach No 4 was burnt out some time prior to May 1937 by a tramp who had made it his home.

At the end of working, No 3 *Blyth* was left in Halesworth Engine Shed (**Fig 176**) – and was manoeuvred out in 1936 for a photograph then

Fig 176: No 3 *Blyth*, derelict and partly vandalised in the remains of Halesworth Engine Shed – November 1935.

Fig 177: Demolition and removal of Halesworth Station shelter – 1940.

returned. No 4 *Wenhaston* was immobile in Southwold Engine Shed and No 1 *Southwold*, which had been withdrawn from service in 1928, was outside that Shed, partly dismantled. It was sold for scrap in May 1929, cut up on the spot and represents the last earning of the line before the company went into receivership (**Fig 173**).

The Railway's slumber was rudely awakened by the Army after the outbreak of the Second World War in September 1939 (**Fig 178**).

Fig 178: Wenhaston Water Mill bridge – rail removed for defence purposes – 1940.

The Government considered the south and east coasts were especially vulnerable because of their nearness to mainland Europe. From May 1940 great efforts were made to defend the area as part of a wider scheme across Britain to create a 'coastal crust' of fortifications. Construction work started on a battery of two six-inch guns near the Harbour North Pier, a pillbox was constructed overlooking the Harbour and hundreds of concrete anti-tank blocks and barbed wire were extended along the Walberswick beaches and the Southwold beaches from Harbour North Pier northwards to the cliffs below the town which provided another anti-tank barrier.

The Harbour was vulnerable to a German attack because it could be used to unload men and supplies and the beaches were suitable for landing armoured vehicles until anti-tank blocks were installed. The mouth of the Blyth was therefore blocked by sinking two wooden trawlers and ultimately a chain boom was placed between the two Harbour piers which could be lowered underwater to permit the passage of shallow-draft vessels.

More seriously for any potential restoration was the destruction of the swing bridge early in 1941. It was subsequently reported in the *East Anglian Magazine*, November 1953, in a colonel's letter to the Editor,

that the Royal Engineers had selected the bridge for a demolition demonstration. The swing section of the bridge was turned to the open position and explosives packed round the central pivot ready for a number of invited guests from all over Eastern Command to watch the bridge blown up at 14.00 on Demonstration Day. During the morning of that day the District Commander visited the site and asked the sapper responsible for wiring the exploder to the fuse on the bridge if all connections had been made and the circuits tested. 'Yes sir,' said the sapper, 'Look.' He pressed down the plunger, the fuse ignited the explosives and the bridge was partially demolished (**Fig 179**).

Demolition of the whole Southwold Railway by Thomas W. Ward Ltd 'the Sheffield contractor' began in earnest in July 1941. Work started at Halesworth with the breaking up of the old rolling stock, followed by lifting of the track; the locomotive shed was pulled down in August, and No 3 *Blyth* was left on a short length of rail in the open (**Fig 180**).

Wenhaston and Blythburgh station buildings were removed but most bridges were left in place. The track for the first four miles from Halesworth was far too overgrown to permit the use of a contractor's locomotive for demolition transport, as was a usual practice when possible, so the rails and other salvage were stacked

Fig 179: Swing bridge open and disabled by Royal Engineers – 1941.

Fig 180: No 3 *BLYTH* in the open air and prey to vandals at Bird's Folly Engine Shed, Halesworth.

at the nearest roadside at intervals for collection. At Southwold Station No 4 *Wenhaston* was cut up, the rails were lifted and sheds not in use were pulled down. By January 1942, the job was done; some of the rails are said to have been sold to a colliery in Yorkshire, but most of the other material was simply scrap and realised about £1,500. Sleepers, sawn up by a retired policeman, were sold for firewood by the Blythburgh grocer at two pence-halfpenny a bundle.

The War Department notified the Railway Company that they had £1,500 from the contractors and asked to whom it should be paid? But the assets and accounts of the Company were still frozen so, in 1945 the War Department put the money on deposit until such time as the Railway could legally claim it.

At the same time, the Receiver of the Railway, after a hard struggle, obtained an Order from the Master of the Court enabling the Company to settle some of its affairs, including the sale of land to the former owners and the payment of long-outstanding debts. A little money was raised from land sales but a newly-appointed Master

of the Court reversed his predecessor's ruling and ordered the cash to be frozen except for the payment of income tax.

The former impasses in the Company's affairs were restored and the Receiver was powerless to do anything else despite some demands for settlement from creditors. For example, complaints were received from Halesworth Urban District Council about the dangerous state of the Southwold Railway bridge spanning Holton Road and adjacent to the LNER bridge over the same road. The SR bridge was now only the main girders and some cross-girders which had carried the SR track and was rightly represented to the Company by the Council as a veritable death-trap for children scrambling up the banks and trying to cross the bridge. Eventually Halesworth UDC paid for the erection of safety fences and applied for a High Court settlement of their bill which included several other small SR-related debts. However, legally the Southwold Railway Company was still in existence and until the High Court chose to consider the Halesworth UDC application, nothing was done.

Fig 181: Southwold Railway bridge over Holton Road, Halesworth. The standard gauge bridge across this road is immediately to the left of this picture so passengers on the main line saw the SR advertised.

For a number of years, the SR Holton Road bridge was a reminder of the Southwold Railway because LNER and subsequently BR travellers on the adjoining bridge could observe the faded letters SOUTHWOLD RAILWAY on the railway side of the SR bridge. At Halesworth, the station name boards once carried the legend 'Halesworth for Southwold' but that went in the 1930s and the footbridge extension and steps to the narrow gauge platform were dismantled. The Southwold platform and the area around it was used for a time as a coal yard and was then comprehensively re-developed into a housing estate along the newly created Bramblewood Way.

The trackbed from Halesworth to Blythburgh remained overgrown but largely extant, including some of the bridges and the foundations, including the inspection pit, in the former Engine Shed. At Blythburgh itself the formation is still well-marked round Blythburgh Church Curve and through the site of Blythburgh Station site. From Blythburgh eastwards to Southwold the formation was much less overgrown and survives, for much of the distance, as a footpath and/or bridleway. The concrete abutments of the Cattle Creep bridge are still in place (**Fig 184**) and at Walberswick Station the concrete base of the timber-framed corrugated iron Station office remains and is marked by a commemorative seat and a plaque (**Fig 183**).

The original swing bridge over the Blyth, initially demolished during the Second World War, survived as a Bailey Bridge on the SR bridge piers and the route across Southwold Marshes and in a cutting through Southwold Common also became a footpath leading to the site of Southwold Station.

Southwold Station building has gone and a Fire Station and Police Station now occupy the site. The whole of the Station Yard has been redeveloped, mainly for houses. Across Station Road the former Pier Avenue Hotel, which was originally Station Hotel and featured in a number of pictures, has survived as The *Blyth* (**Fig 186**).

SOUTHWOLD STATION
as a coal yard c 1935

Fig 182: A final role for the Southwold Station site – as a coal yard.

WALBERSWICK STATION

This commemorative seat is sited on the base of what was once Walberswick Station, one of the five stations connected by the unique narrow gauge Southwold Railway which plied between Halesworth and Southwold from 1879 to 1929. A 3′0″ gauge single line track passed the station on the opposite side to the current footpath and passed in a straight line to the bridge and thence Southwold where the station was opposite what is now called the Pier Avenue Hotel. In the opposite direction it passed through beautiful scenery to Blythburgh and then Wenhaston.

The ten foot by thirty-six foot timber-framed station building was a 1902 replacement for the smaller construction that was initially opened on September 2nd 1881. It contained a clerk's office, booking office and waiting room, plus rather primitive toilet facilities.

This seat, which has been provided by contributions from members of the Southwold Railway Society, was opened by Mrs Margaret Chadd on September 2nd 1996.

Fig 183: Commemorative plaque at Walberswick Station site – 2017.

Fig 184: The SR's very functional concrete abutments and the railway embankment pierced by a cattle creep, on Walberswick Common – 2013.

Fig 185: A Bailey Bridge replacing the SR swing bridge across the River Blyth. The view is towards Walberswick; the massive circular piers and the river-side abutments supporting this bridge are original.

The Harbour Branch was, and is, still traceable from the junction across the marshes (**Fig 187**). The concrete abutments of two small bridges across dykes remain and a fraction of a former headshunt plus the remains of the typical SR central buffer-stop are sometimes discernible. Otherwise, coastal erosion and subsequent Harbour developments have almost entirely covered or otherwise obscured Blackshore Quay and the Harbour Quay at the eastern end of the Branch. The Harbour is still busy with boat builders, small offshore fishing boats, pleasure-boat moorings, the Harbour Inn, a chandlery, Southwold Lifeboat Station and the Alfred Corry Lifeboat Museum, but only the eye of faith can imagine the kipperdrome, steam drifters at Harbour Quay, and the Southwold Railway trying to attract more business with its Harbour Branch.

Fig 186: The *Blyth* was the original Station Hotel. The Police Station on the left of the picture occupies part of the original Southwold Station site and a plaque on the wall, behind the rose, recalls the Railway.

Fig 187: Photographed from the trackbed of the Railway across Woodsend Marshes, the outline of the former Harbour Branch is visible curving away across the field.

So lost, gone forever and forgotten …?

After lingering, almost complete, until 1941, most of the physical remains of the Southwold Railway were cleared away during the Second World War and the prospects of any revival seemed remote. But the Railway was not forgotten and local folk still recalled the shrill whistles of the locomotives echoing over the marshes between Southwold and Blythburgh. A local story is an amusing illustration of the persistence of memory and of Suffolk logic: Elderly Mother: 'I thought I heard the railway whistle again just now.' Daughter: 'It was an owl, Mother.' Mother: 'Yes, those trains sound just like an owl.'

Some smaller Railway items were salvaged from the wartime demolition and clearance by Arnold Barrett Jenkins, photographer in Southwold, Alderman and several times Town Mayor. Initially, the items were displayed in his High Street shop and then, after the business was closed in 1962, were added to the collections of Southwold Museum.

An important large-scale find was made in 1962. It was the body of Van No 14 on private property near Halesworth Station. The discoverer, Mr Lawrence E. Perkins, describes the find:

'A friend decided to drive to Southwold on 19 July 1962 to see the relics of the SR in the care of Mr A.B. Jenkins [before his shop closed]. After this we photographed the remains of Southwold Station and thought we would take a look at the other end of the line at Halesworth.

'We went to the main line station and asked the porter the position of the old narrow gauge station. We went up onto the footbridge over the main line to the point where the steps leading down to the narrow gauge platform had been removed. There was nothing left to see.

'Turning away and looking back over the station yard I saw behind a wall a small van; and the size and cant of the roof reminded me at once of the Southwold stock. A close inspection confirmed that it had once had buffer couplings and the maker's plate was English Bros. Wisbech. We were both certain that it was indeed an SR van. We decided that, since so little remains of the railway at Southwold, Mr Jenkins should be informed in an effort to secure the van for the museum.'

Arnold Barrett Jenkins followed up this wonderful piece of news and in a letter to Mr Perkins dated

25 July 1962 he wrote, 'You will be pleased to hear that I have obtained the first refusal for the local Museum.' For the record, the body was behind a garage in a yard just off Halesworth Down side goods yard, and was moved to a space beside Southwold Station in November 1962; the Museum had to decline the offer of acquisition because it lacked sufficient display space.

Barrett Jenkins set up a Van Restoration Fund; volunteers painted the van body and blocked-in the window inserted when the body was used as a garden shed. He also salvaged about 15ft of SR rail, which he hoped to fix to new sleepers on a concrete base and, if a wheeled underframe could be found, the van would be displayed on this track but otherwise on blocks. The van body did not attract as much interest in Southwold as had been hoped and, because of the encroachments on the station site, it was moved in 1970 to the East Anglian Transport Museum, Carlton Colville, Lowestoft.

Barrett Jenkins was not the only person to try to save elements of the Southwold Railway. Three months after closure, in July 1929, the Directors expressed their willingness to consider an offer for the controlling interest in the railway from Mr Ronald Shephard, a light railway engineer. Shephard lived in Linchmere near Chichester,

West Sussex. He was a member of the Permanent Way Institution and acted as an advisor during the Second World War on the defence of narrow gauge railways. He was consulted frequently by two famous railway authors, O.S. Nock and C. Hamilton-Ellis, was President of the Linchmere Model Railway Club and had an extensive O Gauge model railway in his garden.

Fig 189 is an internal LNER Memo dated 19 February 1930 which outlines Shephard's proposals and includes an interesting observation that the line has been purchased for £4,000 and he hoped to have the line open for Whitsun Holiday traffic.

Shephard proposed to:

- Retain the narrow gauge
- Introduce a fast and frequent passenger service
- Carry passengers in a railcar driven by petrol or a high-pressure vertical-boilered, geared steam engine of the 'Sentinel' type
- Use a 'Sentinel' locomotive for goods traffic
- Eliminate transhipment at Halesworth by the use of narrow-gauge transporter wagons for standard-gauge trucks as on the Ashover and Leek & Manifold Valley narrow gauge railways (**Fig 190**).

Fig 188: SR Van body No 14 conserved, painted and displayed at the East Anglian Transport Museum.

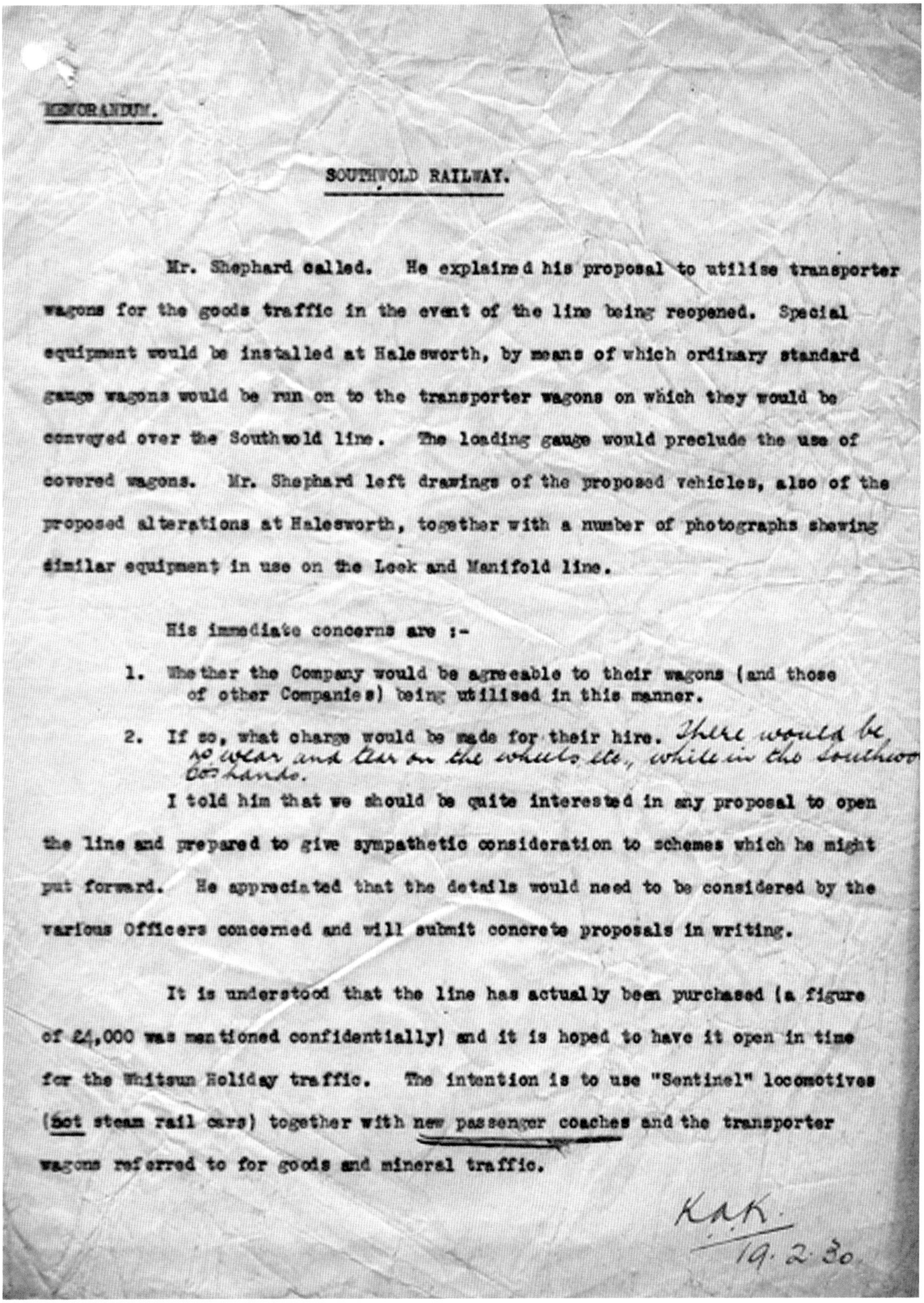

MEMORANDUM.

SOUTHWOLD RAILWAY.

Mr. Shephard called. He explained his proposal to utilise transporter wagons for the goods traffic in the event of the line being reopened. Special equipment would be installed at Halesworth, by means of which ordinary standard gauge wagons would be run on to the transporter wagons on which they would be conveyed over the Southwold line. The loading gauge would preclude the use of covered wagons. Mr. Shephard left drawings of the proposed vehicles, also of the proposed alterations at Halesworth, together with a number of photographs shewing similar equipment in use on the Leek and Manifold line.

His immediate concerns are :-

1. Whether the Company would be agreeable to their wagons (and those of other Companies) being utilised in this manner.

2. If so, what charge would be made for their hire. *There would be no wear and tear on the wheels etc., while in the Southwold hands.*

I told him that we should be quite interested in any proposal to open the line and prepared to give sympathetic consideration to schemes which he might put forward. He appreciated that the details would need to be considered by the various Officers concerned and will submit concrete proposals in writing.

It is understood that the line has actually been purchased (a figure of £4,000 was mentioned confidentially) and it is hoped to have it open in time for the Whitsun Holiday traffic. The intention is to use "Sentinel" locomotives (hot steam rail cars) together with new passenger coaches and the transporter wagons referred to for goods and mineral traffic.

K.A.K.
19.2.30.

Fig 189: LNER Internal Memo *re* Ronald Shephard's negotiations to revive the Southwold Railway.

Shephard stated that the LNER was agreeable to the transporter wagon proposal. He hoped, subject to the necessary capital being forthcoming, to commence operations early in 1930.

The proposal was received in Southwold with considerable enthusiasm, but little financial support, due in part to competition with an alternative scheme propounded by Mr Belcher, the one-time locomotive engineer of the railway and a man of forceful opinions. He advocated conversion to standard gauge and an extension, starting near the Halesworth Engine Shed then via Cratfield and Huntingfield to Laxfield to join the unfinished Mid-Suffolk Light Railway. Mr Belcher maintained that his proposal would put the Southwold Railway and Southwold Harbour in a much more cost-effective position.

Support for the re-opening of the railway being thus divided, neither scheme prospered and negotiations ceased in October 1930.

However, Shephard did not give up and he spent some time walking over and photographing the decaying Southwold Railway. Because he was a Government Adviser on narrow gauge railway matters he managed to photograph – though almost certainly illegally – the Army depredations on the Railway and put together a Schedule of what was lost before formal

scrapping began in 1941. It has survived amongst Shephard's papers which are now in West Sussex Archives, Chichester, and is reproduced full-page as **Fig 191** because it makes interesting and very relevant reading. I do not know whether The Receiver, then Mr Naunton the Southwold Town Clerk, was ever able to recover £1,535 5s 0d.

Shephard also recorded, in a poor photograph and probably taken with a semi-concealed camera, the removal of the mid-river caisson on which the swing bridge revolved (**Fig 192**).

Mr Shephard's interest, and what he tried to achieve, were essentially engineering solutions to the problems he was uncovering. He may not have been fully aware of the legal position of the Railway Company, soon after closure to be in the hands of a Receiver and still a Company created by an Act of Parliament.

In the 18 months that followed the closure, it became clear that no useful outside help was forthcoming and a Board Meeting was convened on 26 November 1930 to consider what should be done. The curious business of Claude Pain's Directorship was noted; it appeared that this appointment was irregular while he also held the position of Engineer, but since he had resigned the latter post on 31 May 1929 he was now eligible as a Director and was officially acclaimed.

Fig 190: An empty narrow gauge transporter wagon as used on the Ashover Light Railway. The standard gauge track on the wagon is visible on either side of the narrow gauge wagon body. Behind is a loaded standard gauge wagon on an Ashover transporter wagon.

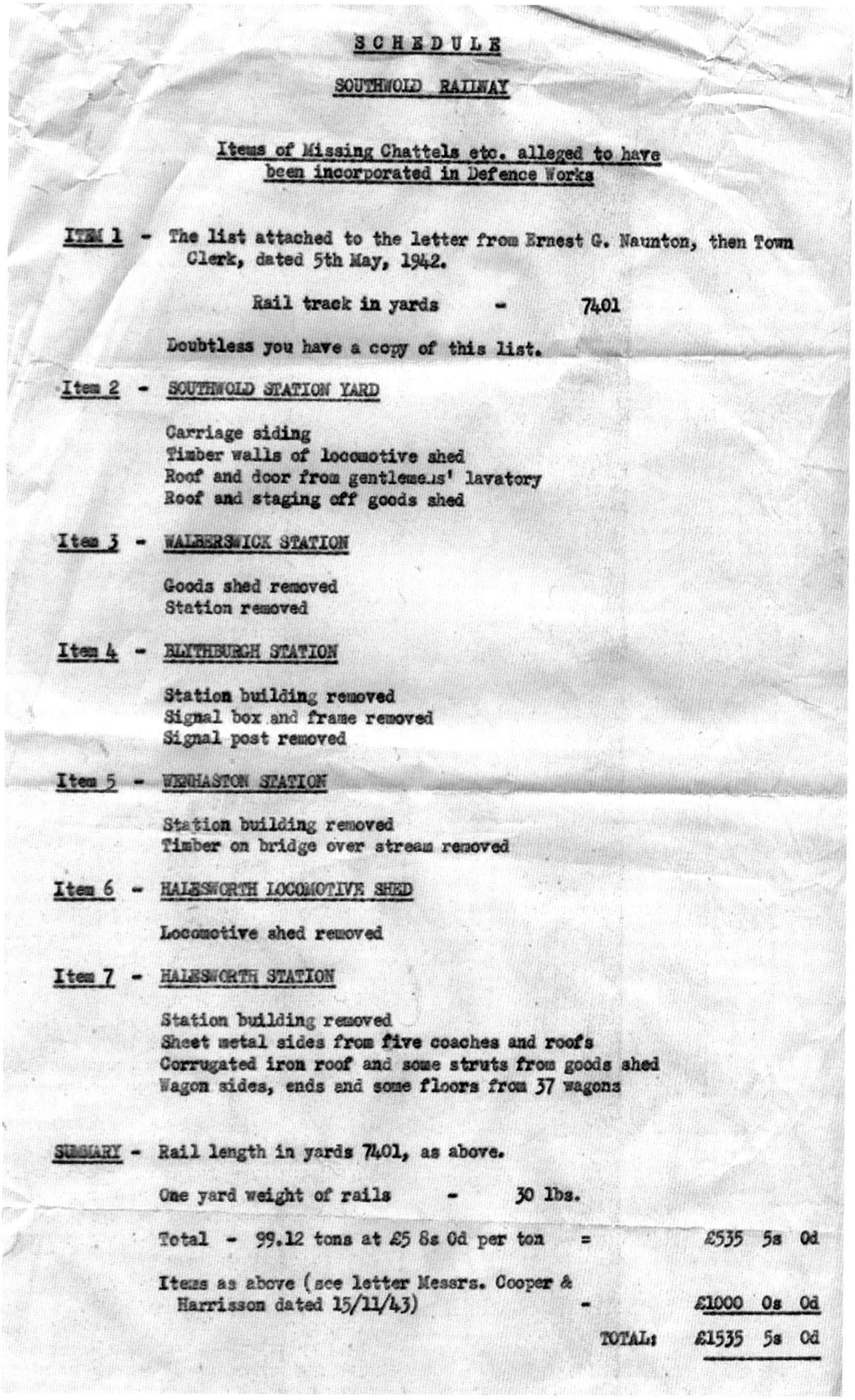

SCHEDULE

SOUTHWOLD RAILWAY

Items of Missing Chattels etc. alleged to have been incorporated in Defence Works

ITEM 1 - The list attached to the letter from Ernest G. Naunton, then Town Clerk, dated 5th May, 1942.

Rail track in yards   -   7401

Doubtless you have a copy of this list.

Item 2 - SOUTHWOLD STATION YARD

Carriage siding
Timber walls of locomotive shed
Roof and door from gentlemens' lavatory
Roof and staging off goods shed

Item 3 - WALBERSWICK STATION

Goods shed removed
Station removed

Item 4 - BLYTHBURGH STATION

Station building removed
Signal box and frame removed
Signal post removed

Item 5 - WENHASTON STATION

Station building removed
Timber on bridge over stream removed

Item 6 - HALESWORTH LOCOMOTIVE SHED

Locomotive shed removed

Item 7 - HALESWORTH STATION

Station building removed
Sheet metal sides from five coaches and roofs
Corrugated iron roof and some struts from goods shed
Wagon sides, ends and some floors from 37 wagons

SUMMARY - Rail length in yards 7401, as above.

One yard weight of rails   -   30 lbs.

Total - 99.12 tons at £5 8s 0d per ton   =   £535 5s 0d

Items as above (see letter Messrs. Cooper & Harrisson dated 15/11/43)   -   £1000 0s 0d

TOTAL: £1535 5s 0d

Fig 191: Schedule of Army depredations on the Southwold Railway.

Fig 192: Ronald Shephard's wartime photograph of the remains of the swing bridge mid-river caisson which has now (2017) completely gone.

Next on the agenda was the appointment of Mr Secretary Ward as Receiver: Mr Justice Maughan on 25 June 1929 had heard a petition brought by a group of creditors to consider the sufficiency of authority of the Halesworth Bench in making that appointment. The strange position of the Railway Company then became apparent; they desired to get the Company wound up but there was no jurisdiction in any Court to enable them to do so. Nobody short of parliament had the authority. His Lordship said that he would order the appointment of the Receiver, though the latter's powers were not those normally associated with his office – he could not sign a valid cheque and it was not in his power to sell a statutory undertaking, the rolling stock or permanent way. Nevertheless, an appointment must be made so Mr Secretary Ward became the Receiver but without any power.

The Board then considered the various offers of help that had been made, including the Shephard and Belcher proposals, and a proposal from Lt Col Boston and Mr P.C. Loftus, both of Southwold. The Board did not consider any of these worth following up. The Solicitor therefore advised that an Act of Abandonment be obtained – though there were no funds for the expensive matter of promotion of this Act – and the application was duly made to the High Court of Justice. Thirty years later, in 1960, this matter was still before the Court.

Ironically, the Company had nothing to gain by abandonment; the Receiver would lose his position and the share and debenture holders whose interest he represented would get practically nothing, since the assets (mostly scrap) would be almost if not wholly absorbed by the legal expenses, which would be about £1,000. The losers were the owners of some of the land – in particular Southwold Corporation – on which the railway was laid, who were unable to obtain rent during the period of dereliction. Eventually this dissatisfaction with the slowness in obtaining permission to abandon the line crystallised in a demand for the removal of Mr Ward from the Receivership and his replacement by someone more impartial. As a result, the Town Clerk of Southwold, E.G. Naunton, was appointed to this position in March 1933, his successors were the subsequent Town Clerks H.A. Liquorish and H. Townsend. Even they, however, found themselves powerless to set in motion the slow machinery of the Law.

Just before the Second World War, Major G.A. Bruce, a consulting engineer with an office in Great Yarmouth and his home at Belton Hall just over the Suffolk border, evolved a project to re-open the Southwold Railway. He carried out surveys and C.D. Brumbley was draughtsman. The scheme seems to have been conducted quietly and little is known of it: Mr Brumbley (from correspondence with David Lee) believes that when Major Bruce sought sanction from Parliament to proceed, the LNER (who had originally raised no objections), bought out his interest and nothing further developed.

Hence year succeeded year and nothing was done, nothing moved, until it seemed that the decaying relics would be left there forever; it was only the urgent demands of war that hastened the end of the silent railway. In the spring of 1940, the Ministry of Supply instituted a nationwide drive for the recovery of scrap metal in the course of which a number of derelict or little-used railways were taken up. In June of 1940, the Southwold Railway effects were requisitioned for scrap, the Emergency Powers overruling the legal considerations that had up till then protected the line.

In 1941, the unhappy state of the Southwold Railway developed into a situation that can only be described as ludicrous. On 3 November 1941, the Council Meeting of Southwold Corporation sent a resolution to Mr Stokes and Mr P.C. Loftus, MPs respectively for Ipswich and Lowestoft:

'The Corporation of the Borough of Southwold desire most emphatically to call attention to the considerable quantity of metal comprising the derelict rolling stock of the Southwold Railway Company … the Corporation asks that you will, in the national interest, again call the attention of the appropriate Department to get this … usefully employed.'

In reply, Mr Stokes, as reported to Council on 7 February 1942, forwarded a letter from the Ministry of Supply to the effect that the requisitioning would take place and tenders would be invited for the sale of the metal, the proceeds to go to the shareholders.

Meanwhile, severe cuts in bus services were causing a good deal of inconvenience and the possibility of re-opening the railway was considered again. In

February 1941, Ronald Shephard again inspected the route, this time in the company of a representative of the War Department, and canvassed the local authorities for support to a Petition to the Minister of Transport. The Petition pointed out that Walberswick and Southwold were connected solely by a row-boat (the vehicle ferry having ceased operation); restrictions on shipping had aggravated the supply of coal to the town, which had now to be transported by lorry from Halesworth or Lowestoft; and farmers were having difficulty in despatching their produce.

When Mr Shephard's initiative was reported to Southwold Council, members received it with enthusiasm as minuted at the 4 April 1941 Council Meeting:

'Strong support was given to a Petition circulating in the District, asking the Minister of Transport to do all in his power to further the re-opening of the Southwold Railway. The Council feel the project will be of the utmost benefit to the Borough and neighbouring parishes'.

However, between collection of signatures and presentation of the Petition, demolition had begun, so the preamble in the Petition was amended to meet the new situation by a proposal to rebuild the railway to standard gauge, to be worked by an LNER Sentinel locomotive on a hiring basis, and the loco to be shedded at Halesworth. The amendments were not as comprehensive or accurate as they should have been because statements like 'station to be tidied up' and 'sidings put in order' implied that the buildings and track were still in position.

An accompanying map of the proposed standard gauge line (**Fig 193**) included two deviations from the original; a short cut-off between Corner Farm and Wenhaston Mill to ease the curvature; and a more considerable alteration, leaving the old route just east of Eastwood Lodge Farm to run due east to Walberswick village then north to cross the Blyth obliquely, join the Harbour Branch at Blackshore Quay and thence into Southwold. It was further proposed to open Halts at Holton, Corner Farm, Wenhaston Mill, Heath Farm, Beaumur Farm and Eastwood Lodge Farm. The proposed deviation between Eastwood Lodge Farm and Walberswick required a new station for Walberswick. It was also proposed to introduce sidings wherever the possibility of traffic warranted them at several of the Halts and to Southwold Gasworks.

The Petition was presented to the Minister of War Transport, Baron Leathers of Purfleet, in the form of a Memorandum dated 26 September 1941 (**Fig 194**).

The Memorandum was unsuccessful, and probably unrealistic because major civil engineering works like the swing bridge, or an alternative which did not open and had limited clearance for boats, would be necessary. The war ended and the Railway Company slumbered on, as a trackbed and a Company still awaiting a High Court response to the 1930 application to obtain an Parliamentary Act of Abandonment.

It was however inconceivable that this impasse should be maintained indefinitely and in 1956 Mr Ronald Shephard, who had always longed to see the old railway restored, put forward the idea of a Preservation Society. This scheme had its origin in the success that had attended the formation of similar bodies founded to look after the narrow gauge Talyllyn and Ffestiniog Railways in North Wales, though in the case of Southwold it would not be a matter of restoring to use a moribund railway. A new Southwold Railway laid on the old route would be a much more expensive business. However,

it was hoped that the existing debenture holders might look favourably on the scheme and that some of the frozen assets could be released in its fulfilment, in the style of the 'Halesworth & Southwold Railway Co Ltd.'

An enthusiastic local helper was Captain J.A. Stedman, the former SR Chief Goods Officer who had retained a nostalgic interest in the railway and had presided at the 1935 Reunion Dinner of former employees. Soon an impressive list of potential voluntary helpers was amassed who would be called upon to work in their spare time in building the railway when plans were further advanced.

At first a miniature railway in the style of the revived 15 inch minimum gauge Ravenglass & Eskdale was envisaged but subsequently 2ft gauge was favoured as it would be easier and cheaper to get second-hand equipment of this type. Nominally, there should be no difficulty in obtaining possession of the land, which was still owned by the railway and, while many sections were heavily overgrown, there was nothing that could not be shifted by a bulldozer. Except for the swing bridge, most larger brick-built bridges were still in place and the wooden bridges over streams could fairly easily be replaced using the surviving concrete abutments like the cattle creep (**Fig 184**). It was intended to begin

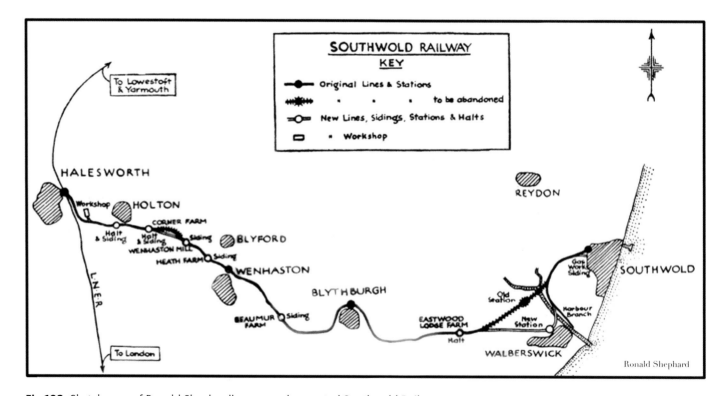

Fig 193: Sketch map of Ronald Shephard's proposed recreated Southwold Railway.

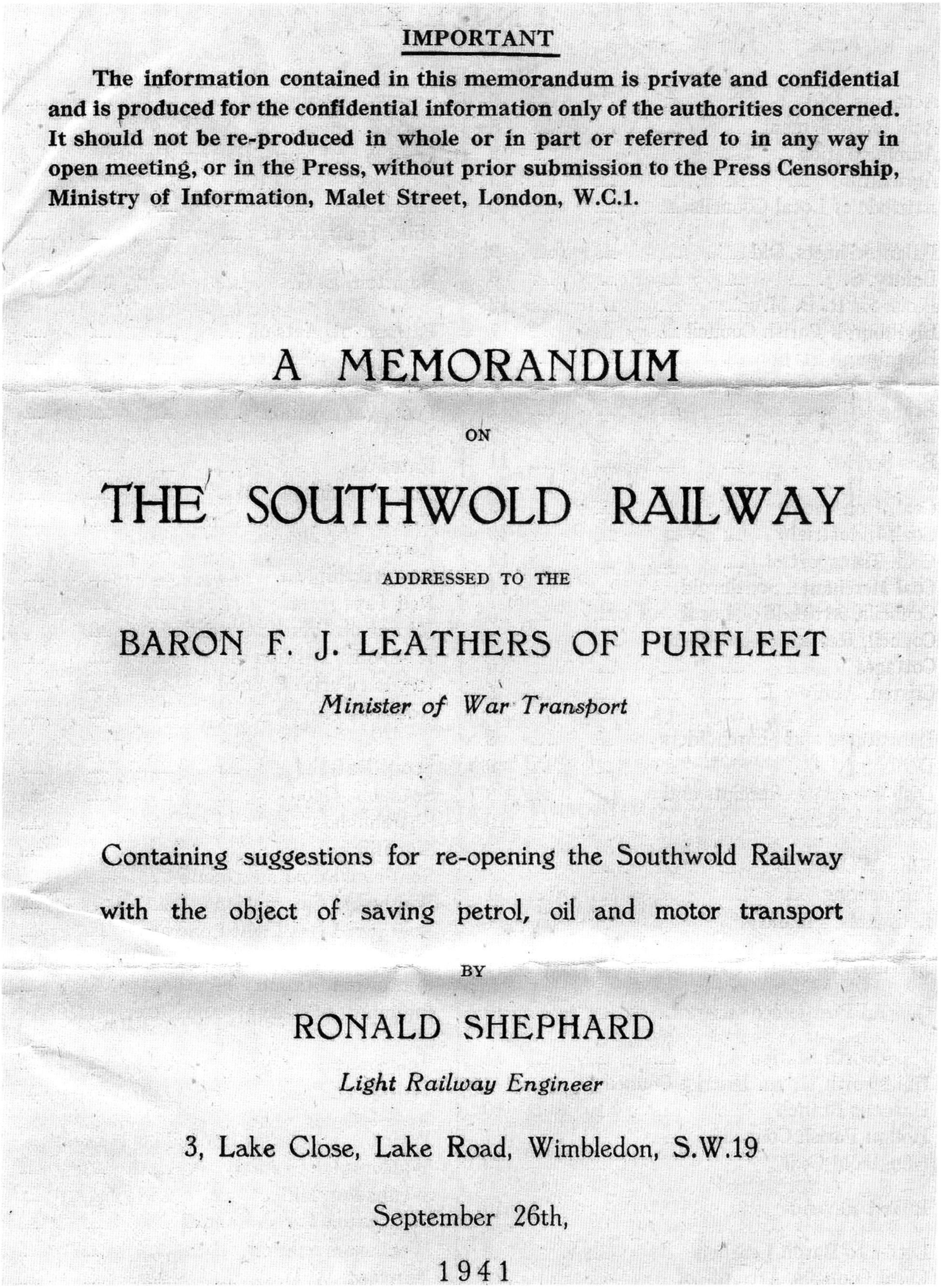

IMPORTANT

The information contained in this memorandum is private and confidential and is produced for the confidential information only of the authorities concerned. It should not be re-produced in whole or in part or referred to in any way in open meeting, or in the Press, without prior submission to the Press Censorship, Ministry of Information, Malet Street, London, W.C.1.

A MEMORANDUM

ON

THE SOUTHWOLD RAILWAY

ADDRESSED TO THE

BARON F. J. LEATHERS OF PURFLEET

Minister of War Transport

Containing suggestions for re-opening the Southwold Railway with the object of saving petrol, oil and motor transport

BY

RONALD SHEPHARD

Light Railway Engineer

3, Lake Close, Lake Road, Wimbledon, S.W.19

September 26th,

1941

Fig 194: Front cover of Ronald Shephard's Memorandum proposing re-opening the Southwold Railway.

reconstruction at Halesworth, whither supplies could more conveniently be delivered. From a railway business point of view Southwold was the more attractive end and it was believed that the pleasure traffic on which the line would rely would mainly originate there.

Although plans and hopes were quite high, no official approach had been made to the existing Southwold Railway Company by 1959. In that year, unaware of the Stedman scheme, the Company instituted proceedings which, if brought to fruition, would mean the end of any hopes of revival. This course had been urged on the Company primarily by Southwold Corporation to whom a large sum was owing in rent, but whose chief anxiety was to obtain possession of the derelict land leased to the railway. The sole surviving Director was Claude Pain, to whom the Company's books had been entrusted at their last Board Meeting on 18 July 1933. In the capacity of Chairman, he addressed an Extraordinary Meeting convened at Haslemere in Surrey – where he lived – on 26 February 1960. The Notice of the Meeting was to discuss the following:

(1) To reduce the number of Directors to three.
(2) To elect three Directors.
(3) To move the principal office to the Town Hall, Southwold.
(4) To register the Company under Part VIII of the Companies Act, 1948.

The nature of the meeting may best be explained by the Chairman's address:

'This is a meeting of the shareholders of the Southwold Railway Company. As required by the relevant Acts of Parliament, notice of the Meeting has been given by newspaper advertisement.

'The present position of the Company is this: It has an issued capital of £49,000, the capital being divided into shares of £10 each. It has debentures outstanding and unsatisfied and a Receiver of the Company's revenue was appointed on behalf of the debenture holders. I, alas, am the sole survivor of the Board of Directors.

'By way of assets, the Company appears to have a sum of money in the High Court of London, representing compensation for the requisitioning for war purposes in about 1941 of the Company's remaining rolling stock and track. It is in Court because, at the time of the requisitioning there was nobody able, in the name of the Company, to give a good receipt for the money to the requisitioning authority, the Ministry of Supply.

'The Company also owns some land, notably the disused station sites, sidings and track sites.

'For many years the Company has been no more than a shell. Its records have been out of date and it has had no proper office and no officer except myself. This was a most unsatisfactory state of affairs, not helped by the fact that, as the last surviving Director, I am of the age mentioned in the notice of this meeting. It seemed sensible therefore that steps should be taken during my lifetime to put the Company's affairs in order.

'The Company's special Act of Parliament and the Companies Clauses Consolidation Acts of 1845 and 1889 are a little out-of-date and provide no ready and simple means of putting the Company's affairs in order. The present legal code for Companies, however, is the Companies Act of 1948 and Counsel has advised that the Company should apply for registration as a Joint Stock Company under that Act. Counsel was Mr Denys Buckley, long regarded as the leading authority on company matters in this country. Since the date of his Opinion, viz July 1959, he has in fact been made a Judge of the Chancery Division. It is on the authority of his Opinion that this meeting has been convened by myself as sole surviving Director. It is on the authority of his Opinion also that the first stage has been taken to bring the Register of Shareholders up to date.

'I am advised that I ought, before closing these remarks, to make one matter clear to the meeting. By Section 69 of the Companies Clauses Act of 1845 it is provided that "No Extraordinary Meeting shall enter upon any business not set forth in the notice upon which it shall have been convened". For the moment, therefore, however, interesting and exciting it may be to hold the first formal meeting of this old Company to be held for many years, the law prohibits us from discussing any business other than that contained in the Notice of this meeting.

'You will all be aware, however, that once the steps on the agenda have been duly taken, the Company will live again, the shareholders will have the opportunity of becoming an articulate body again and the Board will be reconstituted. There will be a few important decisions affecting the Company which could henceforth be taken without reference to any Extraordinary General Meeting of the Shareholders.'

Is the key to the history of the Southwold Railway to be perceived here? The former Engineer speaks nostalgically of the 'interesting and exciting event' of 'holding the first formal meeting of this old Company for many years'. What hollow joy could be obtained from the formation of a new Company whose sole purpose was to destroy the last vestiges of the old? But perhaps the SR Directors' interest was confined to the Boardroom; to them it was 'the Company' that mattered – shareholders and debenture holders, accounts and notices. It had nothing to do with a train puffing up the grade through Blythburgh Woods on a wet rail; that was 100 miles away from a meeting in Haselmere and a Company which could 'live again' without the problems of running a railway.

The resolutions were put and carried. Mr Pain, however, declined a seat on the new Board and N.A. Loftus became the new Chairman. H. Townsend, the Town Clerk of Southwold and the Official Receiver, became Secretary, and he was authorised at a subsequent meeting on 16 June 1960 to register the Company and transfer debentures. The Board were also to concur with Southwold Corporation on appointment of liquidators.

The new Company was registered as a Limited Company on 15 September 1960, with its principal office at the Town Hall, Southwold, and a Compulsory Winding up Order was obtained in the High Court on the application of the Corporation on 17 April 1961.

Following the first meeting of Creditors and Contributories on 11 May 1961, the Official Receiver acted as Liquidator with the task of realising the Company's assets and distributing any monies left over after liabilities had been met (about £1,600 was due to Southwold Corporation in respect of rent charges and rates).

A further incident in the Company's final demise began at Easter 1962 with the compulsory purchase by Suffolk County Council, through the Ministry of Transport, of Southwold Railway land at Blythburgh, including demolition of the A12 railway bridge for road levelling and widening. The new SR Company stated

that they had 'no power to relinquish the Company's Statutory Rights under the 1876 Act' but the bridge was duly demolished. It was a curious reservation – retaining the old Company's 'rights' on the one hand and trying to get rid of them with the other!

The Company records were handed over to the Liquidator, who in the autumn of 1963 appointed Messrs Notcutt & Son, Solicitors of Ipswich, to dispose of the railway land, including the eviction of 'squatters'. As it happens most of the trackbed still survives and can be followed, sometimes by nearby footpaths and, particularly east of Blythburgh, along the railway with lovely views of the Blyth estuary. The larger earthworks – like Lists's Cutting (**Fig 60**) – still have a railway ambience and the coverts are rich in birdlife.

The later twentieth century, and the present time, have seen many railways restored and working again and the question has often been asked: why did the Southwold Railway close? This chapter, and much of this book, has addressed many answers to that question so, to conclude the story of the historic Southwold Railway, here is a summary in no special order of priority:

- The Railway provided passenger transport through a relatively thinly populated area to Southwold which was a popular seaside resort so ticket revenue was very seasonal.
- Goods traffic, especially fish, was also very seasonal and the SR Company's reluctance to build a Harbour Branch meant that Southwold Harbour could never compete with Lowestoft.
- When a Harbour Branch was finally completed it missed in its first year the end of the herring season and the Directors seem not to have known that nearly 90 per cent of the herring catches landed at East Anglian ports was shipped out again to European markets so business in tolls for the Harbour but very little for the Harbour Branch.
- Transhipment – from the Harbour to the Railway and at Halesworth from standard gauge to narrow gauge wagons, and vice versa – was slow, inconvenient and under-staffed. As motor lorries and motor buses were developed the need for transhipment, of passengers and goods, became a fatal weakness.

- In April 1928 Southwold Corporation licensed motor buses to operate within its boundaries which meant the Railway lost much of its passenger traffic. The railway speed limit was 16MPH, buses were allowed 20MPH and, in Southwold, they went to and from the market place in the commercial centre of the town and near the seafront.

- Passenger carriages, especially Third Class, were very functional; hard wooden seats and straw on the floor for winter heating were not very attractive to passengers after the initial novelty of the 'little railway' had been superseded (**Fig 195**).

- The SR Company never had, or earned from the Railway, sufficient capital to carry out extensive improvements to locomotives, rolling stock or permanent way.

- SR Company management was very distant from the Railway. It was sensibly economic in using shared offices in London but needed a senior working representative on the spot, capable of seizing traffic opportunities as readily as the local omnibus management and taking operating decisions swiftly with good local knowledge and contacts.

Fig 195: Interior of a Third Class carriage.

Had the will to restore the Southwold as a Heritage Railway been present in the 1930s, it might have been 'saved'. **Fig 196** is the stock at Halesworth in the mid-1930s and it is the sort of image that generated enthusiasm to restore narrow gauge moribund railways in North Wales, for instance, but it was 20 years too soon.

Fig 196: Goods wagons and carriages at Halesworth in the mid-1930s. Instead, the SR trackbed offers country walks (**Fig 197**) and, perhaps, a new beginning.

Fig 197: List's Cutting; the SR trackbed as a footpath looking towards Blythburgh, 2013.

PART 6

A NEW BEGINNING

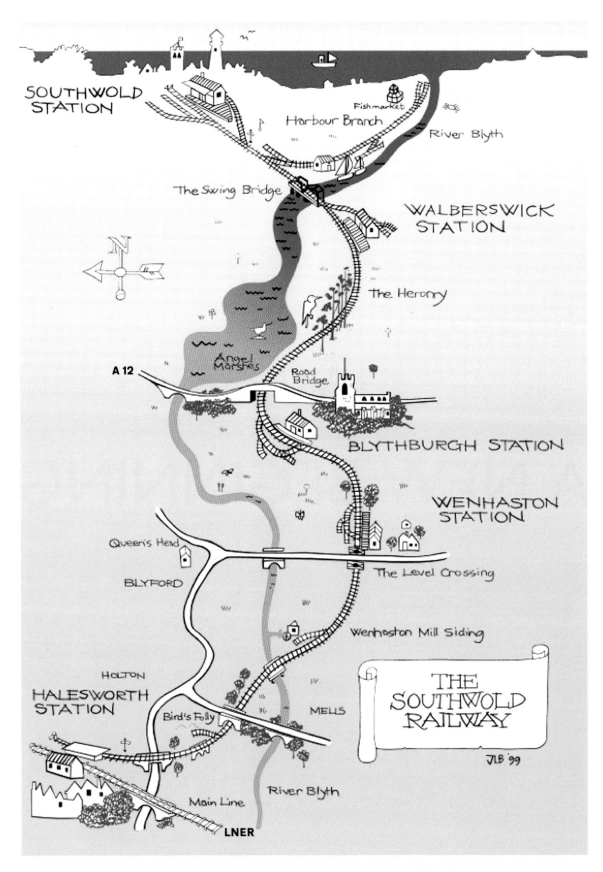

Fig 198: A visualisation of the Southwold Railway and its environs by Southwold architect John Bennett. Can it be built again?

CHAPTER 18

RECREATING THE SOUTHWOLD RAILWAY

'We must not lose sight – through … our enthusiasm
… for [the essence of railway]– that the working
railway is one of the most important dimensions of
our cultural history.
SIR NEIL COSSONS OBE FSA FMA `-
geographer; museum director;
trustee of NHMF

I have agreed with David Lee that I will write this concluding chapter of our book. Like Neil, whom I have known since the 1970s, I am a geographer and a great believer in the holistic vision which geography explores. The subject embraces the physical and the human landscapes in which our cultural history has evolved.

The Southwold Railway was part of the East Suffolk cultural history for fifty years while it was operating and, remarkably, for another ninety years – to the present – in the memory of the area. The physical railway remained almost complete, though becoming over-grown and derelict, until the Second World War; the Railway Company survived until 1963; some buildings – like Southwold Station – remained until the 1980s and the trackbed, including some bridges, is largely extant today. Many folk, like me, recall exploring these remains, walking along the former trackbed and occasionally discovering a little more – like the fragment of track not quite buried in vegetation near Blythburgh (**Fig 199**).

Research uncovered more of the railway story but in Southwold in the late twentieth century there were still fragments of oral history to hear – for instance in some of the town's pubs and in the Sailors' Reading Room. The Sailors' Reading Room was a teetotal place of refuge and relaxation overlooking the sea on East Cliff Southwold.

Fig 199: Rob Shorland-Ball discovers an SR rail-end on the former trackbed near Blythburgh, 2004.

It opened in June 1864, as a gift from the widow of Captain Charles Rayley RN (1780-1863) and became:

'A well managed Institution for the benefit of mariners, liberally supplied with books and newspapers, and with such attractive features as billiards and bagatelle boards. The Rooms are open at a small fee for the use of residents and visitors.'

Remarkably, and I like to think an omen for the recreated Southwold Railway, the Rooms are still open today and offer a snug and quiet retreat from cold onshore winds and the bustle of the town (**Fig 200**).

I know from personal experience that some elderly Southwold residents still come in regularly for a 'warm' and a 'sit down'. Many, if not rushed, are happy to recall times past and that includes memories and stories of the Southwold Railway; not all the recollections are entirely accurate, but they are entertaining and the tellers are part of the town's cultural history.

In Chapter 17, we have outlined some of the proposals to re-open, and subsequently to recreate, the Southwold Railway. Once the original Company was finally wound-up in the autumn of 1963, planning for a recreated Southwold Railway became feasible but the 1960s were not good times for existing railways let alone for the re-opening of long-closed ones. Dr Richard Beeching's two seminal documents *The Reshaping of British Railways* and *The Development of the Major Railway Trunk Routes* were published in 1963 and 1965, respectively. But railways and especially heritage railways and community railways are now, more than 50 years after Beeching, offering prospects for development, for social transport services, educational resources and for enhancing well-being in rural areas where volunteer involvement can bring about projects once thought to be impossible.

It is helpful, too, to review the course of the Southwold Railway and the particular difficulties which would have to be addressed if a re-creation was possible. The map (**Fig 201**) from David Lee's extensive reference files gives a useful overview. The numbered yellow squares are explained below:

1. The Southwold Railway's Halesworth station, which adjoined the main-line station, has gone and the site is now occupied by a housing development. And, even if Halesworth (SR) could be recreated, the SR bridge over Holton Road has been removed. Until it could be replaced there would be no link between a

Fig 200: Sailors Reading Room, East Cliff, Southwold. 2010. Where oral history lives! (from: *The Sailors' Reading Room. The First 150 Years from 2nd June 1864*. Douglas R. Pope, COMPILIER. The Southwold Trust. 2013).

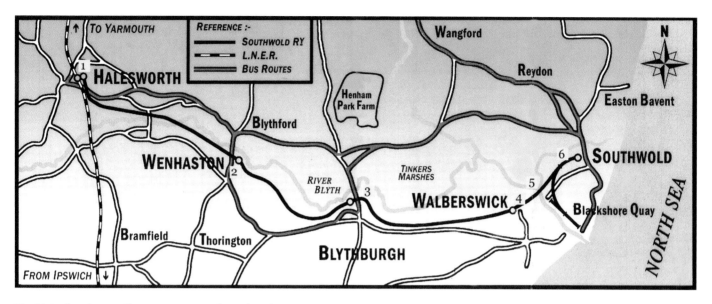

Fig 201: Sketch map illustrating routes by rail and road to Southwold and, by numbered yellow squares, difficulties to be addressed if the Southwold Railway is recreated on its original route.

recreated Halesworth (SR) station and the SR trackbed across the road.

2. The road leading to Wenhaston village is narrow and includes some poor sightlines for drivers seeking to pass oncoming traffic. The SR's only public road level crossing was here and restoring it may be possible but needs careful and extensive negotiation with the Highway Authority and the Office of Rail & Road.

3. At Blythburgh the SR bridge has been removed and the A12 widened. The road is very busy and although there is an existing Level Crossing on the A12 at Darsham, south of Blythburgh, it seems unlikely that a new Level Crossing would be permitted at Blythburgh.

4. Walberswick Station is over a mile's walk on a rutted and, in winter, muddy track from the facilities in Walberswick village and the beach south of the Harbour mouth.

5. The SR swing bridge has gone, and the cylindrical caisson on which it revolved. The current bridge is a relatively light-weight structure which can only carry foot traffic and bicycles. A new railway and footpath bridge is possible in engineering terms but likely to be expensive.

6. Southwold Station site has now been built on so any terminus will be more than half-a-mile from Southwold Pier, the Market Square or the cliffs and beach.

If one believes that 'difficulties' are really opportunities for new thinking, then all the six points listed from the map can be overcome given the will, the resources, the support of landowners, residents, and of local authorities. The Southwold Railway Project needed an engine to drive it and that finally came about in 1994. The Southwold Railway Society (SRS) was set up in 1994.

A brief history of the SRS, and the several possible schemes which were explored, is in the Society's own publication *Southwold Railway News* August 2005. Ostensibly the Project was – in the words of the header of the *News* - 'To restore the Southwold Railway from Halesworth to Southwold' but the 2005 Phase I proposal ignored the Halesworth end of the line, by-passed Blythburgh and then followed an entirely new route on the northern side of the River Blyth to a station near Southwold Pier (**Fig 202**).

I had a personal interest in the SRS because in 2003 I had read of their activities in the *Heritage Railway* magazine so, in the course of an autumn bird-watching holiday in Southwold, I arranged to meet SRS Chairman John Bennett, a Southwold architect. I explained to John my railway, museums and freelance consultancy background, agreed to join the SRS and offered my services to the Project. John was very courteous, seemed very interested in what I might offer, and agreed to contact me when I could be useful. Apparently I was not useful because I heard no more and when I learned

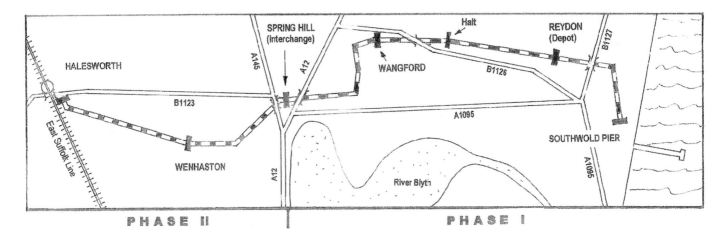

Fig 202: Southwold Railway Society's (SRS) proposed new route for a 'Southwold Railway' following a very different course than the original railway shown in **Fig 201**. Published by SRS in *Southwold Railway News* August 2005.

that the SRS planned to build *a* Southwold Railway and not to recreate *the* Southwold Railway I ceased to be an SRS member.

Perhaps I was not alone because in 2006 SRS became Southwold Railway Trust and, in due course, new thinking agreed that the new railway should be, so far as was practicable, a replica of the Southwold Railway in its main particulars. The recreated Railway was to be 3ft gauge again – unique for passenger services in the British Isles except for the original Ravenglass & Eskdale Railway (no longer extant at that gauge), Southend Pier Railway and the Isle of Man Railways which still operate one steam line from Douglas to Castletown and Port Erin and the Manx Electric Railway at the original 3ft gauge. It was to follow, wherever possible, the original trackbed and, by clever civil engineering at Blythburgh, pass under the A12 and continue through the Heronry and Tinker's Woods to Walberswick Common and, perhaps, to a Southwold terminus not too far from the original station site.

Some of this new thinking may be attributed to James Hewett who became Chairman of SRT in 2015. He was born and raised in Suffolk, a Cambridge University graduate and involved in heritage railway development and operation for much of his life inspired, he says, when as an eight-year old he saw the decaying but surviving Southwold Railway Station building. James decided (as young but determined children do) that the unique, historic and classic Victorian narrow gauge railway must be recreated. He told the *Southwold Organ* local news journal in July 2015:

'I will certainly not live to see the restored SR Victorian train meandering gently down the Blyth Valley between Southwold and Halesworth, as it did in 1879. Heritage railways are expensive in time, effort and cash; my last railway, the Welsh Highland Railway which runs through the Snowdonia National Park, took 60 years and several tens of millions to rebuild. But I very much hope, before I am no longer able to enjoy it, to see the Southwold Railway on its way to do for Southwold, Halesworth, Wenhaston and Blythburgh what the North Norfolk Railway does for Sheringham, Weybourne and Holt.

'The British invented railways; it is only right that we celebrate that fact.'

I agree with James and, although I did not become a paid-up member of the Southwold Railway Trust until 2015, I followed their activities and liked what I read. I have been interested in railway history, operation and preservation for more than sixty years but I am a realist, too. As older men still say in Yorkshire, 'Yer cannot mek owt wi' nowt' so the idea of a recreated Southwold Railway may be an attractive one but the reality of it means the sort of thinking and forward planning that SRT advocates:

The Southwold Railway Trust exists to promote awareness of the heritage of the old Southwold Railway (which closed in 1929), preserve any remaining artefacts of the railway and instigate re-instatement of the railway as a local community & public amenity connecting Southwold to the main line at Halesworth.

Company Aims: The Southwold Railway Trust…

- is determined to build an operating railway on part or all of the original Southwold Railway trackbed, and will therefore continue to pursue such re-instatement until that end is attained
- will to this end (as opportunity arises and where practical) purchase or otherwise acquire any sections of the original trackbed that become available
- will promote, enable and provide environmentally-friendly visitor access to the Southwold Railway trackbed (e.g. guided vintage bus tours between Southwold & Halesworth), and also by promoting public access along the trackbed for walkers and cyclists
- will promote the memory of the SR and foster wider interest therein
- will research, collate and add to the information about the SR, augmenting our existing collection of artefacts and memorabilia in anticipation of the establishment of an Accredited Museum at Wenhaston, or other suitable site
- will publish and otherwise disseminate information via displays at exhibitions and other public events
- will initiate and promote other such activities as may be determined.

I hope this book may be a small contribution to the history and heritage ambitions of the SRT, but David Lee and I know it is a very small contribution and the SRT are progressing with important developments on the ground. Volunteer working parties have researched, explored and where appropriate restored elements of the former SR including: Bird's Folly bridge; the excavated foundations of the Engine Shed at Bird's Folly (**Figs 35** and **205**); Wenhaston station site where some land has been acquired, clearance done, SR-style fences erected and a length of track relayed and Southwold Steam Works created on a site acquired beside the former railway track in Southwold. A 3ft gauge steam locomotive – *Scaldwell* – is now at the Steam Works site as are replica Wagon No 41 and Covered Luggage Van no 40 and work is progressing on new-build locomotive 2-4-0T *Blyth*.

News of the SRT is readily available from the Trust's website: www.southwoldrailway.co.uk and that leads to the SR Blog and many pictures and news of the Trust's work and progress.

Two items already accomplished and mentioned above are the fencing at Wenhaston (**Fig 203**) and the Engine Shed foundations (**Fig 205**).

The quality of the fencing work is apparent in the picture (**Fig 203**) and all done by volunteer working parties. It was good enough to win a Certificate in the 2016 National Railway Heritage Awards – **Fig 204**.

Fig 203: SR trackbed site at Wenhaston owned by the Southwold Railway Trust; SR-style fencing and driftway accomodation crossing gate with some 3ft gauge sleepers and track laid out.

National Railway Heritage Awards

NRHA

The Supporters Award

Highly Commended Certificate
presented to

Southwold Railway Trust
for
Southwold Railway Trackside Fencing

by Paul Maynard MP, Rail Minister
on the 7th December 2016

Fig 204: NRHA Certificate presented to the SRT for SR-style trackside fencing at Wenhaston.

Another achievement, though at the moment less in the public view, is the clearing of the site of the former SR Bird's Folly Engine Shed near Halesworth and the careful excavation of the remaining brick foundations and the inspection pit. The site is owned by the Halesworth Millennium Green Trust – the largest Millennium Green in the country – and the SRT is liaising with them to enhance the public access, safety and educational resource which the Engine Shed site provides.

And finally, the Southwold Railway Steam Works development in Southwold. Planning consent was granted in 2016 for a Visitor Centre, Railway and Nature Reserve on a site in Blyth Road, Southwold IP18 6AZ. **Fig 206** is an edited OS map extract from the 1904 County Survey showing the SR route into Southwold Station and, as a hatched area superimposed on the map, the site. The OS map also shows the original Southwold Gasworks, near to but never rail-connected to the SR despite the daily need for coal to produce gas which was

Fig 205: SRT volunteer working party clearing the foundations of the former Southwold Railway Engine Shed at Bird's Folly Quarry near Halesworth. The outline of the shed, inspection pit and small workshop are at the back of the picture; at the front is an ash pit outside the shed.

piped round Southwold. As Southwold grew, a need for more Gas Holders (sometimes wrongly referred to as 'gasometers') were built on the hatched site on Blyth Road. As natural gas replaced coal gas, the former Gas Works closed and the Blyth Road site was often referred to as 'Southwold Gasworks' though gas was no longer made there. As gas distribution methods improved in the twentieth century the Eastern Gas Board dismantled the Gas Holders and sold off the site. It had several uses,

including by a car dismantler, so the change-of-use the SRT proposed was much more attractive, adjoining the SR trackbed and only about 500 yards from the original SR Station site in Station Road.

Fig 207 is the planning proposal layout including a Visitor Centre; a 7¼ inch gauge miniature railway running around the site; parking for blue badge holders, a landscaped Nature Reserve containing ponds, a wild flower meadow and woodland.

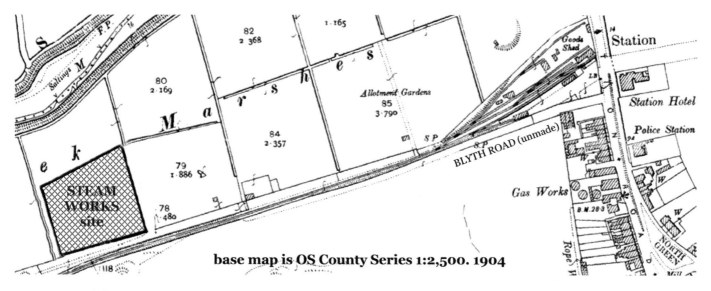

Fig 206: Site of the SRT Steam Works development on Blyth Road 'Southwold' superimposed on a 1904 OS map which shows the course of the Southwold Railway and Southwold Station.

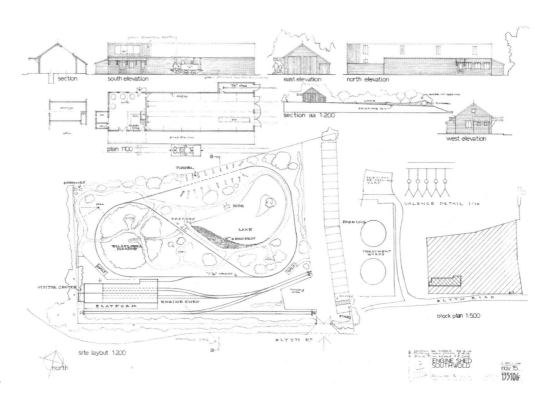

Fig 207: Planning proposal for the SRT Steam Works development submitted November 2015 *from*: John Bennett Architect, Southwold.

After various conditions applicable to the planning permission were discharged, the SRT was able to complete the purchase of the site outlined in **Fig 206** and, almost a year after the application was granted, to begin development work. By August, the first part (about a third) of the main building was broadly complete, with 3ft gauge Peckett saddle tank *Scaldwell* inside. The architect's plan of the 3ft Southwold Railway platform is included in **Fig 207**. And detailed in **Fig 208**.

While this book was being completed in the final months of 2017, the Steam Works site was rapidly developing so it is appropriate to conclude with another 'Architect's vision' of the site which will soon be open for visitors.

If the Southwold Railway Trust's development sites at Halesworth, Wenhaston and Southwold are seen as the parts of a greater whole, there is the beginning of both a Heritage Railway and a Minor Railway replicating the former Southwold Railway. Unlike the 1960s, when the Southwold Railway Company was finally wound up and Beeching was taking his economic surgeon's knife to much of British Railways, the twenty-first century is a time of resurgence and development for railways.

The Government's Office of Roads & Railways (ORR) states that minor railways and heritage railways are 'lines of local interest,' and many are museum railways or tourist railways that have retained or assumed the character, appearance and operating practices of railways of former times. Several lines that operate in isolation provide genuine transport facilities, providing community links. Most lines constitute tourist or educational attractions in their own right.

The principal support body for Heritage Railways is the Heritage Railway Association or HRA. It is a voluntary-run trade association representing Heritage & Tourist railways, related Museums, Tramways, Cliff Lifts, Railway Preservation Groups and related organisations, so over 300 corporate members in total. The HRA assists and guides Members, who may be any organisation that is heritage-rail related, and is preserving, or helping their visitors understand, or just enjoy, the UK's rich rail-based history. HRA- funded research has shown that Heritage Railways make a major contribution to the economies of the areas they serve both in terms of attracting tourism and of substantial spending on local services. The research suggests a mean benefit to the local economy of around 2.7 times the railway's turnover. In aggregate, this would suggest that the economic benefit nationally is just under £250m.

The SRT is at the beginning of a lengthy volunteer and community project for a recreated Southwold Railway which will benefit the lower Blyth Valley area and enhance the tourist offer in East Suffolk. In 2016 the DCMS funded a £1M competition for rail tourism

Fig 208: Architect's vision of the SR Platform and the Heritage Train shown on **Fig 207** Plan. Note the characteristic SR buffer stop. *from*: John Bennett Architect, Southwold.

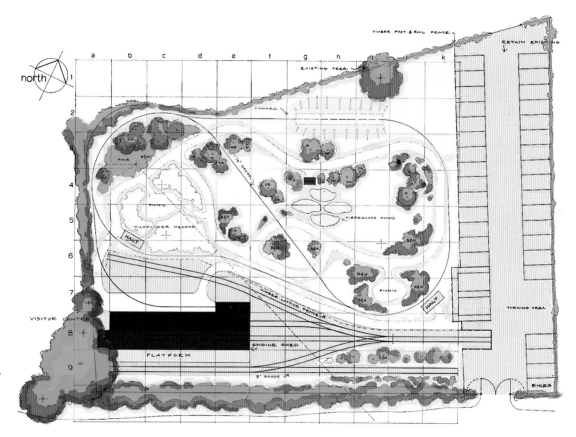

Fig 209: Architect's impression of the developed Steam Works site, Blyth Road, Southwold. *from*: John Bennett Architect, Southwold.

providers and the words of one of the judges, Deirdre Wells OBE, Chief Executive *UK Inbound,* are a fitting ending to this chapter and an ambition for the SRT:

'Heritage and community railways play a vital role in our vibrant and often quirky tourism industry. We want to do all we can to encourage more of the 36M annual inbound visitors to the UK to explore more of our beautiful country by rail.'

And a final picture is the re-born Southwold Railway's seaside terminus (**Fig 210**).

Fig 210: Panorama of Southwold from a boat just offshore. Harbour entrance off to the left, beaches and cliffs across the picture; Lighthouse nearly central; guesthouses, apartments and hotels overlooking the sea and the Pier off to the right. Enjoy Southwold, and one day visit on the re-created Southwold Railway.

LIST OF ILLUSTRATIONS

From my memories of Southwold from the 1950s onwards to the present; time working for BR in the 1950s and 1960s; research in Southwold and Suffolk for my University Dissertation: *A Geographical Study of the Borough of Southwold, Suffolk* (University of Nottingham 1964); time at the National Railway Museum (1987-94) and as Museums Adviser to the HRA, I have been a keen photographer and collector of railway photographs. For this book I have drawn on the extensive picture collections put together by David Lee and the late Alan Taylor; both have checked ownerships and copyright and given me permission to use their pictures in this book. Others have helped too, thank you, and are acknowledged below.

Where there has been any doubt I have tried to contact all possible copyright holders and have checked any unacknowledged images with forensic image search engines. If any have been missed my sincere apologies and would those concerned please contact me at robsb@ wfmyork.demon.co.uk

Fig Nos	Title	Acknowledgements
COVER	Train with some Station staff at Southwold on a busy day. (early 1900s).	David Lee's collection
1	**Frontispiece**: a mixed down train passing through Deadman's Covert between Blythburgh and Walberswick Stations. This image was used by the Railway Company on the 1914 Timetable because it was one of the most attractive sections of the 8.5 mile route.	Author's collection
2	Southwold Station building in the early 1950s.	© Rob Shorland-Ball
3	A peremptory letter from Secretary, and subsequently Manager, H. Ward in London to the operating staff in Suffolk.	RSB and David Lee's collection
4	SR No 1 *SOUTHWOLD* heading the 6.30pm mixed down train at Halesworth, 3 July 1920.	Ken Nunn collection, courtesy John Scott-Morgan
5	1960 sketch map, shows the River Blyth winding its way through extensive marshes to the sea at Southwold.	© Rob Shorland-Ball
6	Sketch plan of GER from LNER Encyclopaedia online. Edited with additions for this book.	Author's collection
7	Notice from the *Suffolk Chronicle . . etc*. expressing concern about EUR proposals to build more branch lines in East Anglia. 3 March 1855.	RSB and David Lee's collection
8	Advertisement of public meeting in Town Hall, Southwold.	From *Halesworth Times* on 19 December 1865. Author's collection
9	Advertisement for private omnibus services running from Southwold to Darsham by Mrs Jane Catton, proprietress of the Swan Hotel, Southwold.	David Lee's collection
10	Copy of Report by C.J. Wall, formerly manager of the Bristol & Exeter Railway, on the traffic expectations of the proposed Southwold railway.	RSB and David Lee's collection
11	First page of Secretary Jellicoe's Report to Shareholders of the Southwold Railway Company.	RSB and David Lee's collection

Fig Nos	Title	Acknowledgements
12	Poster advertising Southwold Railway Opening Day – Wednesday 24 September 1879.	David Lee's collection
13	The *Ipswich Journal* header. Saturday 27 September 1879.	Author's collection
14	The opening of the Woosung Railway in China. The gauge was 2ft 6ins but there are similarities to the 3ft gauge Southwold Railway and some of these similarities are explored later in this book.	© *Illustrated London News*. Author's collection
15	Southwold Railway Prospectus map (undated) Printed by the Southwold Press, 6 & 8 Church Street, Southwold.	RSB and David Lee's collection
16	Pencil sketch of keels on the Blyth. H. Davy c1824.	Author's collection
17	Table illustrating tonnages of goods traffic on the Southwold Railway, 1880 to 1913.	David Lee's research
18	BoT Licence for the maintenance and working of the Southwold Railway 'as a light railway' with a speed limit of 16MPH but less than the 25MPH speed limit permitted on Light Railways defined in the Regulation of Railways Act 1868.	RSB and David Lee's collection
19	Map illustrating a standard gauge extension from Southwold to Kessingland proposed by the Southwold Railway Company.	Author's collection
20	Southwold was a popular holiday resort in the early 1900s.	RSB and David Lee's collection
21	**Fig 21 (above)**: Reg Carter (Southwold artist) keeps up-to-date on English affairs so subsequently – **Fig 21** (below) has to air-brush out 'Votes for Women,' the suffragette, and the branch on which she was sitting!	Stewart Green's collection
22	Front page of: 'Particulars of a proposed Application to Parliament for an Act to authorize the construction of a Railway from Cambridge to Southwold'.	Author's collection
23	Halesworth GER Station and the transhipment facilities from standard gauge to narrow gauge for Southwold Railway in the 1880s. The GER was using heavy horses for shunting which was helpful but slow when one of the problems between the two companies was emptying and releasing the standard gauge wagons.	RSB and David Lee's collection
24	The GER's First Cost Estimate of the civil engineering which had been necessary to create the Southwold Railway.	Author's collection
25	Map which shows the ambitions of the Mid-Suffolk Light Railway Company [MSLR]. This copy is an edited extract from a 1901 MAP SHEWING [sic] ROUTE which was issued with an MSLR Company Prospectus.	RSB and Southwold Museum Archives
26	The MSLR was a standard gauge 'country railway' still operating in the 1950s and very like the Southwold Railway was 30 years earlier. At a level crossing the guard has opened the gates; he then returns to the footplate and the guard, at the back of the train, closes them.	RSB – Courtesy of John Scott-Morgan
27	Layout at Halesworth Station, GER and SR, 1884.	Author's collection
28	A mixed up train arriving at SR's Halesworth Station c1920.	Ken Ledran Penrose's collection
29	Final layout at Halesworth Station, GER and SR, 1922.	Author's collection

Fig Nos	Title	Acknowledgements
30	The SR transhipment platform and goods shed on the right and the GER Halesworth Station platforms on the left.	David Lee's collection
31	Halesworth Station level crossing gates which also include a platform section, on wheels, to provide a lengthened platform for the greater number of passengers travelling to and from Southwold.	David Lee's collection
32	1 – 2,500 OS map extract 1904.	Author's collection
33	Dismantling SR Bridge No 1 over Holton road, Halesworth, in 1962	David Lee's collection
34	Bird's Folly gravel pit: 1 – 2,500 OS 1904 map extract shows both the siding to the pit and the subsequent addition of an engine shed which was required in 1914 to accommodate an additional locomotive.	Author's collection
35	Foundations and inspection pit of the SR Halesworth Engine Shed uncovered and stabilised by a Southwold Railway Trust working party.	SRT – courtesy James Hewett
36	An up mixed train passing a typical accommodation crossing on the way from Southwold in the early 1900s. The railway fences are sound, the crossing gates painted white and the track well-ballasted and weed-free so, it seems, this was a railway proud of its standards, maintenance and appearance.	David Lee's collection
37	SR Bridge No 4, Mells Bridge, under an unclassified road near Corner Farm on what is now the B1123 – photographed in 1994.	© Rob Shorland-Ball
38	Elevation of SR Bridge No 6 near Wenhaston Mill.	Author's collection
39	Steel RSJs and timber baulks supporting the SR track on Wenhaston Mill bridge.	David Lee's collection
40	Edited map extract from 1904 1 – 2,500 OS map.	© Rob Shorland-Ball
41	SR Bridge across the Mill Pond and Wenhaston Water Mill in the background.	David Lee's collection
42	Edited map extract from 1927 1 – 2,500 OS map.	© Rob Shorland-Ball
43	Wenhaston Water Mill and house 1920s.	Author's collection
44	Wenhaston Station and adjoining level crossing – 1880s.	David Lee's collection
45	Final layout of Wenhaston Station, 1921.	Author's collection
46	Picture undated but probably taken in the 1920s and a useful contrast to **Fig 44** from the 1880s. One addition is the telegraph pole which carries telephone wires to the all-stations circuit that was installed in 1899 enabling the Station Masters to communicate with each other for safe working and for dealing with any emergencies which might arise.	David Lee's collection
47	An up mixed train arriving at Wenhaston in 1902 to pick up a number of passengers or, perhaps some villagers meeting friends returning from Blythburgh, Walberswick or Southwold.	David Lee's collection
48	Blythburgh church in 1898. In the middle foreground is an accommodation crossing and Southwold Railway fencing – which is clearly not lamb-proof!	Southwold Museum collections

Fig Nos	Title	Acknowledgements
49	Edited map extract from 1904 1 – 2,500 OS map.	Author's collection
50	Final layout of Blythburgh Station – 1909.	Author's collection
51	View of Blythburgh Station looking towards Southwold and illustrating some of the details on the Station plan, probably from the 1890s.	David Lee's collection
52	Blythburgh Station photographed after 1908 because the brick abutments of the Railway bridge carrying the Yarmouth Turnpike road have replaced the timber props (in **Fig 51**) which were the Company's first response to concerns expressed about the carrying capacity of the bridge as heavy motorised road traffic replaced the horse-drawn traffic of the later nineteenth century.	David Lee's collection
53	Blythburgh Station: the photographer is further back from the road bridge than **Fig 51** and has captured an up mixed train on the platform road, the passing loop empty, the Coal Shed, and four sheeted wagons on the goods siding to the north of the Coal Shed; note that there was no rail connection into the Shed. The churns on the platform, like the single churn in **Fig 52**, show the milk traffic which was probably in both directions and a timbered barrow crossing which would make moving full churns a little easier.	David Lee's collection
54	Blythburgh Station, viewed from the road bridge, shows the carriages of a Southwold bound down train and Odam's shed. This view (**Fig 54**) must date from before September 1908 when the passing loop shown in the Station plan was completed and inspected by the BoT. Here it is a siding for Odam's shed and unloading platform. The functional simplicity of the buffer-stop at the end of the siding is typical of the Southwold Railway and can also be found in an illustration of the Harbour Branch.	David Lee's collection
55	Blythburgh Station, viewed from the road bridge and after 1908 when Odam's Manure Co. had sold their shed to the Railway Company. A down mixed train and a crowded platform perhaps in the 1910s.	David Lee's collection
56	Edited OS map extract from a 1-10,560 (or 1 inch) map dated 1938 but still showing the Southwold Railway, and its Harbour Branch, which had been disused since 1927.	© Rob Shorland-Ball
57	A mixed down train passing through Deadman's Covert between Blythburgh and Walberswick Stations – 1900s.	Author's collection
58	Accommodation crossing and adjoining gradient post in Tinker's Covert looking towards Southwold.	David Lee's collection
59	List's embankment, 2015.	© Rob Shorland-Ball
60	List's cutting, 2015.	© Rob Shorland-Ball
61	The original Walberswick Station – 1890s.	David Lee's collection
62	Walberswick Station enlarged in 1902.	David Lee's collection
63	Final layout Walberswick Station 1902.	Author's collection

Fig Nos	Title	Acknowledgements
64	Original swing bridge across the River Blyth – 1879 to 1907.	David Lee's collection
65	Footbridge over Southwold Cutting for members of Southwold Golf Club – and used by folk enjoying the sunshine.	David Lee's collection
66	Original layout for Southwold Station – 1879.	David Lee's collection
67	Final layout for Southwold Station until closure in 1929.	Author's collection
68	Elevation and Plan of Southwold Station building from GER Valuation of 1892 & 1894.	Author's collection
69	Panoramic view of Southwold Station approach and, in the background, Pier Avenue Hotel in the early twentieth century.	Ken Ledran Penrose's collection
70	Southwold Station: the busy platform and the well-dressed passengers show the relative prosperity of Southwold, and of the Railway, in the early 1900s. However, the problems brought by the First World War and the growing competition from motor buses – and from motor lorries – did not bode well for the Railway's long-term sustainability.	David Lee's collection
71	GER motor bus from and to Lowestoft outside the Swan Hotel, Southwold Market Place.	Author's collection
72	SR Edmundson card tickets, for bicycles and dogs accompanying passengers.	Southwold Museum & Archive
73	Map based on and edited from a map in Thomas Gardner's book, *History of Dunwich* which shows the coastal changes engendered by erosion that have almost obliterated Dunwich and given Southwold its present sea-scape.	© Rob Shorland-Ball
74	Southwold Harbour on map extract edited from OS County Series 1- 2,500 for 1904.	© Rob Shorland-Ball
75	Southwold Harbour on map extract edited from OS County Series 1- 2,500 for 1927.	© Rob Shorland-Ball
76	Southwold Harbour Fish Quay and the Kipperdrome with several Scottish steam drifters alongside.	Author's collection
77	Blyth steam-powered chain ferry lands on the Southwold shore in 1904.	© Alfred John ('Jack') Bootman; Mike Bootman's collection
78	Aerial view of the inner Southwold Harbour area in the 1980s showing the high-lighted ground-shadow of the SR main line and the Harbour Branch.	© Rob Shorland-Ball
79	Farrow of Brixton were the contractors who laid the Harbour Branch – using this temporary railway on the line of the Branch (see embankment in background).	David Lee's collection
80	Sketch plan, from OS maps, of the Southwold Harbour Branch junction.	© Rob Shorland-Ball
81	Southwold Railway Harbour Branch multi-gauge weighbridge on the Fish Quay – early 1920s but already boarded up.	David Lee's collection
82	Southwold Railway Harbour Branch track to the Fish Quay – mid 1920s. The fence to the left is beside the Ferry path.	David Lee's collection

Fig Nos	Title	Acknowledgements
83	Remains of Blackshore Quay siding and a timber buffer-stop similar to the one shown at Blythburgh in **Fig.54**.	David Lee's collection
84	Wealthy passengers and 'quality' luggage at Southwold c1900.	David Lee's collection
85	Opening paragraphs of the Railway Act 1921 which, by grouping together most railway companies, created four principal companies – LNER, SR, GWR, LMS.	Courtesy Michael Perrins
86	List's bank and the Heronry on the banks of the River Blyth between Blythburgh and Walberswick Stations.	David Lee's collection
87	Unloading goods traffic at Southwold Station – 1920s.	David Lee's collection
88	Loading goods at Southwold Station – 1920s. Staff, left to right at front of picture are: Porter Stannard; Guard Burley; Porter Fisk.	David Lee's collection
89	Closure of the Southwold Railway announced in a front page Notice, *Halesworth Times*, Wednesday 10 April 1929.	Author's collection
90	The 5.23pm ex-Southwold was the last Southwold Railway up passenger train on 11 April 1929.	David Lee's collection
91	Last Southwold Railway up train, 11 April 1929. Major Debney is on the carriage steps; he also travelled on the first train in September 1879. On the platform is Mr Hurst, Southwold Borough Council Surveyor.	David Lee's collection
92	Station Master Girling's farewell to his staff at Southwold, April 1929. From left to right: FRONT ROW Guard Burley; Fireman Adamson; Station Master Girling; Porter Aldis; Doy's driver Self. BACK ROW GPO Telegraph Clerk Marchant; Porter Fisk; and Arnold Barrett Jenkins (with camera).	David Lee's collection
93	Former Station Master Girling on the platform of Southwold Station in the early 1980s. Mr Girling's memories have been very helpful in telling this story of the Southwold Railway's history and operation. It was a sad but pertinent chance that there is an Eastern Counties bus in the background of this picture.	David Lee's collection
94	Well ballasted SR track and wayside fencing east of Blythburgh	David Lee's collection
95	Track through Southwold Common cutting illustrating superelevation on a curve and quality of track-laying and ballast. The footbridge was a later addition in 1903.	David Lee's collection
96	Detailed drawing of SR track from GER Survey of the Southwold Line carried out in 1892 / 1894 in preparation for a possible take-over purchase by the GER.	Author's collection
97	Southwold Railway bridge under the A12 at Blythburgh from the GER Survey of the Southwold Railway 1892 / 1894 by which time it had been necessary to place substantial props under the bridge and to improve the decking.	Author's collection
98	Section of SR 30lb per yard rail.	© Rob Shorland-Ball
99	SR permanent way fastenings – dog-spike, fang bolt and triangular fanged nut.	© Rob Shorland-Ball

Fig Nos	Title	Acknowledgements
100	Original swing bridge 1879 to 1907.	David Lee's collection
101	GER Civil Engineer drawing of the original swing bridge - 1892.	Author's collection
102	Rebuilt swing bridge open in September 1907 while testing. Although there has always been general public interest in the swing bridge, it was opened so infrequently that pictures like this are rare and unusual. The men on the bank in the left foreground are holding a hawser attached to the bridge which is the only means of swinging it open, and closed. Note the bowler-hatted figure on the bridge; typically, if he is the Foreman, he is only supervising, not pulling on the rope!	David Lee's collection
103	The rebuilt and widened swing bridge showing the radiused cross-bracings between the two side spans which identify and date the rebuilt bridge in pictures.	David Lee's collection
104	Morton's workmen rebuilding the swing bridge – 4 September 1906.	David Lee's collection
105	Track-side view of Morton's workforce on the rebuilt swing bridge.	David Lee's collection
106	Track over Woodsend Marshes towards Southwold Common cutting in the distance. Any standard gauge Lengthsman would be proud of this length: well ballasted, superelevation on the curve, no weeds, fences at the foot of the low embankment, clear drainage ditches, gradient post to the LHS and milepost to the RHS.	David Lee's collection
107	No 1 SOUTHWOLD working the 3.30pm down train near Halesworth 3 July 1910.	David Lee's collection
108	Southwold Railway Timetable [facsimile] 4 October 1914 to 31 March 1915 – page 20. **UP TRAINS – TRAIN SERVICE TO LONDON.**	© Rob Shorland-Ball
109	Southwold Railway Timetable [facsimile] 4 October 1914 to 31 March 1915 – page 29. **DOWN TRAINS – TRAIN SERVICE FROM LONDON.**	© Rob Shorland-Ball
110	Final layout for Southwold Station until closure in 1929.	Author's collection
111	No 1 SOUTHWOLD on the 6.30pm mixed down train at Halesworth 3 July 1920.	Ken Nunn collection, courtesy John Scott-Morgan
112	Wenhaston Station Master demonstrates a signal – lamp has been lowered.	David Lee's collection
113	A down train approaching Southwold Station Advance Home signal. 1920s.	David Lee's collection
114	The left hand staff is for the Southwold to Blythburgh block section and that on the right hand for Blythburgh to Halesworth so two blocks with Blythburgh as a mid-point and change of staffs for a through train, which nearly all were.	RSB & David Lee's collection
115	A Walberswick / Blythburgh Train Staff Ticket.	RSB & David Lee's collection

Fig Nos	Title	Acknowledgements
116	The short-lived Walberswick / Blythburgh staff with a hexagonal head and no Annetts key.	RSB & David Lee's collection
117	Royal insignia at head of Act to Amend the Regulation of Railways Acts – 30 August 1899.	Author's collection
118	Southwold Railway Working Timetable and Staff Instructions 1 July to 30 September 1913 – **Private: for use of the Company's Servants only**.	Author's collection
119	Memorial in St Edmund's Churchyard, Southwold, recording the death of Edward Court 'WHO LOST HIS LIFE ON THE SOUTHWOLD RAILWAY NOV 14 1885 AGED 17 YEARS'.	© Rob Shorland-Ball
120	An up mixed train arriving at Halesworth SR Station with, in this example, five 4-wheel wagons, two 4-wheel vans and at least two of the Cleminson Patent 6-wheel carriages. No record now exists of the consist of the up train in the Wenhaston accident but let us suppose it was the same as the train at Halesworth.	Ken Ledran Penrose's collection
121	Wenhaston Station layout sketch map illustrating some elements of Station Master Harry Girling's fatal accident, 24 December 1926.	© Rob Shorland-Ball
122	Elevation and Plan of SR underbridge No 8 at Wenhaston.	Author's collection
123	Figure-of-eight coupling link.	RSB & David Lee's collection
124	Sketch of 'chopper'-type buffer coupling.	© Rob Shorland-Ball
125	Southwold Railway gradient profile annotated to show where a too-rapid closing of the loco regulator caused a sudden buffering-up of the train which disengaged a chopper coupling near Walberswick, 3 August 1921.	© RSB / Negus
126	A view from the swing bridge (behind the photographer) towards the Southwold Common cutting after the 1897 gale and floods scoured out the Woods End Marshes embankment.	David Lee's collection
127	Workmen re-ballasting the Woods End Marshes embankment.	David Lee's collection
128	'We are not complaining.' Mothers, perambulator, children, dog beside carriage at Southwold Station.	RSB & David Lee's collection
129	'We are not complaining – but we wish we could get away to the beach . . .' Mother and two young children getting off carriage at Southwold Station.	RSB & David Lee's collection
130	Portrait of Arthur Pain in retirement loaned by his great-grandson, Simon Pain.	Courtesy of Simon Pain
131	Southwold Railway Guard Wright in his frock-coat uniform.	RSB & David Lee's collection
132	No 3 BLYTH on up train with Station staff: left to right – Finch [Booking Clerk]; Stannard [Driver on footplate]; Moore [Fireman]; Self [Doy's dray driver]; Cox [Porter / Shunter]; Case [Lad Porter]; Calver [Southwold SM 1900 to1908]; Bailey [Goods Porter - under tree].	David Lee's collection

Fig Nos	Title	Acknowledgements
133	Southwold Station staff on the goods stage: - left to right – King [Porter]; Stannard [Driver]; Steadman [Goods Clerk]; Fisk [Porter]; Moore [Foreman Porter]; Jackson [Loco Foreman].	David Lee's collection
134	Doy's dray and driver George Self in Southwold Station yard	David Lee's collection
135	List of Southwold Railway Directors, Auditors, Manager and Secretary with London office address from page 5, Southwold Railway Timetable 4 October 1914 to 31 March 1915.	Author's collection
136	Front cover of Halesworth Station Master's Wet Copy Letter Book. The book belongs to David Lee and he has had it professionally rebound because it was falling apart; the hard front shown here illustrates the long-service wear and tear on a book over 100 years old.	© Rob Shorland-Ball
137	Letter from Halesworth Station Master W. Calver's Wet Copy Letter Book to SR Secretary Carne 15 July 1890. Calver wrote a neat, round hand but deciphering this letter is not easy!	RSB & David Lee's collection
138	Fireman Albert Stannard and Driver Nealey Fiske on their footplate.	RSB & David Lee's collection
139	Drawing No 1: The first three Sharp, Stewart locomotives.	Alan Taylor's collection © D. Clayton
140	No 1 SOUTHWOLD 1879 to 1883.	Alan Taylor's collection © D. Clayton
141	No 2 HALESWORTH in maker's lined grey 1879.	Alan Taylor's collection © D. Clayton
142	Ex-Southwold Railway No 1 working on the Santa Marta Railway, Colombia c1900.	David Lee's collection
143	No 2 HALESWORTH in steam on a GER flat wagon after overhaul and awaiting return from Stratford Works to Halesworth. 1909.	David Lee's collection
144	No 4 WENHASTON. Manning Wardle works photo. 1914.	David Lee's collection
145	Drawing No 2: No 4 WENHASTON 0-6-2T was a more powerful locomotive than the Sharp, Stewarts and liked by footplate crews. It became the last working locomotive on the railway.	Alan Taylor's collection © D. Clayton
146	No 3 BLYTH shunting at Southwold on an apparently windless day.	David Lee's collection
147	Fireman Adamson on No 4 WENHASTON footplate and A N Others.	David Lee's collection
148	Southwold Railway Locomotive Foreman William Jackson on the SR from 1879 to 1916.	David Lee's collection
149	0-4-2T No 1 SOUTHWOLD outside Southwold Engine Shed. Driver Collett on footplate, Fireman Moor on step and Driver Stannard with oil can c1908.	David Lee's collection
150	2-4-0T HALESWORTH heads a mixed down train at Southwold.	RSB – Courtesy of John Scott-Morgan

Fig Nos	Title	Acknowledgements
151	Interior & exterior views of 1st class carriages for railways of 2ft 6ins – (Shanghai & Woosung Railway [S&WR]) – to 3ft 6ins gauge. from: Richard Rapier. *Remunerative Railways for New Countries* (E. & F. N. Spon 1878).	Author's collection
152	SR carriages after unloading from standard gauge flat wagons at Halesworth in 1879.	David Lee's collection
153	Drawing No 3: Measured drawing of Carriages 1 to 6 as originally delivered with open verandahs.	Alan Taylor's collection © D. Clayton
154	Detail of an SR carriage coupling showing the weight securing the pin which locked the chopper coupling in a closed position.	David Lee's collection
155	Third class carriage No 2 as built with an open end; it was never rebuilt. The next carriage has an enclosed verandah-end which improved conditions inside, especially in winter.	David Lee's collection
156	Carriage No 1 First Third composite in the 1920s. It was converted from Third in 1912.	David Lee's collection
157	Drawing No 4: Measured drawing of carriages 1,3 & 6 as rebuilt after the First World War with the former verandahs enclosed.	Alan Taylor's collection © D. Clayton
158	Passenger comfort. Interior of a third class carriage; note the strip of carpet along the wooden benches.	RSB – Courtesy of John Scott-Morgan
159	Drawing No 5: Measured drawings of original and rebuilt vans and the 4-wheel wagons. 6-wheel wagon dimensions are on Drawing 4 – **Fig 157**.	Alan Taylor's collection © D. Clayton
160	4-wheel van 13, delivered new in 1885 and shown before rebuilding in 1918.	David Lee's collection
161	4-wheel van no 14 as rebuilt and lengthened in 1918. The van body was discovered and returned to the Southwold Station site in 1962 then subsequently moved to the East Anglian Transport Museum, near Lowestoft.	David Lee's collection
162	4-wheeled dropside open wagon No 4 of 1879 with high ends. Behind is a standard gauge Southern Railway wagon. Photographed at Halesworth in the 1920s.	David Lee's collection
163	Maker's photo of 4-wheel, four plank drop-side wagon No 16.	David Lee's collection
164	6-wheeled three plank wagons nos 31 & 37 of 1899 and 1922 respectively being shunted by No 3 *BLYTH* at Southwold in 1928.	David Lee's collection
165	4-wheeled open wagon loaded with coal on a mixed train. The photographer was on the open verandah of the carriage behind the wagon.	David Lee's collection
166	Private-owner 6-wheeled wagon No 1511. Maker's photograph mid-1880s.	David Lee's collection
167	No 3 *BLYTH* with an up goods train in the siding at Southwold Station c1908.	David Lee's collection
168	'Eyore' would not welcome a fence across 'his' railway!	Author's collection

Fig Nos	Title	Acknowledgements
169	Walberswick Station, looking towards Southwold, in 1935.	David Lee's collection
170	Wenhaston Station level crossing c1935.	David Lee's collection
171	Wenhaston Station building, boarded-up and desolate; the Station nameboard survives – c1932.	David Lee's collection
172	Southwold Station 1931. In the background is the Southwold HomeKnit factory and the Station Hotel.	David Lee's collection
173	No 1 *SOUTHWOLD* partially dismantled and subsequently scrapped on site at Southwold Station in May 1929.	David Lee's collection
174	Southwold Station detail – L to R: Water tank; Engine Shed; Goods Office. 1937.	David Lee's collection
175	Winter at Halesworth Station 1937. Carriages at the platform and SR goods wagons in the engine run-round loop. The second carriage in this view was accidentally (?) burnt out by a tramp who had a home in it.	Ken Ledran Penrose collection
176	No 3 *BLYTH* derelict and partly vandalised in the remains of Halesworth Engine Shed – November 1935.	Ronald Shephard collection – © WSCC
177	Demolition and removal of Halesworth Station shelter – 1940.	Ronald Shephard collection – © WSCC
178	Wenhaston Water Mill bridge – rail removed for defence purposes – 1940.	Ronald Shephard collection – © WSCC
179	Swing bridge open and disabled by Royal Engineers – 1941.	Ronald Shephard collection – © WSCC
180	No 3 *BLYTH* in the open air and prey to vandals at Bird's Folly Engine Shed, Halesworth.	Ronald Shephard collection – © WSCC
181	Southwold Railway bridge over Holton Road, Halesworth. The standard gauge bridge across this road is immediately to the left of this picture so passengers on the main line saw the SR advertised.	Ronald Shephard collection – © WSCC
182	A final role for the Southwold Station site – as a coal yard c1935.	David Lee's collection
183	Commemorative plaque at Walberswick Station site – 2017.	© Rob Shorland-Ball
184	SR's very functional concrete abutments and the railway embankment pierced by a cattle creep, on Walberswick Common – 2013.	© Rob Shorland-Ball
185	A Bailey Bridge replacing the SR swing bridge across the River Blyth. The view is towards Walberswick: the massive circular piers and the river-side abutments supporting this bridge are original.	© Rob Shorland-Ball
186	**Fig 186**: The *Blyth* was the original Station Hotel. The Police Station on the left of the picture occupies part of the original Southwold Station site and a plaque on the wall, behind the rose, recalls the Railway.	© Rob Shorland-Ball
187	Photographed from the trackbed of the Railway across Woodsend Marshes, the outline of the former Harbour Branch is visible curving away across the field.	© Rob Shorland-Ball

Fig Nos	Title	Acknowledgements
188	SR Van body No 14 conserved, painted and displayed at the East Anglian Transport Museum.	David Lee's collection
189	LNER Internal Memo re Ronald Shephard's negotiations to revive the Southwold Railway.	Author's collection
190	An empty narrow gauge transporter wagon as used on the Ashover Light Railway. The standard gauge track on the wagon is visible on either side of the narrow gauge wagon body. Behind is a loaded standard gauge wagon on an Ashover transporter wagon.	Ronald Shephard collection – © WSCC
191	Schedule of Army depredations on the Southwold Railway.	Author's collection
192	Ronald Shephard's wartime photograph of the remains of the swing bridge mid-river caisson which has now (2017) completely gone.	Ronald Shephard collection – © WSCC
193	Sketch map of Ronald Shephard's proposed recreated Southwold Railway.	Ronald Shephard collection – © WSCC
194	Front cover of Ronald Shephard's 1941 Memorandum proposing re-opening Southwold Railway.	Ronald Shephard collection – © WSCC
195	Interior of a Third Class carriage.	Ronald Shephard collection – © WSCC
196	Goods wagons and carriages at Halesworth in the mid-1930s.	Ronald Shephard collection – © WSCC
197	List's Cutting; the SR trackbed as a footpath looking towards Blythburgh, 2013.	© Rob Shorland-Ball
198	A visualisation of the Southwold Railway and its environs by Southwold architect John Bennett. Can it be built again?	© John Bennett
199	Rob Shorland-Ball discovers an SR rail-end on the former track-bed near Blythburgh, 2004.	© Rob Shorland-Ball
200	Sailors Reading Room, East Cliff, Southwold. 2010. Where oral history lives! (from: *The Sailors' Reading Room. The First 150 Years from 2nd June 1864.* Douglas R. Pope, COMPILIER. The Southwold Trust. 2013).	Author's collection
201	Sketch map illustrating routes by rail and road to Southwold and, by numbered yellow squares, difficulties to be addressed if the Southwold Railway is recreated on its original route.	Author's collection
202	The Southwold Railway Society's (SRS) proposed new route for a 'Southwold Railway' following a very different course than the original railway shown in **Fig 201**.	Southwold Railway Society –Published by SRS in *SOUTHWOLD RAILWAY NEWS* August 2005.
203	SR trackbed site at Wenhaston owned by the Southwold Railway Trust; SR-style fencing and driftway accommodation crossing gate with some 3ft gauge sleepers and track laid out.	Courtesy James Hewett (SRT)
204	NRHA Certificate presented to the SRT for SR-style trackside fencing at Wenhaston.	Courtesy James Hewett (SRT)

Fig Nos	Title	Acknowledgements
205	SRT volunteer working party clearing the foundations of the former Southwold Railway Engine Shed at Bird's Folly Quarry near Halesworth. The outline of the shed, inspection pit and small workshop are at the back of the picture; at the front is an ash pit outside the shed.	Courtesy James Hewett (SRT)
206	Site of the SRT Steam Works development on Blyth Road 'Southwold' superimposed on a 1904 OS map which shows the course of the Southwold Railway and Southwold Station.	© Rob Shorland-Ball
207	Planning proposal for the SRT Steam Works development submitted November 2015 *from*: John Bennett Architect, Southwold.	© John Bennett
208	Architect's vision of the SR Platform and the Heritage Train shown on **Fig 207** Plan. Note the characteristic SR buffer stop. *from*: John Bennett Architect, Southwold.	© John Bennett
209	Architect's impression of the developed Steam Works site, Blyth Road, Southwold. *from*: John Bennett Architect, Southwold.	© John Bennett
210	Panorama of Southwold from a boat just offshore. Harbour entrance off to the left, beaches and cliffs across the picture; Lighthouse nearly central; guesthouses, apartments and hotels overlooking the sea and the Pier off to the right. Enjoy Southwold, and one day visit on the re-created Southwold Railway.	Author's collection
211	Southwold up train approaches Halesworth alongside GER Claud Hamilton 4-4-0 express locomotive. Painted for this book by the late Joe Crowfoot (1946– 2017).	

SOUTHWOLD RAILWAY BRIDGES 1879 TO 1929

DEFINITIONS:

UNDERLINE bridge: a structure carrying the railway *over* whatever is beneath the structure

OVERLINE bridge: a structure built *over the railway* so may need to be protected from the consequences of being struck by derailed railway vehicles

Bridge No	Location (miles & chains from Halesworth)	Type of bridge	Span (in ft and ins)	Abutments	Bridge Construction	Remarks
1	0m 14ch	UNDERLINE – Holton Road	45ft	Brick faced	Lattice, wrought iron	Rebuilt in steel plate in 1907
2	0m 30ch	UNDERLINE – accommodation road	2 x 20ft	Concrete	Concrete – widened in brick in 1907	
3	1m 0.5ch	UNDERLINE – over stream	9ft 5ins	Concrete	Concrete baulks under rails	
4	1m 22.5ch	OVERLINE – Mells Road (*unclassified*)	19ft 7ins	Concrete	Concrete top	'Balls Bridge'
5	1m 56.5ch	UNDERLINE – over stream	17ft	Timber	Timber baulks under rails	
5a	1m 58ch	UNDERLINE – flood relief	*not known*	*not known*	*not known*	20/03/1914 Cost £25.00
6	1m 63ch	UNDERLINE – viaduct over River Blyth and New Cut	92ft 8ins	Timber	Timber baulks under rails	15/09/1911 Strengthened by 9 new piles
7	1m 65ch	UNDERLINE – Mill leat	30ft	Timber	Rolled steel joints supporting sleepers	'Ketts Bridge' also known as 'Water Mill Bridge'
8	2m 49ch	UNDERLINE – over stream	16ft 3ins	Concrete (west) Timber (east)	Baulks under rails	
9	2m 64ch	UNDERLINE – over stream	16ft 8ins	Concrete (west) Timber (east)	Baulks under rails	Culvert
10	3m 61ch	UNDERLINE – over stream	48ft	None	Timber baulks under rails	'Youngs Bridge'

Bridge No	Location (miles & chains from Halesworth)	Type of bridge	Span (in ft and ins)	Abutments	Bridge Construction	Remarks
11	4m 72ch	OVERLINE – A12 road	18ft approx (later reduced)	Concrete	Timber deck	Yarmouth Turnpike Demolished 1962
12	7m 19ch	UNDERLINE	14ft 7ins	Concrete	Rolled steel joints supporting sleepers	Cattle creep
13	7m 74.5ch	UNDERLINE – Swing bridge over River Blyth	146ft	Concrete (Walberswick side) 2 cast iron cylinders (Southwold side)	Wrought iron Rebuilt in steel 1906 / 07	Centre span swings open to clear 57ft for river traffic. Each side spans in timber, replaced in steel 1914
14	9m 25ch	OVERLINE – footbridge over Southwold Common Cutting for Golf Course	66ft approx	Concrete with steps	Scrap rail	Built at the expense of Southwold Golf Club

© David Lee

courtesy of Alan Taylor

NOTES ON LINE DRAWINGS OF LOCOMOTIVES AND ROLLING STOCK IN CHAPTERS 15 AND 16

(ORIGINAL © DOUGLAS CLAYTON)

These drawings– which are all in Chapters 14 and 15 – have been prepared from several sources:

- Locomotives from makers' drawings
- Rolling stock from the sketches and measurements made by Arnold Barrett Jenkins when the stock was lying derelict at Halesworth
- Careful scrutiny of all available photographs.
- Data obtained from the 1962 find of the surviving body of van 14.

The aim has been twofold: to make a permanent record of the Southwold Railway stock within the limits of information available, and to provide modellers with reasonably accurate data.

In addition to original differences between batches of coaches or wagons, many were modified on repair or rebuild. Known major differences are indicated on the drawings but it is possible that some small details of individual stock may have escaped record; readers requiring fullest details of a particular vehicle are advised to study appropriate photographs. In SR train formation vehicles, the buffer couplings ensured close coupling so photographs cannot usually reveal details of carriage, wagon or van ends.

On all the drawings, an arrow indicates the direction of view of the end and relates either to Halesworth or to Southwold. The Railway never possessed a turntable, so stock was always the same way round in operation, and therefore in photographs. All rolling stock wheels are assumed to be two feet diameter.

DRAWING No. 1 (Page: xxx): Locomotives *Blyth, Halesworth, Southwold*. This shows the basic outline of the 2-4-0T and the rear of the 2-4-2T (where different from the former) and is based on Sharp, Stewart Drawings 6853 dated 13/3/1874 and 8886 dated 5/4/1893, each of which have only a sectional side elevation and a sectional plan view. The external views of the ends and some of the plan have been built up by projection with confirmation from photographs. Each half of the end views shows either the one type or the other as noted, and a section through a locomotive tank is of the LH side to rear in front of the tank filler. The dimensions are as given on the Sharp, Stewart drawings, except where marked X which have been obtained by addition or subtraction. Details to be noted from the drawings are:

- Buffer beams are not single plates, but each side of the frame are separate pieces thinner than the central section
- As built the 2-4-0T had solid bushed ends for coupling and connecting rods but 2 and 3 were later altered to marine type as supplied new to the 2-4-2T
- The sand box added to the front of the tank was placed on the RH side only. Size is estimated from photographs
- Front and rear carrying wheels are mounted in radial axle boxes.

DRAWING No. 2 (Page: 169): Locomotive *Wenhaston*. This is based on an undated Manning Wardle drawing for Order No. 70000, which gives only a side view and half-section plan. The external end views and plan have been built up by projection with confirmation from photographs where possible, though full details of tank tops (especially the filler) are not known. Only RH photographs seem to be available, hence, though the connection between the sandboxes was removed at some time, it is uncertain if the LH sandbox was removed or left in position but out of use. Most dimensions are from the Manning Wardle drawing, with some by addition or subtraction. The height of couplers is as dimensioned on the original drawing and is 12in different from the Sharp, Stewart locos.

In the *Locomotive* of 15 June 1916, p. 120, the cylinders are quoted as 82in. x 15in. rigid wheelbase 7ft 4ins and total wheelbase 11ft 4ins. An alternative Manning Wardle drawing No. 14647, dated 25/2/1914, shows only an outline of side and front but confirms the dimensions of drawing 70000. However, this earlier tracing is otherwise different in many points of detail and is possibly a proposal, the loco being built to the completed and dimensioned drawing No. 70000. Both drawings scale to the dimensions thereon.

DRAWINGS Nos. 3 and 4 (Page: 176 and 180): : Coaches. These drawings are based on Arnold Barrett Jenkins' sketches and dimensions (probably measured from No. 3), supplemented by a close scrutiny of photographs. The 6ft height is obtained by summation – though it is not quite clear how each individual measurement applied – and the other dimensions are based on this 6ft. The length is given as 30ft body and 36ft over headstocks, but as the top step is given as 2ft 6ins with the platform clearly the same length the overall length is estimated as 35ft. The platform length is confirmed by the transposition of the saloon end doors to the platform side of the enclosed vestibule on rebuilding; these doors are understood to have been 2ft wide, from which the width of the body is estimated as 6ft 6ins which is in proportion to the 6ft height. Steps were on south (platform) side only.

Before rebuilding, the main differences were the odd non-opening top-lights, on Nos. 1 and 2 at the Halesworth end and on 3 to 6 at the Southwold end; this feature was retained on rebuilding. The rebuilt coaches 1 and 3 to 6 showed slight differences, mostly as illustrated in drawing No. 4, though different forms of moulding were used also – some flat, some half round, and some were wider

and reached to the bottom of the body. These differences doubtless arose from the fact that only one coach was rebuilt per year. One of the 3 to 6 batch in unrebuilt form ran for a time without the vertical moulding.

In original condition there were three composite coaches: 1, 4 and 5. Coach 1 had the FIRST CLASS at the Halesworth end and the other two at the Southwold end and these characteristics appear to have survived re-building. The position of handbrakes and associated rigging, however, cause considerable difficulty; no photo studied shows clearly this feature on a coach where the number can be read. It is probable that all in fact did have brakes, three at the Halesworth end and three at the Southwold end; with coaches in pairs this would facilitate adjustment. The notes below summarise the knowledge which underpins my assumptions and reflects the difficulty of being definitive from photographic evidence:

- No. 1: As rebuilt had a brake at the Southwold (THIRD CLASS) end, and presumably was built so.
- No. 2: Photograph shows no brake at the Southwold end as built and a dereliction period photo of the Halesworth end shows no brake either. One photograph suggests that No 2 may have had a brake at this end originally, possibly removed when the coach was derelict.
- No. 3: Had a brake at the Southwold end. A photo of an unrebuilt THIRD CLASS coach of the 3 to 6 series [but the number is not visible] shows a brake at the Southwold end but another photo, of No. 6 rebuilt, shows that rebuilt No 6 did *not* have a brake at the Southwold end.
- Nos. 4 and 5: Are both understood to have had brakes. Before re-building one of them had the brake at the Halesworth (THIRD CLASS) end, presumably No. 5 as a photo shows this with no brake at the Southwold end. No. 4, if fitted, must have had the brake at the Southwold (FIRST CLASS) end.
- No. 6: Had no brake at the Southwold end after rebuilding but may have been so fitted at the Halesworth end.

In all cases, the brake fitting was presumably on the off side, the screwed rod being operated by a vertical handwheel via bevel gears in the rebuilt coaches and presumably all similar to No. 1 at appropriate ends. It is unlikely that the position of brakes was altered by re-building.

After re-building no really adequate photographic view shows the offside but it is believed that drawing 3 gives a reasonable approach to the appearance of the closed end corner. The position of partitions is given as far as could be ascertained from photographs and appears to be retained after re-building. However, an exception is No. 1 which did not have a partition at the Southwold end after re-building so the one indicated at the Southwold end must be uncertain in No 1's original form.

Rain strips over windows and possibly on roofs are not visible in early photos and are presumed to have been added a little later. The main window pillars have been drawn slightly over-scale for clarity; Barrett Jenkins' sketch gives the windows as 1ft 9ins long with 3ins timber, but the latter probably applied only to the body corner pillars, the intermediate ones appearing to be no more than 22-2ins wide, which would slightly increase the window length. The 3ins corner pillars would possibly exclude the 2ins window moulding and the summation of pillar and window dimensions seems to confirm the 30ft body length.

DRAWING No. 4 (Page: 180): : Six-wheeled wagons. The dimensions given are taken from Barrett Jenkins' sketches; the actual vehicle he measured is not known and variations are known to exist, probably between batches and possibly within batches. The height in Barrett Jenkin's sketches was probably rounded off to the nearest inch. Two types of door (shown as A or B on the drawing) and three types of end (A B C) existed and examples of variants are as follows:

No	Door type	End type	Details
24 and 25	A	B	Square wooden door-stop to end doors only (platform side and, presumed, for off-side)
27	A	C	No door-stops on offside at least
28	A	C (probably)	Wooden stop to end door only, platform side at least
33	B	B (probably)	
Moy 1507	A	A	Wooden door-stops as for 24 and 25
Moy 1511	B	B	One steel stop on each door, platform side at least
It is possible that 24 to 26 (1896 batch), 27 to 32 (1899 batch) and 33 to 36 (1914 batch) were similar			

DRAWING No. 5 (Page: 181): : Four-wheeled vehicles 1 to 23. Vans 13 and 14. The dimensions have been obtained from the van body recently discovered at Halesworth. The right-hand half plan is as after re-building and both doors open the way shown, towards Southwold as far as is known. The left-hand half plan shows the original length, estimated at 10ft based in particular on the door runner length, assumed to be original and also presumably the same length as the wagons, for which reason the wheelbase of 5ft is suggested as applying. As built, no diagonal bracing was fitted and on one van at least the lower door runner had been fitted inverted for a period. Also, as shown, the existing rebuilt van at least had what appears to be a lamp bracket fitted at the Southwold end only (compare carriage); this may apply to the other van but probably, not before rebuilding, to either van.

Wagons 1 to 8, 15 to 23: Dimensions are from Barrett Jenkins' sketches, supplemented by information from the van body where applicable. Of the dimensions quoted for 18 to 23, the length is certain and the height believed to apply to these, though the vehicle from which his measurements were obtained was not recorded by Barrett Jenkins. Apparently one end view only was sketched for both 4- and 6- wheeled wagons. Wagons 1 to 8 were similar except for the maximum height of the curved ends, which are definitely higher except for at least one which was either built – or more probably rebuilt – with level ends as shown.

No width is quoted but all wagons appear to be of the same width as the vans 15 to 17 and were probably similar to 18 to 23. There may be variations, particularly in height and in width of planking, between individual wagons and the dimensions given by Barrett Jenkins may have been rounded off to the nearest inch. Door stops on all these wagons seem to vary considerably but in almost every case in photos each wagon and its contents are shrouded under a tarpaulin, effectively hiding the number so that details cannot be specified. Some wagons ran for some time with protective covers over the axle boxes.

Wagons 9 and 10: These two two-plank dropside wagons call for no comment beyond saying that their

sizes are presumably the same as for 1 to 8, except for height (estimated).

Wagons 11 and 12: These are quoted as timber wagons but no bolsters are to be seen in photographs, where they always appear as open wagons. Sizes are assumed to be as for 1 to 8 except for height, again estimated. The coupler socket on these, and on 9 and 10, were most likely as for 1 to 8.

Fig 211: Southwold up train approaches Halesworth alongside GER Claud Hamilton 4-4-0 express locomotive. Painted for this book by the late Joe Crowfoot (1946– 2017).

SELECT BIBLIOGRAPHY

The principal reference sources which underpin this book are listed on page 7 so are not repeated here. The following books provide a substantive context for the story of Southwold and its environs, the Southwold Railway, other railways in East Anglia, and UK railways history and heritage.

Branches & Byways – East Anglia	John Brodribb. OPC: Ian Allan Publishing. 2000
Illustrated History of the East Suffolk Railway. An	John Brodribb. OPC: Ian Allan Publishing. 2003
Impact of the Railway on Society in England. Essays in honour of Jack Simmons	A.K.B.Evans and J.V.Gough (Editors). Ashgate. 2003
Light Railways in England and Wales	Peter Bosley. Manchester University Press. 1990
Light Railways of Britain and Ireland. The	Anthony Burton & John Scott-Morgan. Pen & Sword Transport. 2015
Making Waves – Artists in Southwold	Ian Collins. Black Dog Books. 2005
Mid-Suffolk Light Railway. The	Peter Paye. Wild Swan Publications Ltd. 1986
Narrow Gauge Adventure – A model making journey	Peter Kayzer. Wild Swan Publications Ltd. 2012
Railway Atlas Then and Now	Paul Smith and Keith Turner. Ian Allan Publishing. 2012
Railways – Nation, Network and People	Simon Bradley. Profile Books. 2015
Railways in the Landscape. How they transformed the face of Britain	Gordon Biddle. Pen & Sword Transport. 2016
Remunerative Railways for New Countries	Richard C. Rapier. E. & F. N. Spon. 1878 [Kessinger Legacy Reprint. nd]
Southwold – An Earthly Paradise	Geoffrey C. Munn. Antique Collectors' Club. 2006
Southwold 1927. Old Ordnance Survey Maps	Alan Godfrey Maps. 1999
Southwold as an Industrial Town	Paul Scriven. Southwold Museum. 2007
Southwold Railway Children. The	John Bennett & Geoffrey Crab (Collators & Editors). Southwold Railway Society. 1999
Southwold River. Georgian Life in the Blyth Valley	Rachel Lawrence. Moxon (Southwold). 1990
Suffolk Transport – Britain in Old Photographs.	Robert Malster. Lucas Books. 2003
Will They Ever Learn? A History of Southwold Harbour	John Winter. 2013

INDEX

The list of CONTENTS on pages 5 and 6 is a useful general guide to the whole book. Because the specific subject of the book is the Southwold Railway that is not an Index subject, but 'Southwold' is where the reference is to the town or the harbour.

The SR served the villages of Wenhaston, Blythburgh and Walberswick with intermediate stations, mentioned frequently in the book so not separately indexed.

A suggestion for enjoying the Index, as well as using it for reference, is to glance through the entries and follow up one or two which may seem quirky or unusual. For instance:

Lion in the waiting room; Kipperdrome; A ". . . typical and paltry letter."; Phonographs not on wheels; Case dismissed?; 'Eyore.'

References to Southwold Railway in the Index use the abbreviation SR.